Moral Vision

*for
my mother,
who first encouraged me
to study philosophy*

Moral Vision

An Introduction to Ethics

DAVID MCNAUGHTON

BLACKWELL
Oxford UK & Cambridge USA

First published 1988
Reprinted 1991, 1992, 1994 (twice), 1995, 1996, 1998

Blackwell Publishers Ltd
108 Cowley Road, Oxford OX4 1JF, UK

Blackwell Publishers Inc.
350 Main Street
Malden, Massachusetts 02148, USA

British Library Cataloguing in Publication Data
McNaughton, David
   Moral vision: an introduction to ethics.
   1. Ethics
   I. Title
   170
   ISBN 0-631-15945-2 Pbk

Library of Congress Cataloging in Publication Data
McNaughton, David, 1946–
   Moral vision: an introduction to ethics/David McNaughton.
     p. cm.
   Bibliography: p.
   Includes index.
   ISBN 0-631-15945-2 (pbk.)
   1. Ethics I. Title
BJ1012.M42 1988
170-dc19   88-5101
                                                   CIP

Typeset in 10½ on 12½ pt Times
by Joshua Associates Ltd, Oxford
Printed and bound in Great Britain by MPG Books Ltd,
Bodmin, Cornwall

This book is printed on acid-free paper

Contents

Preface

This book springs from a final year undergraduate course that Jonathan Dancy and I have been giving for some years at the University of Keele. I have benefited greatly from discussion with students during that time; I owe special thanks to David Bakhurst, Paula Boddington and Cathy McDaniel. Eric Steinberg, Helen Brownbill, Bobbie Farsides and three anonymous Blackwell referees read all, or parts, of the book, and I am grateful to them all for encouragement, and for positive suggestions for improvement. Michael Smith and David Brink both took time and trouble to correspond with me on themes in the book, and to them too I am grateful. My intellectual debt to John McDowell is obvious throughout. I must also thank my parents-in-law, Milton and Evelyn Hunt, whose quiet hospitality enabled me to finish the main work on this book among the beauties of the hills of South Carolina.

Two people deserve special mention. The first is my friend and colleague, Jonathan Dancy, from whom I have learnt much that is in this book. With great patience, he has read every draft and made detailed and perceptive comments on all of them.

The second is my wife, Lee, who provided constant support and encouragement throughout the writing. She also took on the role of the general reader, forcing me to remove many barbaric sentences and clarify many points. Without her help this book could not have been written.

Introduction

This book provides an introduction to ethics. It does so by exploring a central, and perennial, debate between two sharply contrasting views of morality. On the one side are ranged those who think, roughly, that we live in a world which contains no objective values. How, then, do we acquire our ideas about moral value? Because we are creatures with certain feelings, needs and desires, we react favourably to some actions and unfavourably to others. The source of value is thus in ourselves. This position goes naturally with the view that there are no moral truths. For reasons that are made clear in the book, this view of morality is usually called non-cognitivism.

Opposed to the non-cognitivist is the moral realist, who claims that moral values are to be found in the world, and that there are moral truths which we can discover. What is morally right or wrong does not depend, in the way that the non-cognitivist suggests, on how we feel about it.

Although the debate is an old one, it has recently flared into active life, and is now at the forefront of moral philosophy. Unfortunately, much of the material in the current debate is complex and difficult. So this book will serve, not only as an introduction to ethics in general, but also as a guide to this confusing area of modern philosophy.

This book aims to be genuinely introductory, and presupposes no prior knowledge of philosophy. It should be accessible, not only to the first-year philosophy student, but also to that character who may only exist on the dust-jackets of books – the interested general reader.

Philosophers, like other academics, delight in the use of technical terms. While I have tried to avoid these as much as possible, the introduction of some of them is inevitable, especially if the reader is to gain enough familiarity with them to be able to tackle primary sources after reading this book. I have taken care to explain each term as it is introduced. I am conscious, from my own case, that it is often difficult to remember what a strange term means when it is next encountered.

One solution to this problem is a glossary. But glossaries have drawbacks as well as advantages. They encourage the erroneous belief that a complex position can be captured in a sentence or two. This tendency is especially pernicious when a position, which may have been simply described when first introduced, is later refined and qualified as the result of subsequent discussion. I have opted instead for an analytical index, which will draw attention to the first occurrence of a term, and then to places where it is attacked, defended or qualified.

At the end of each chapter there are suggestions for further reading. Given the nature of the writing in this field, some of these are quite difficult. I have indicated where this is the case. References in the text are by the author–date method; full references are found at the end of the book.

Finally, a word should be said about the protagonists in this debate. Both figures, as they appear in this book, are composites. No one person ever held all the views attributed, at one stage or another in this book, to either the non-cognitivist or the realist. This is more true in the case of the non-cognitivist, for reasons that are worth a brief mention. Moral realism has enjoyed a resurgence of late and, in its present form, has a comparatively short intellectual history. (Of course, it has many respectable ancestors.) It has not had time, therefore, to develop and branch into competing factions, although there are signs that this is now happening. To those familiar with his work it will be obvious that the philosopher whom the realist most resembles is John McDowell.

Non-cognitivism, by contrast, has been in vogue since the 1930s, and has gone through many transmutations since then. I wished to show how it has developed from the crude statement in A. J. Ayer's *Language, Truth and Logic* to the sophisticated doctrine it has become in the hands of Simon Blackburn. The views of many authors are utilized in tracing that development.

Although my account of these rival schools draws on many sources, I have been less concerned with the question of who said what, and whether they have been interpreted correctly, than with developing the arguments in whatever way seemed most fruitful. I have, therefore, been sparing in my use of references in the text, preferring to leave it uncluttered. This necessarily means that the sources of many of my ideas go unacknowledged (though this defect is partly remedied in the suggestions for futher reading). Worse perhaps, from their point of view, because of the need to keep the lines of the argument fairly clear, defences and qualifications of their positions go unmentioned. For both of these necessary omissions I apologize to all concerned.

1

Morality – Invention or Discovery?

1.1 TWO VIEWS OF MORALITY

The experience of value is a constant feature of our life. Any adequate understanding both of ourselves and of the world – the kind of understanding which philosophy traditionally seeks to provide – must take account of that experience. We find things of value both in nature, such as a beautiful sunset or a majestic mountain view, and in the products of human art – music, painting, dance or literature. Philosophical study of these aspects of our experience of value has traditionally been the province of aesthetics. We also judge the value of the lives and actions of ourselves and others: sometimes in the most general terms, as when we think of a person as good or bad or an action as right or wrong; sometimes in more specific ways – assessing a person or an action as just or unjust, cruel or kind. It is with this dimension of our experience of value, with our moral thought, that ethics is concerned.

There are two contrasting feelings about our moral life that all of us share to some extent. On the one side, we often feel that morality is an area of personal decision; a realm in which each of us has the right to make up his or her own mind about what to do. While other people may offer advice on what we should do and what moral principles we should adopt they have no authority to tell us how to live our lives. There are no moral experts. This feeling finds expression in many aspects of our social life. For example, on what are considered to be questions of conscience, British Members of Parliament are usually given a free vote; pacifists are not now forced to act against their sincerely held convictions by joining the armed forces. In the campaign to legalize abortion probably the single most persuasive argument was the claim that each woman had the right to make this moral choice for herself.

In this mood, we may feel that what matters is not that we make the right decision – for who is to determine what is the right decision? – but that each of us makes his *own* decision. Each of us has to determine, as it is sometimes put, what is the right thing for him or her. Each of us has to decide what values he is to live his life by and the rest of us should respect the sincerity of those choices.

This view of moral choice sits unhappily with the second feeling that we all share, namely that it is often difficult, when faced with some pressing and perplexing moral problem, to discover which answer is the right one. If I am puzzled as to what I ought to do then I am likely to feel that what matters is not that the answer I arrive at should be mine, one for which I am prepared to assume ultimate responsibility, but that it be the correct answer. I do not think of my choice as determining the right answer; on the contrary, I wish my choice to be determined by the right answer. It is because I fear that I may choose wrongly that I find the decision so difficult.

These feelings are in tension: the first appears to lead to the view that there is nothing independent of our moral opinions that determines whether or not they are correct; the second runs counter to that conclusion. Once people begin to reflect on these positions and try to develop either of them then that tension is likely to generate a debate between the two sides. Each will probe weaknesses in the other and thereby provoke a response which will in turn evoke a further challenge. As this dialogue or dialectic develops, what were at first fairly inchoate feelings will turn into more elaborate theories about the nature of moral thought. Philosophical theories about the nature of value can thus be seen as developing naturally from reflection on feelings that we all have about ethics.

While philosophers have tried to do justice to both feelings in their theories they tend to veer to one side or the other. Those who are impressed by the first line of thought will probably picture moral thinking as a method for deciding what values we should *place* on things. (Mackie's influential recent book (1977) in this tradition is subtitled 'Inventing Right and Wrong'.) Those more under the influence of the second feeling will see moral experience as a matter of trying to *find* a value that is already there. So the issue for debate becomes: are we to picture ethical thinking as a matter of creating or inventing values or rather as a matter of discovering or recognizing values that exist independently of us?

1.2 JUSTIFICATION AND TRUTH

If we look at an obvious difficulty raised by the first line of thought, the one that pictures us as creating value, we can see a typical pattern of challenge and counter-challenge emerging. If each of us has to decide for himself what his values are then it might seem that no moral opinion could ever be questioned, still less refuted. *I* can determine what *my* values are but not what yours should be; only you can do that. It looks as if the moral views of each of us would be exempt from criticism – any view would be as good as any other. Yet this seems to conflict with the feeling that some moral positions are better founded than others. Surely, if we are to take someone's moral views seriously he should be able to produce some justification for them.

The advocate of the view that we create our values may well respond to this objection by reminding us that, in his opinion, what each of us is choosing is a set of values that he fully accepts and which is going to govern the whole of his life. We are all familiar with the moral hypocrite; the person who pretends to accept a set of moral principles he does not really believe in. But we are asking what is involved in sincerely adopting some set of values, as distinct from merely claiming to have them. Firstly, having some moral convictions is surely more a matter of what a person *does* than of what he *says*, so they have to be values that he can actually live by. Whatever moral principles he adopts must be ones that he is prepared to follow himself. Secondly, his moral views must be consistent, otherwise he will find himself committed to conflicting moral positions and so, when it comes to putting them into action, he will not be able to live by them.

The upholder of the view that each of us has to decide what our values are is now in a position to claim that there is room in his ethical system for criticism of another's moral views. We can always try to show him that his views are internally inconsistent, and so force him to change them to bring them into line with each other. Philosophers of this persuasion have exercised a great deal of ingenuity in showing that what we might call the sincerity conditions for moral commitment – that a person's principles be consistent and that he be prepared to live by them – place severe limits on the kinds of system of moral value that are available to each of us.

This reply is unlikely entirely to satisfy his opponent, who sees moral thinking in terms of discovering the correct values rather than creating them. It seems perfectly possible that there might be many moral systems that are internally consistent but inconsistent with each other.

Indeed, it might appear that there actually are several such ready-made systems available in the moral market-place. Christians, Buddhists, Marxists, utilitarians and others all ask their adherents to subscribe to a complete moral system, and it is at least conceivable that more than one of these systems is internally consistent, or could be made so. Someone who thinks that we invent our value systems seems committed to the view that any consistent position is as good as any other, since the only grounds for criticizing a value system is its internal inconsistency. His opponent will seize on this point.

Suppose I am trying to decide between two or more such competing but consistent systems. It seems to matter very much which one I choose. As we saw earlier, the second feeling that we have about difficult moral choices is that if I am puzzled about which one to choose it is because I want to choose the best one and I don't yet know which that is. The same objection reappears even if I am choosing systems of moral principles rather than just making individual moral decisions. I don't want to choose just any consistent system of values by which I can live my life; I want to choose the right system. The picture of each of us creating our own values leaves no room for the question of which system is the correct one to choose; any consistent system is as good as any other.

An alternative way of putting this objection would be in terms of truth. People often have conflicting beliefs about a whole range of matters. Consistency in a person's set of beliefs is certainly a necessary condition of their being true but it is not sufficient for their truth. There can be many internally consistent though competing sets of beliefs, but we normally think that not more than one set can be true. It is natural to suppose that what determines whether a belief is true is the way things are in the world. My belief that milk contains vitamin D is true just if milk *does* contain vitamin D. So the true set of beliefs will be the one that accurately reflects the way things are. We might now express the worry in the last paragraph by saying that, when I am presented with competing but internally consistent ethical systems, what I want is to select the set that is actually true.

If we express the objection in this way then we can see that a further difference between the two lines of approach has emerged. The feeling that we have to discover which moral values are correct, rather than invent them, leads naturally to the view that there are moral truths. Moral truth is thought of as independent of whatever moral decisions we may happen to reach. What we aspire to in our moral thinking, on that view, is to get to that moral truth. On the other side, the feeling that values are a product of our choices leads equally naturally to the contrary view that there is no moral truth; there is nothing independent of our choices that could possibly determine which consistent system of moral values is the correct one.

1.3 MORAL REALISM

In developing the view that the answers to moral questions are independent of us and need to be discovered, it was natural to draw on the interrelated concepts of truth, belief and reality. The notion of truth is intimately connected with that of belief. Beliefs aim at truth; they are true if they hit their mark, false if they miss it. If we discover that two of our beliefs are inconsistent then we must abandon at least one of them because two inconsistent beliefs cannot both be true. That our beliefs are consistent is a necessary condition for their being true, but is not, as we have just seen, sufficient for truth. Consistency within our system of beliefs is thus no guarantee that they are true. Whether or not our beliefs are true depends on something independent of them, namely reality: the way things are, the way the world is. It follows that our moral beliefs will be true if things are, morally, as we suppose they are.

This view, which springs from the second feeling about ethics, might best be called *moral realism*, for it insists that there is a moral reality which is independent of our moral beliefs and which determines whether or not they are true or false. It holds that moral properties are genuine properties of things or actions; they are, as it is sometimes picturesquely put, part of the furniture of the world. We may or may not be sensitive to a particular moral property, but whether or not that property is present does not depend on what *we* think about the matter.

We saw that it was natural to see the opposing view as denying that there is any moral truth. Since the concepts of truth, belief and reality are so closely tied, this denial naturally goes with moral *ir*realism – the claim that there is no moral reality – and with the suggestion that moral convictions are not best thought of as beliefs. If each of us has to invent his own moral values then they are not appropriately thought of as features of an independent world. We cannot, on this view, be sensitive to the way things are, morally speaking, for there is no moral reality. If our moral opinions cannot be true or false then they cannot be beliefs, for to believe something is to believe that it is *true*. There is nothing in the world for them to be true or false of.

This account of the view that we create our values is so far entirely negative: it denies that there is a moral reality, that there can be moral truth, that moral commitments are to be seen as beliefs. Can the moral irrealist produce some more positive characterization of what a moral conviction is?

1.4 MORAL NON-COGNITIVISM

Being in a particular *cognitive* state, such as believing something, or doubting it or knowing it, does not seem to be essentially connected with feeling. Of course, I may care very much about some belief of mine, I may very much want it to be true. But it seems perfectly possible, maybe even desirable, that we should be dispassionate about our beliefs. After all, what matters in the end is whether or not they are true, and that depends on how things are not on how we feel about them. By contrast, our moral views do seem to involve our feelings in a direct manner. It is surely not possible to have a deeply held moral conviction about some issue and yet not care about it. The very terms we use to describe actions that we morally condemn, such as 'outrageous', 'appalling' or 'intolerable', betray the link with feeling.

The moral irrealist stresses this connection between our feelings and our moral convictions and suggests that we should think of moral commitments as being like feelings or emotions. By adopting this account, he claims, he can explain this connection in a way that his opponent cannot. If moral views are just beliefs, as the moral realist holds, why is there this close connection between those views and our feelings? Surely, on the realist account, someone might have a set of moral beliefs and yet be emotionally entirely detached about them. This appears to be a defect in the realist position.

The irrealist is now in a position to develop his suggestion into a positive account of the nature of moral commitment. We can best explain his views by means of an example. Suppose that I see some children throwing stones at an injured dog. Because of what I see I acquire a whole variety of beliefs – that there are three children, that the dog is bleeding, and so on. I am horrified by what I see; I am sure that such behaviour is cruel and wrong. What is it to make such a moral judgement? According to the irrealist I am not, as the realist supposes, forming a further belief about what the children are doing, namely that what they are doing is wrong. Rather, I am reacting emotionally to what I see. My moral condemnation is to be thought of as an *affective* response – a reaction of the feeling side of my nature – *to* my beliefs about the way things are. The close connection between feeling and moral judgement is thus explained. To hold that something is wrong just is to have a negative emotional reaction to it; to tell others that it is wrong is to express that feeling.

This account explains why we cannot be emotionally detached when considering an issue which we think is morally important. To have a strong moral conviction about some issue is to care about it. This account also explains something else on which the irrealist laid stress. Sincerely held moral principles, it will be recalled, were taken to be ones on which we act, ones by which we live. We can now show why our moral views have an influence on our actions. Caring about some issue and wanting various things to happen go together. If I really care about animal welfare then I shall characteristically want a range of things to be the case: that factory farming be stopped; that money be provided for animal clinics etc. Since I want these things I shall be motivated to bring them about, as far as I can. The more I care, the stronger my desires and the more motivated I will be. Since to have a moral conviction is to care, it is also to be motivated to act in accordance with it.

The moral realist thinks of moral views as being purely cognitive; they are simply beliefs about the way the world is, morally speaking. His irrealist opponent claims that what is distinctive about moral views is that they contain a non-cognitive element, an element from the feeling or emotional side of our natures. We may, therefore, call such a position *moral non-cognitivism*. Since the non-cognitivist denies that moral views are to be thought of as beliefs about the facts he must find some other term to describe them. Let us introduce the concept of an *attitude*. To adopt an attitude is not to form a belief about the facts but to evaluate those facts. Attitudes can be positive or negative, pro or con. Terms of assessment tend to come in pairs (for instance, right/wrong, good/bad) enabling us to express either a favourable or an unfavourable attitude to whatever we are evaluating. I can, of course, evaluate things from standpoints other than the moral one. If I find opera dull, lifeless and artificial then I am certainly condemning it, but my objections to it are not moral ones. A moral attitude is one kind of attitude; not all questions of value are moral questions.

The non-cognitivist sees evaluative thought in general, and moral experience in particular, as possessing two quite distinct aspects. We can illustrate this by referring to our example of the children throwing stones at the dog. First, we have some beliefs about what we take the facts to be; we might acquire these by actually seeing the children behaving this way or by being told about it. If our beliefs about the facts are inaccurate or incomplete then this may invalidate the moral judgement we form on the basis of those beliefs. Our beliefs need to be sensitive to the facts, to the way the world is. Second, we are so constituted, whether by nature or upbringing, that we react to this behaviour with revulsion. This reaction is the work of our feelings and it reveals something about *us*, but nothing about the world. Since people differ in their emotional make-up, it is possible for two people to agree about all the facts and yet differ in the values they assign to those facts. We might express this by saying that people can agree in belief but disagree in moral attitude.

In 1.1, I said that the first approach to ethics, which developed into moral non-cognitivism, appealed to a common belief that there are no moral experts. The non-cognitivist is now in a position to offer support for this belief. Where factual questions are involved I may safely appeal to an expert who is in a better position than I am to know what is true. However, the notion of a *moral* expert makes no sense on the non-cognitivist view. There are no moral facts about which he or she might have special knowledge. What I need to know when I am making a moral judgement is what I feel about the situation; on such questions each of us is his own expert.

1.5 MORAL FREEDOM AND THE MEANING OF LIFE

Non-cognitivism can be cast in a very attractive light. It can appear as a doctrine of liberation, as an affirmation of individual human freedom in the face of determined attempts, by people who think they know what is best for us, to run our lives for us. The knowledge explosion has led to an expert explosion. In an increasingly complex society, in which no single person can grasp a fraction of the knowledge that is available, there are experts on everything, telling us what we should believe and do. While we have to bow to expert opinion in many areas of life, in the realm of moral choice we at last find an area from which expertise is excluded. Here we have the freedom to make up our own minds about how to live our own lives.

Non-cognitivism preserves an area of life in which feeling and emotion come into their own. On factual questions it is not what we feel that matters but what reasoned evidence suggests to be the truth. Such reasoning is often seen as cold and impersonal; an abstract method of determining truth which can be applied by any thinker. In moral thought, however, it is personal feelings that are crucial.

The non-cognitivist thus rejects the philosophy of life and the theory of education put forward by Mr Gradgrind at the beginning of Dickens's *Hard Times*: 'Now what I want is, Facts. Teach these boys and girls nothing but Facts. Facts alone are wanted in life. Plant nothing else, and root out everything else.' Each of us needs feelings, as well as knowledge of the facts, if he is to have any grounds for preferring one way of life to another. And what feelings I have is up to me, whereas what is a fact and what is not is something outside my control. In claiming that moral questions are factual questions moral realism may appear to threaten our moral autonomy, our freedom to decide moral questions for ourselves.

Non-cognitivism can also appear as a doctrine of toleration. If no one is in a better position than anyone else to decide what is the right thing to do then no one has the authority to interfere with other people's choices. Each of us should be allowed to do his own thing. The realist, by contrast, may look like a dogmatist. From saying that there is a moral truth to be known it seems but a short step to claiming that you have found it and that other people are just wrong because they do not see it the way you do.

It is a mistake, however, to think that tolerance falls out of non-cognitivism in such a direct way. For that would be to claim that non-cognitivism can show that an attitude of toleration is preferable to an attitude of intolerance. However, it would be inconsistent, as most non-cognitivists have recognized, to hold both that we are free to choose what moral attitudes to take and also that we can demonstrate that an attitude of tolerance is superior to one of intolerance. Furthermore, a little reflection will show that toleration cannot be limitless. If you hold, for example, that fox-hunting is morally perfectly acceptable and I feel that it is cruel and barbaric then I cannot tolerate your hunting without abandoning my attitude. To have a moral attitude is to act in appropriate circumstances. I cannot, therefore, be committed to preventing cruelty to foxes and, at the same time, think nothing should be done to stop it, without being inconsistent. And the same goes for many other moral attitudes.

This realization may make the freedom of which non-cognitivism boasts appear less attractive. If moral questions are not questions of fact and there are no correct answers, how are clashes of attitude to be resolved? If it cannot be shown that one attitude is superior to another then moral disagreements will have to be settled by such non-rational methods as persuasion, threats and, ultimately, force. In reply, the non-cognitivist can remind us that we can show a moral position to be unjustified if it is inconsistent and that we have not yet explored how far that strategy will take us. If, however, at the end of the day, there are irreconcilable clashes of attitude then it may well be that we shall just have to fight for what we believe in, as men have fought down the ages.

This answer serves, however, only to raise another doubt. Can non-cognitivism make sense of people's commitment to a moral ideal in which they believe and for which they are, perhaps, even prepared to die? The difficulty is this. Non-cognitivism invites us to stand outside our own evaluative commitments and recognize that, from this external standpoint, nothing is intrinsically valuable, for values are no part of the real world but are created or invented by us. Can our commitment to various values survive this recognition? That is, once we have realized that there are no objective values can we go on caring about and fighting for the things we value, or shall we become convinced that nothing matters?

The usual non-cognitivist response to this worry rests on a distinction between what is *logically possible* and what is *psychologically possible*. There may be positions which it is logically possible, but psychologically difficult, or even impossible, to accept. It is logically possible to maintain a position if it contains no contradictions or incoherences. The non-cognitivist maintains that there is nothing incoherent in believing that there are no objective values *and* caring passionately about various issues. Thus A. J. Ayer, a lifelong proponent of non-cognitivism, is always writing letters of protest to *The Times* and he is not being untrue to his philosophical beliefs in doing so. No belief, not even a philosophical belief, can dictate what attitudes we may or may not take, since attitudes are independent of beliefs. The non-cognitivist is quite prepared to concede that someone who has been an unreflective moral realist may, on being exposed to the arguments for moral irrealism, experience feelings of disquiet and a sense of alienation from his own value-system. Such qualms are, however, of merely psychological interest and do not raise any logical difficulties for non-cognitivism.

The disquiet to which irrealism about values often gives rise is not so easily allayed. We desire something because we believe it to be valuable; we do not think it is desirable or valuable because we desire it. We find meaning in various activities because we think of those activities as being worthwhile, and by that we do not mean that they are worth pursuing solely because we want to pursue them. Only the conviction that what we are doing is objectively worthwhile may make it reasonable for us to accept the sacrifices and hardships which may be involved in bringing any major project, such as raising children or writing a book, to fruition. Non-cognitivism threatens to undermine the beliefs about the nature of value which give many of our activities their point. If we do not believe that our most cherished goals have any value independent of our desire to see them succeed, then those projects, and even life itself, may cease to have any meaning. The non-cognitivist has yet to show that he can allow room for a conception of value that would enable us to see life as having any point.

While most non-cognitivists in the Anglo-American tradition have tried to show that the truth of their theory would not make life meaningless – often by the disingenuous method of pretending that they can make no sense of the question of whether life has a meaning – some European philosophers in the existentialist tradition have embraced the conclusion that life has no meaning. Like the non-cognitivist the existentialist denies that there are objective values and holds that each of us is responsible, from moment to moment, for choosing how he should live. It is bad faith to try and avoid the agony of that choice by pretending that there are objective values or external duties. Whatever we decided yesterday cannot be simply carried over to today; we must either reaffirm that choice or choose anew. Life is absurd; once we have recognized that fact we either have to live by a never-ending series of radical choices or make the final, irrevocable, choice of suicide.

1.6 REALISM, NON-COGNITIVISM AND THE MORAL TRADITION

The two feelings about ethics with which we started have already developed into starkly contrasted theories. The realist holds that there is an independent moral reality of which we can be aware; the non-cognitivist denies this. The realist thinks of moral views as beliefs about the way the world is; his opponent conceives of them as attitudes which we take towards the facts. The realist insists that there is moral truth; the non-cognitivist rejects the notion.

Both theories are still in a fairly crude state. As they are refined, in response to obvious difficulties and objections, the contrast between them will become less clear cut. The main difference between the two, which remains through all the twists and turns of their development, concerns the status of moral properties. The central pillar of the realist position is the insistence, as the name implies, that there is a moral reality; in moral experience we are genuinely sensitive to moral properties which are as much a part of the real world as any other properties. Although the details of non-cognitivist accounts of moral experience may vary they are all committed to irrealism, to denying that moral properties are part of the furniture of the world. It is because the non-cognitivist denies that there is a moral reality of which we can come to be aware that he holds that moral experience cannot be purely cognitive, but must involve a non-cognitive element.

As the last remark suggests, there are various forms that our two theories might take. It is with the debate between them that this book is mainly concerned. I shall not explore all these forms, but try to develop the most plausible version of each so that we are in a position to judge the strengths and weaknesses of the best representatives of the two approaches. It would be misleading to imply that these are the only theories in the field. In particular, moral realism does not represent the only possible response to what may seem the most disturbing aspect of the non-cognitivist position – its denial that there is anything objective, anything independent of our moral reactions, in which those responses are grounded. The claim that there is a moral reality is one attempt to provide such an objective grounding for ethics, but there are others.

One such tradition stems from the ethical theory of the eighteenth-century German philosopher Immanuel Kant. Kant was, in part, reacting to the views of another eighteenth-century philosopher, David Hume, whose ideas supply the main inspiration for much modern non-cognitivist thinking. Kant seeks to ground morality in the nature of reason. We not only use reason theoretically, to discover what the world is like, but also practically, to discover what we ought to do. Kant argues that there are limitations, not only on which beliefs it is rational to accept, but also on which plans of action it is rational to adopt. It would be irrational, for example, to pursue a goal in such a way that I undermined any chance I might have of achieving it. By a series of ingenious but highly dubious arguments Kant tries to establish that immoral action is irrational. Kant agrees with the non-cognitivist that claims about what we ought to do are not statements about the way things are and cannot be true or false in virtue of the way the world is. He differs from him in holding that reason requires that we do certain actions and refrain from others, quite independently of our desires. What we *ought* to do is independent of what we *want* to do. We can show which moral principles are objectively justified and which are not by reflection on the nature of practical rationality. Immoral principles of action are rationally untenable and we therefore have good reason not to adopt them.

Although some version of Kantianism is often put forward as the chief rival to non-cognitivism I do not believe that it represents a viable alternative. There are serious objections to Kant's own theory and many philosophers are agreed that, interesting and stimulating though the Kantian approach to ethics may be, it is deeply flawed. One feature of Kant's theory does, however, play a central role in our debate. For, as we shall see, the moral realist agrees with Kant that moral requirements have a claim on our compliance which is independent of what we happen to desire.

Moral realism and non-cognitivism are, in my opinion, the two most plausible theories about the nature of ethics. They are also the most topical, in that the debate between them is at the forefront of recent discussion. Indeed, ethics in the twentieth century, at least in the English speaking world, can be seen as a prolonged debate between the two, with first one side gaining favour and then the other. In the first thirty years of the century a species of realism, often known as intuitionism, held sway; among its leading advocates were G. E. Moore, W. D. Ross, H. A. Prichard and C. D. Broad. (Representative works will be found in the References.) During the 1930s non-cognitivists, such as Ayer and Stevenson, launched a blistering attack on the prevailing realist tradition and since then non-cognitivism has tended to dominate Anglo-Saxon moral philosophy, with occasional resistance from authors in the realist and Kantian traditions. The leading non-cognitivist has undoubtedly been Hare, but the theory has had many able supporters on both sides of the Atlantic including, more recently, John Mackie, Simon Blackburn, Gilbert Harman and, to an extent, Bernard Williams. Moral realism has re-emerged of late as the strongest challenger to the non-cognitivist tradition. As well as its British proponents, John McDowell, David Wiggins, Mark Platts, John Finnis and Jonathan Dancy, it does not want for supporters in the United States, such as Hilary Putnam, Thomas Nagel, Nicholas Sturgeon, Richard Werner and David Brink. The debate between the two ethical theories is still developing, but one trend that will be prominent in this book has already emerged; the effect of the renewed interest in moral realism has been to challenge received views, not only in ethics, but in other areas of philosophy as well.

1.7 MORALITY AND ETHICAL THEORY

Moral philosophy can be divided into at least three branches. First, there is *practical ethics*, the study of specific moral problems: Is abortion ever morally acceptable? What structures would we find in a perfectly just society? Second, there is *moral theory*, the attempt to develop a theory of morality that will give us a general method for answering all the specific moral questions that are raised in practical ethics. Third, there are questions about the nature and status of our moral thought: Are there any moral truths? Is it possible to show that one moral view is better than another? It is with this third sort of question that this book is primarily concerned. Thinking about the status of moral thought is sometimes called *meta*-ethics to distinguish this last approach from practical ethics and the construction of moral theories. I shall avoid this clumsy modern coinage and use the traditional term 'ethics'.

These three areas are not, of course, entirely separate; someone's opinions in one area cannot be isolated from his views in the other two. Ethical questions are basic; the conclusions we come to about the nature and status of our moral thought are bound to have an effect on our views about how we may set about determining the correct solution to some moral problem, or even whether there is such a thing as a correct answer. Towards the end of the book we shall see what implications for moral theory follow from adopting non-cognitivism or realism.

Nor can ethics be kept separate from other areas of philosophy; we have already seen that our debate raises questions about truth, the nature of reality, the motivation of action and the meaning of life – all of them major areas of philosophical controversy in their own right. Any satisfactory ethical theory must have things to say in all these areas and so form an integrated picture of the world and of our place in it which is much wider than the field of ethics.

While both our theories are primarily attempting to understand the nature of *moral* value any such project must be seen as part of a wider enterprise of making sense of our experience of value in general. Thus many of the themes of this book will be relevant to problems in other areas of value, especially aesthetics. Both of our theories find important parallels, as well as differences, between moral and aesthetic experience. Moral realism, in particular, often appeals to aesthetic experience as a model for moral experience. A detailed comparison of both areas can only help our understanding of each.

FURTHER READING

Williams (1973b) provides a good short introduction to the area. Warnock (1967) is a lively, clear and critical account of moral philosophy in the first half of the twentieth century. Richard Norman (1983) provides an excellent introduction to the main historical figures in ethics.

On 1.5 A vigorous defence of the view that we are free to make up our own minds about morality can be found in Hare (1963, ch. 1). A classic, though slightly misleading, statement of the existentialist view is found in Sartre (1970). Camus (1955) discusses absurdity and suicide. See Wiggins (1976, pp. 331–49) for a discussion of the relation between non-cognitivism and the meaning of life.

2

Moral Non-Cognitivism – an Outline

A. J. Ayer once said that the whole of ethics could be written on the back of a postcard. In the case of the simplest non-cognitivist theory this is scarcely an exaggeration. On that view, to say that stealing is wrong is merely to voice one's disapproval of stealing, so the remark could be more revealingly rewritten as: 'Stealing – Boo!'. Similarly, 'God is good' could be translated as 'Hurrah for God'. Not surprisingly, this view was dubbed the Boo–Hurrah theory of ethics. There is, in fact, a great deal more to be said in elaboration and defence than Ayer suggested, but we should not lose sight of the appealing simplicity of the basic theory, amid all the complexities of some of the more sophisticated versions of the doctrine.

According to the non-cognitivist, factual questions are very different from evaluative ones. The facts are determined by the way the world is. We can find out what the facts are by observation and experiment. Our beliefs about the facts are constantly subject to revision in the light of further observations. If our beliefs fit the facts they are true; if not, they are false.

Values are not determined by the way the world is, because value is not to be found in the world. A complete account of the world would not mention any evaluative properties, such as beauty or evil. Our moral evaluations, like all our evaluations, are not beliefs about the way the world is; rather, they are affective responses to the way we take things to be. As such they cannot be true or false, for there is nothing for them to be true or false of. It seems perfectly possible that two people might agree about all the facts and yet still disagree about moral values because they had different attitudes to those facts. Such purely evaluative disagreements could not be settled by observation and experiment because the dispute is not about things that can be observed. The disputants do not have conflicting beliefs about the facts; rather, they have different attitudes towards the facts.

Evaluative questions are practical in a way that factual questions are not. To settle on an answer to an evaluative problem is to decide what to *do*; to discover an answer to a factual question is to find out what to *believe*. We can find out which moral principles someone is really committed to, rather than the ones he merely pays lip-service to, by watching what he does. This close connection between someone's moral commitments and their actions is explained by appealing to the fact that moral opinions are attitudes rather than beliefs. To have an unfavourable attitude towards some course of action is to be opposed to it; it is to be motivated to avoid it oneself and to discourage others from taking it. When we adopt a moral attitude our feelings are necessarily engaged.

This division between fact and value runs right through non-cognitivism finding expression in many distinctions, such as the one between belief and attitude which we have just employed. Its influence can be traced in the non-cognitivist accounts of moral motivation, moral language and the nature of our experience of moral value.

2.2 FOUR CHALLENGES TO NON-COGNITIVISM

It is the non-cognitivist's claim that values are not to be found in the world that motivates the sharp distinction between fact and value which runs through his account. Not surprisingly, many of the doubts about non-cognitivism focus on this irrealism and its consequences. There are four main challenges that will emerge in the rest of the chapter.

Truth

As we saw in 1.2 the denial of a moral reality seems to render the notion of moral truth problematic. If there is no moral reality then there is nothing for our moral opinions to be true of. Yet the claim that moral judgements do not have a truth-value – that is, cannot be properly said to be true or false – seems to fly in the face of our normal thought and speech. The non-cognitivist has either to show that this radical departure from our normal way of thinking is justified, or else explain how, on his account, we can retain the right to speak of moral judgements having a truth-value.

Scepticism

Secondly, if there is nothing in the world for our moral opinions to be true of, to what can we point if we wish to justify our moral views? If our moral convictions are challenged can we produce any good reasons in support of them? Non-cognitivism appears to face the threat of moral scepticism. Scepticism is by no means confined to ethics. The sceptic typically claims that all the proffered justifications for our beliefs in some area are inadequate.

Someone may be a moral sceptic without being a sceptic in other areas. The moral sceptic claims that there is something distinctive about moral claims which makes it impossible to show one to be more justified than another. Non-cognitivism tends towards moral scepticism for two reasons. Firstly, because of its irrealism about values. If there is no moral reality then our moral opinions cannot be justified by observation or experiment. But these are our main tools for establishing and checking our opinions. Secondly, while I may be able to produce good reasons for my beliefs, it is hard to see how I could have good reasons for my attitudes. What attitudes I have depends on how I feel – and it does not seem to make sense to ask someone to justify their feelings, any more than it makes sense to ask me to give good reasons to support my dislike of cold rice pudding. But isn't the fact that it leads to moral scepticism a reason for being wary of the non-cognitivist account of morals?

Observation

Thirdly, as we have just seen, it looks as if the non-cognitivist must deny that we can observe value, for there is nothing there to observe. This claim is counter-intuitive. Our experience of the world does seem to involve experience of value, both moral and non-moral: we hear the beauty of Mozart's music; we see the children's cruelty to the dog; we witness McEnroe's rudeness on the tennis courts. Can the non-cognitivist give an account of our experience of value which is true to the nature of that experience while denying value any place in the world?

Appearance and reality

Finally, the claim that there is no moral reality, that moral properties form no part of the furniture of the world, itself stands in need of justification. By what criterion do we decide what properties there are in the world? How do we determine whether some aspect of our experience represents, or fails to represent, a real property to us? Non-cognitivism faces the challenge of providing a general account of the distinction between what is really there and what only appears to be there – an account which not only gets the answer the non-cognitivist wants in the moral case, but which also gives plausible answers elsewhere.

If the non-cognitivist can meet these challenges then he will have gone a long way towards substantiating his theory. That theory draws on philosophical positions in other areas for support. To gauge its success we need to trace out its consequences in philosophically contentious areas, such as the explanation of action, the theory of language and the nature of reality. We can only make full sense of it within this wider philosophical picture; we can only reach a final assessment of its plausibility when we have made up our minds about what views to take in related areas of philosophy.

2.3 EXPLANATION OF ACTION AND MORAL MOTIVATION

Moral questions are, as we have seen, questions about what to do. We would not accept a person's claim to have a moral conviction if he never acted on it. We seek to change the views of those we believe to be mistaken on some moral issue because we wish to alter the way they act. Any moral theory that fails to give a convincing account of this close relation between our moral commitments and our actions must be unsatisfactory. The non-cognitivist claims not only that his theory can provide such an account but also that the realist cannot do so.

We will sometimes appeal to an agent's moral commitments in explaining why he acted in the way he did. How can such an appeal help us to understand what he was doing? The best way to get to grips with that issue is to subsume it under the wider question: How do we explain intentional human action? When an agent acts intentionally we presume that he has reasons for what he does; that he has certain aims or purposes which could be spelled out. We explain his action by setting out the reasons that he had for acting that way.

His reasons may not be good ones; but appeal to them will help us to understand what he was doing even if we do not think they justified him in doing what he did. I understand why Karen spent thousands of pounds at the orthodontist getting her teeth straightened when I realize that she wants to be attractive to the opposite sex, even if I do not think that this is a very good reason for spending so much money. Sometimes it is obvious what the agent's reasons were; sometimes we may be puzzled. Kremlin watchers make their living by supplying reasons that make the Soviet leaders' actions understandable to the rest of us in the West.

What is it for an agent to have reason to act; what sort of explanation do we need to supply to make someone's action intelligible? An obvious answer claims that an agent has reason to act if he has both beliefs and desires of appropriate kinds. If either is absent the agent will have no reason to act. In a complete explanation of any action, therefore, both would need to be mentioned.

This view of action explanation, which we may dub the *belief–desire theory*, was advocated by Hume who often expounded it in terms of a hydraulic metaphor. For example, the desire to eat an apple provides the motivational push which drives the agent to act but furnishes no information about how to satisfy that desire. Beliefs, which are themselves lacking in motive force, supply that information and thus guide or channel that push in appropriate directions. Thus the belief that I can buy apples at the local store channels the latent energy in my desire for apples in the direction of the shops. The combination of belief and desire is required to motivate the agent to act. Desires without beliefs are blind; beliefs without desires are inert.

What the use of this hydraulic metaphor illustrates is the common belief that we should think of beliefs and desires as radically different kinds of state. Beliefs, as we have already seen, are cognitive states – they are representations of the way we take the world to be. Desires, by contrast, are typically thought of as non-cognitive states – a desire is not a passive state that reflects the world but an active state which leads its possessor to seek to change it.

Internalism and the belief–desire theory

We can express that close connection between an agent's moral commitments and his actions, on which the non-cognitivist has laid such stress, in terms of reasons for action. A moral conviction, in conjunction with appropriate beliefs, might be thought to be sufficient to supply an agent with reason to act. For example, my conviction that I ought to visit my sick grandmother, coupled with my belief that she lives in Birmingham, gives me reason to travel there. Since we explain an agent's actions by appeal to his reasons it would appear that we can sometimes fully explain a person's action by citing some moral view of his in conjunction with some of his beliefs. My trip to Birmingham is completely explained once attention has been drawn to my beliefs about my grandmother's location and my sense of family duty.

The view that a moral conviction, coupled with suitable beliefs, is sufficient to supply the agent with reason to act, and thus to motivate him to act, is often called *internalism* because it postulates an internal or conceptual connection between an agent's moral attitude and his choice of action. Internalism appears plausible; moral convictions appear to be essentially action-guiding. How could someone genuinely hold that a particular action was wrong and yet see no reason not to act in that way?

The combination of internalism and the belief–desire theory of action provides the non-cognitivist with a powerful argument in favour of his position. Internalism tells us that we can give a complete explanation of my trip to Birmingham by ascribing to me a moral opinion – that I took it to be my moral duty to visit my grandmother – and some obvious beliefs about where my grandmother lived and how to get to Birmingham. The belief–desire theory tells us that a complete explanation of any action must mention a desire as well as some beliefs, since only desires are suitably motivational. But where in the explanation of my trip to Birmingham do we find reference to a desire? Since, obviously, my beliefs about where my grandmother lives, or how to get to Birmingham, are not desires, the only place left where a desire could be lurking is in my moral conviction. So my moral opinion cannot be purely cognitive, cannot be just a belief about what I ought to do. It must contain a non-cognitive element because it is motivational, and pure beliefs cannot motivate. It must either itself be a desire or somehow incorporate a desire.

This argument appears to confirm the claim that moral convictions are attitudes and not beliefs and it gives us more detail about what an attitude must be, since to have an attitude must be a form of wanting or desiring. To have an attitude of disapproval towards, say, abortion is to want there to be no abortions.

The threat to moral realism

We can now see why the combination of internalism and the belief–desire theory threatens moral realism. The moral realist rejects the non-cognitivist distinction between factual beliefs and moral attitudes. He holds that a moral opinion is a purely cognitive state; it is simply and solely a belief. That claim stems from his realism. In moral experience, we are sensitive to a moral reality – we acquire beliefs about the way things are, morally speaking. Just as moral properties are, for the realist, genuine features of the world, so moral opinions will be genuinely beliefs about the world. However, the belief–desire thesis tells us that if an agent's moral opinion is purely cognitive then it is not sufficient, when combined with other beliefs of his, to give him any reason for acting.

If the moral realist accepts the belief–desire theory of what it is to have a reason to act then he is committed to *externalism* about moral motivation. That is, he must admit that someone might firmly believe that some action was morally required of him and yet see no reason at all why he should act in accordance with it. Yet externalism appears counter-intuitive.

We can exhibit the non-cognitivist's challenge to the realist in the form of an inconsistent triad of propositions; that is, three propositions which cannot all be true, although any two of them may be true. In presenting his opponent with such a triad the non-cognitivist forces him to say which one he is prepared to reject, for he cannot hold all three without inconsistency.

1 The belief–desire theory of action is valid.
2 A moral opinion, when combined with other beliefs of the agent, can motivate him by providing him with reason to act. (Internalism)
3 Moral opinions are purely cognitive.

The non-cognitivist accepts 1 and 2 and uses them to unseat 3. Since the realist must accept 3 he has to reject 1 or 2. Yet the first two propositions, as the non-cognitivist insists, are highly plausible.

The non-cognitive nature of attitudes

It is essential to this non-cognitivist argument that a moral attitude is either solely a desire or at least incorporates a desire. How does this square with the earlier claim that moral attitudes are non-cognitive because they are feelings or emotions? These two suggestions are not necessarily in conflict. Emotions and feelings are complex states and many of them incorporate desires as an essential part. Thus it is in the nature of fear to want to escape from the object of fear. To love someone involves wanting him or her to be happy. It is characteristic of a feeling of depression that there is little or nothing that the agent cares about or wants to do. A feeling of pain is something we shun. There is no reason why moral attitudes should not be thought of as feelings or emotions which themselves incorporate an element of desire.

Such a theory makes room for a wide range of moral response within a simple overall framework. Our attitude towards any course of action must take one of three basic forms: in favour, opposed or neutral. But within those three basic categories of reaction there is room for a wealth of detailed and subtle variation. We can be displeased by the wrong action of another, or outraged and indignant, or merely disappointed and hurt. What all these have in common is that they are all forms of disapproval; where they differ is in the precise nature of the emotional response.

2.4 MORAL LANGUAGE

In 1.3 we saw how the concepts of belief, truth and reality are intimately connected. A belief is true just if things are, in reality, the way they are believed to be; otherwise it is false. An alternative way of making the point would be to talk about how things are, about the facts. Thus a belief is true just if it fits the facts. These concepts are also intimately connected to the linguistic notion of a *statement*. A statement is true just if things are the way it states them to be – if it fits the facts – and false otherwise. A statement is the natural linguistic expression of a belief.

We have seen that the non-cognitivist believes that

1 there is no moral reality;
2 moral convictions are attitudes and not beliefs;
3 moral attitudes cannot be true or false;
4 moral issues are questions of value, not of fact.

It is not surprising that, having rejected the idea of a moral reality, of moral truth and of moral facts many non-cognitivists have also held that moral utterances cannot be statements or, more plausibly, not *merely* statements. The search for an adequate alternative account helped philosophers to recognize that there are a great many things we can do with words; we can not only make statements but also give promises, christen children, and ask questions. Some kinds of speech act seem particularly suggestive in relation to moral language: we can use words to vent our feelings, express our preferences, issue orders and offer advice. If we recall that non-cognitivists have closely linked moral attitudes to action via the notions of feeling and desire then we shall not be surprised by the range of options that they have come up with. It has been variously suggested that moral utterances are used to: express the feelings of approval or disapproval of the speaker (Ayer and Stevenson); arouse feelings in the hearer or persuade him to act in a way approved of by the speaker (Stevenson); offer advice on what to do (Hare).

It may look therefore as if, at the point where it needs to give a positive account of the function of moral language, non-cognitivism fragments into a bewildering array of proposals. However, all the plausible accounts have a common structure which underlies the differences in detail. The division between fact and value, with which we are now becoming familiar, finds linguistic expression in a distinction between two radically different kinds of utterance or speech act: describing and evaluating. The former is allied to the notion of a statement; in describing something I state how things *are*. As we have seen, a statement is the natural expression of a belief. In evaluating we express not our beliefs but our attitudes. To evaluate something is to assess it favourably or unfavourably. We are not just describing the facts but reacting to them in a positive or negative manner.

To have a favourable attitude to a course of action is, as we have seen, to have a desire or preference that that course of action be taken. It seems natural, therefore, to suppose that the purpose of evaluation is to provide guidance on what to choose. Evaluating, we might suggest, is closely related to advising or ordering; that is, telling people what to do, or *prescribing* some course of action. If I am buying a car or a home computer I may ask you for advice. In pointing out the good and bad features of each make and coming to an overall conclusion about which is the best buy you will be evaluating the competitors in order to give me the guidance I requested.

Language offers a host of ways in which I can express my evaluations and there is no particular grammatical form that signals that I am evaluating. However, there are a good many words that speakers typically use when they are evaluating and their presence is often the signal that enables the hearer to interpret correctly the force of the speaker's remarks. There are not only very general terms of evaluation such as 'good', 'bad', 'right' and 'wrong' but also a wealth of terms that enable us to evaluate things in very specific ways – 'intelligent', 'courageous', 'gaudy', 'imaginative' and so on. We might say of these terms that they have *evaluative meaning* as well as *descriptive meaning*.

To understand the descriptive meaning of a term is to grasp the range of things that it picks out. I understand the descriptive meaning of 'panda' when I know that it picks out an animal of a certain kind. Some words only have descriptive meaning. To call something a panda is simply to describe it, not to evaluate it. We have fully grasped the meaning of the word 'panda' when we have grasped what an animal must be like in order for it to have that term correctly applied to it.

A word has evaluative meaning if its use implies a favourable or unfavourable attitude on the part of the speaker. If I read a reference on a candidate described as intelligent, conscientious and loyal then I know that the writer approves of him or her, at least in those respects. Terms that have evaluative meaning normally have descriptive meaning as well. I have not understood what is meant by intelligence unless I understand what sort of skills and attributes someone needs to display to have that term applied to him or her. In the case of evaluative terms, however, a grasp of the descriptive meaning is not sufficient for a full understanding of the term. A speaker who did not grasp that such terms are normally applied only to things which the speaker evaluates favourably (or unfavourably, depending on the term in question) would show an inadequate understanding of the language. For example, a foreigner who was learning English would have shown that he had a grip on the descriptive meaning of the word 'nigger' if he correctly applied it to blacks and withheld it from whites and coloureds. But he would show the incompleteness of his mastery of his new language and risk considerable embarrassment, or worse, if he failed to realize that it is a term of racial abuse. There is a difference of meaning between 'nigger' and 'black', but it is not a difference in descriptive meaning.

Of course, a word can change its evaluative meaning over time. To describe a political system as democratic has not always been to praise it; 'hussy' was once a term of endearment. This does not show, however, that the evaluative nuance is too impermanent to be part of its meaning, for the descriptive meaning of a word can change just as quickly. A word can also come to acquire an evaluative meaning because it picks out features which some group of speakers find desirable. Thus the word 'tubular', which might be thought to be a clear case of a word with precise descriptive meaning and no evaluative meaning, has become, among surfers on the west coast of the USA, a term of general approbation without specific descriptive force. The reason for this change lies in the preference of surfers for waves that are tubular in shape; a tubular wave makes for a good surf-ride, and so, by extension, (almost) anything good can be called tubular, whatever its shape.

Putting 'inverted commas' round an evaluative term

As we have seen, when a speaker applies a term which has favourable evaluative meaning to some object, person or course of action there is an implication that he is thereby expressing his approval of whatever it is. And similarly with terms of disapproval. That implication can, however, be cancelled. This can be done explicitly; a hard-line Conservative might retort to a common criticism of Margaret Thatcher by saying 'I admit she is ruthless, but I don't think that is necessarily a bad thing.' Or it may be done implicitly. Irony can be used to achieve the effect of distancing the speaker from the normal evaluative implications of his words. I may agree with my well-meaning vicar that the village busybody is a very pious person, but in such a way that it would be obvious to anyone except, I hope, the vicar, that I do not regard that brand of piety as a good thing. In ironic usage one can almost hear the inverted commas round the word.

Where the speaker uses a term of approval, but does not use it to approve, he is not, on the non-cognitivist account, using it in its normal or primary sense. For it is standardly used to express approval and the speaker is not using it in that way, but is indicating by his tone of voice or the context that he dissociates himself from the evaluative stance which its use normally implies. He is using the term only to describe and not to evaluate. So we might say that he is using the word in what Hare called (see, for instance, 1952, ch. 7.5) an 'off-colour' or 'inverted-commas' sense of the term.

Describing and evaluating

Evaluative terms standardly have descriptive as well as evaluative meaning. It follows that we should not think of evaluating and describing as exclusive activities, so that if I am doing one I cannot also be doing the other. If I call your action generous or courageous then I am both describing it as being of a certain type, and expressing my approval of it. To evaluate *is* to make a statement, but it is to do *more* than just make a statement.

The recognition that a speaker can use a moral utterance both to describe and to evaluate has consequences for the account of the distinction between beliefs and attitudes. Non-cognitivism is not committed to the view that, since a moral utterance expresses an attitude, it cannot also express a belief. It can do both. If I hold that Captain Oates' sacrifice at the South Pole was courageous then I both have a belief about what kind of thing he did and also have an attitude of approval towards it. What distinguishes a purely factual opinion from an evaluative one is that the former is solely a belief, whereas the latter involves having an attitude as well as holding a belief.

Meaning and the fact-value gap

The non-cognitivist alleges that there is a connection between his theory that evaluative terms have a special kind of meaning and his scepticism about the possibility of justifying an evaluative stance. To trace this connection we need to look more closely at the way we would normally set about justifying our moral views.

When someone challenges one of my moral opinions I may seek to defend it by citing reasons that support it. I may mention various facts which I believe establish my case. I am, say, a vegetarian and wish to convince you that eating meat is morally wrong. There are a whole host of things I might mention: I could draw attention to the suffering of animals in factory farm units, on cattle trucks or in the slaughter-house; I could point out that cattle rearing is an inefficient way of producing protein and that if humans ate the grain now fed to beef cattle world starvation could be eliminated. This raises an important question in ethics: What is the relation between the facts that I cite as evidence for my moral opinions and those opinions themselves? I offer these facts as evidence for my conclusions, but could someone accept the evidence and reject the conclusion?

It might be thought that, at least in favourable cases, I could prove that some moral judgement was the correct one. There might be well-established factual evidence which conclusively established my contention. Suppose someone suggested that it was morally acceptable to induce heroin addiction in young children. There is a wealth of medical evidence that heroin addiction causes pain, illness and, eventually, early death. Once we accept the medical evidence how could we resist the conclusion that inducing heroin addiction in young children is morally wrong? Surely, if morality forbids anything it forbids causing great suffering to helpless people without any conceivable gain.

The non-cognitivist, however, denies that any set of factual premises could ever *conclusively* establish an evaluative conclusion. To accept an evaluative conclusion is to be motivated to act on it. To accept a piece of factual evidence is to form a belief. But however many beliefs an agent forms they will never motivate him. For beliefs alone are not, according to the belief–desire thesis, sufficient to motivate the agent. From believing some factual evidence to accepting an evaluative conclusion is always an extra step – a step the agent can rationally refuse to take. As we saw in 1.2, he has to decide what values to accept, what attitudes to adopt; no amount of factual evidence can force him to make that decision one way rather than another.

The point is often put more technically as the claim that no set of factual premises can *entail* an evaluative conclusion. If one statement entails another then one cannot consistently accept the first but reject the second. A relation of entailment between two propositions is often held to rest on meaning. Take a simple example: 'The Pope is a bachelor' entails 'The Pope is unmarried'. Given that 'bachelor' means 'unmarried man' someone who accepted the first and denied the second would be contradicting himself. Accepting the second proposition commits one to nothing over and above what was involved in accepting the first and that is why it is inconsistent to accept the first and reject the second.

How can we be certain, in advance of looking at particular examples, that no descriptive premises can entail an evaluative conclusion? Since entailment depends on meaning, the non-cognitivist can use the division between descriptive and evaluative meaning to explain and justify his claim that there is a gap between any set of factual premises and an evaluative conclusion, a gap which no entailment relation can ever bridge. In the case of an argument with factual premises and an evaluative conclusion the premises will only have descriptive meaning. But the conclusion, as well as having descriptive meaning, will also have evaluative meaning. Hence, accepting an evaluative conclusion would always commit one to accepting something that one was not committed to in accepting the descriptive premises. To accept the evaluative conclusion would, as we have seen, commit one to taking up a particular evaluative attitude, whereas accepting the descriptive premises is compatible with adopting any attitude, or none. The claim that there is a fact–value gap turns out to be the reflection, in terms of logic, of the claim that accepting a set of beliefs does not commit one to taking up any particular attitude.

For the greater part of this century the claim that there is a fact–value gap took on the status of holy writ. The importance of the claim lies in the limitation it seems to place on the bringing forward of factual information as a means of settling moral disagreement. One's opponent might accept every factual statement that one made and yet consistently refuse to accept one's moral conclusion. Thus moral disagreements, unlike factual disagreements, do not seem to be rationally resolvable merely by the production of further factual evidence. But that leaves the question: How are moral disagreements to be resolved? Before we can answer that we need to tackle the more basic question: What, on this theory, *is* moral disagreement?

2.5 TRUTH

In 1.2 we saw that, because non-cognitivism denies that there is a moral reality and insists that moral opinions are attitudes rather than beliefs, it seems committed to denying that there can be moral truth. The non-cognitivist account of moral language appears to reinforce that commitment. If evaluating is thought of as more closely related to ordering or advising than to stating or describing then we have further grounds for claiming that non-cognitivism leaves no room for moral truth. A statement or a description is always assessable as true or false; if an utterance cannot have a truth-value then it is not a statement. Advice, on the other hand, can be sound or unsound, timely or misplaced, but it cannot be true. An order can be legitimate or unauthorized, reasonable or absurd, but not true or false.

We saw in the last section that it would be a mistake to suppose that describing and evaluating are mutually exclusive activities. If I describe someone in a reference as honest and trustworthy then I am both describing the sort of person he is and expressing my approval of that trait in his character. This may seem to leave a loophole for truth. It seems natural to suppose that the descriptive aspect of my utterance is assessable for truth or falsity in just the way any other statement is; the factual information I am relaying to my audience may be true or false. If it later turns out that he has been embezzling a fortune from his employer and spreading malicious gossip about his colleagues then my *description* of him was just false.

This admission does not, however, give the non-cognitivist the right to talk of moral utterances as being true or false. For what is distinctive about moral judgements is not their descriptive aspect, which they share with factual judgements, but their evaluative function. If it is natural to suppose that the descriptive element in a moral judgement can be assessed for truth or falsity it is equally natural to suppose that the evaluative element cannot have a truth-value. In so far as moral judgements are expressions of attitude, rather than of belief, they cannot be assessed as true or false. So there still seems to be no room for *moral* truth; there is no question of a moral attitude being true or false. In trying to decide between conflicting moral attitudes about some moral issue, such as whether abortion is morally permissible, we cannot suppose that one attitude is the true one.

Moral disagreement without truth

We have seen that the non-cognitivist faces a sceptical challenge about justification; we may doubt whether, on his account, there is any way in which moral disagreements can be rationally resolved. However, if there is no room for moral truth then non-cognitivism faces an even more fundamental challenge: Can it even make sense of the suggestion that there are moral disagreements?

Suppose we take disagreement about the facts as our model. To disagree with someone on a factual question is to hold that the other person is mistaken or in error; to hold, in short, that he has false beliefs. When two people disagree about some factual question their beliefs are inconsistent with one another in the sense that both of them cannot be true. But if reference to truth is essential in an explanation of what it is to disagree then, if there is no moral truth, there is no room for moral disagreement. We can make room for a conflict of moral views only if we can give an account of moral disagreement that does not appeal to the concept of truth.

The non-cognitivist answers this objection by distinguishing between disagreement in belief and disagreement in attitude. The former type of disagreement is to be spelled out in terms of truth but the latter is not. What other sort of disagreement can there be? The non-cognitivist once again appeals to the connection between a moral attitude and action. As well as disagreeing about what is the case, the facts, we can disagree about what to do. If we are on a date and you want to go to the cinema and I want to go dancing then we do genuinely disagree. We can use the latter type of conflict as a model for moral disagreement. When two people disagree about a moral question then they are disagreeing about what is to be done, rather than about the facts. Such disagreements, though different from disagreements in belief, are clearly important and often need to be resolved if decisions about what to do are to be made.

Some disagreements in attitude may be based on disagreement in belief. It may be that the only reason why we disagree about whether taxes should be cut is because we disagree about the effect of that measure on the rates of unemployment. If we could get agreement in belief we would have agreement in attitude also. Even where the disagreement in attitude can be resolved in this way we can still distinguish the two sorts of disagreement: disagreement in belief is a difference of opinion on the facts; disagreement in attitude is, at least potentially, a conflict about what should be done.

Reinstating moral truth

Many non-cognitivists have shown an understandable reluctance to abandon the notion of moral truth. We do speak of moral opinions as being true or false; is there any way that the non-cognitivist can allow that, despite the arguments we have encountered, such talk is legitimate? He might begin by reminding us that responding to what someone else says by saying 'That's true' has the down to earth function of expressing agreement with the speaker. If the speaker is expressing a belief then my saying that his statement is true simply avoids the long-winded effort of repeating what he said. Since beliefs can be true or false this way of expressing agreement is entirely appropriate. But it is also the case, as we have just seen, that two people may agree in attitude as well as in belief. By a natural extension, the non-cognitivist suggests, it is unexceptionable to use the expression 'That's true' to express agreement in attitude with the speaker. So we can *talk* of moral attitudes as being true or false. In using such expressions we are doing nothing more than expressing our assent to, or rejection of, the attitudes in question. This usage does not commit us to abandoning any of the tenets the non-cognitivist holds dear. In particular, it does not commit us to the existence of a moral reality or to the view that moral opinions are purely cognitive.

While this neat solution may explain why it is permissible to talk of moral truth it may appear simply to bypass the kinds of worry that were raised by the original suggestion that there is no room in moral thought for the notion of truth. We are still left, for example, with the possibility, first raised in 1.2, that there might be an indefinite number of internally consistent but incompatible moral systems.

This non-cognitivist response to the first challenge to the theory (see 2.2) explains why we employ the notion of moral truth but insists that no realist conclusions should be drawn from this fact. This concession should not disguise the fact that ethics is still seen, on this view, as an area in which there is no room for the idea of truth as something independent of the views of any individual.

2.6 JUSTIFICATION AND SCEPTICISM

If there are no moral facts then there is nothing external to which I can appeal to justify my moral position. I cannot simply appeal to the non-moral facts, because the non-moral facts do not themselves determine what attitudes I should take. Even if, however, there are no external constraints on what moral views I may justifiably hold there may yet be internal constraints. The non-cognitivist maintains that a person's moral attitudes must be internally consistent. How are we to understand consistency here? The non-cognitivist conceives of a value judgement as the selection, by the judger, of some non-evaluative features for favourable or unfavourable evaluation. Consistency is then naturally thought of as continuing to apply the same evaluation to the same features wherever and whenever they occur.

As an illustration of how this works, in an area of non-moral choice, take the attempts by consumer magazines to evaluate different makes of car. The writers have a set of features which they regard as desirable in cars – a car is good if it has low fuel consumption, is comfortable, holds the road when cornering, and so on. Each car is assessed for each of these features. Consistency demands that if one car is praised for its low fuel consumption then so should any car which is equally, or even more, economical. Consistency also demands that where two cars are alike in all the features which are being evaluated they should get the same overall rating. Thus it would be inconsistent for the magazine to say that the Honda was a better buy than the Ford if they were alike in all the relevant features.

If we apply this model to moral thought we see that it would be inconsistent to think that truth-telling or loyalty was a good trait in one person but not in another. Furthermore, if there were two actions which were exactly alike in all the morally relevant respects then consistency requires that I make the same moral judgement about both of them. These constraints appear unexceptionable but undemanding, for two reasons. Firstly, they do not tell me what I must say in any one case, they only tell me that whatever I say in the one case I must go on and say the same thing in the next similar case. Or, if I do not wish to say the same in the second case then I must, in consistency, change my first judgement to conform to my views about the second. Secondly, since my final choice between courses of action is likely to depend on weighing up a whole range of factors, some of which favour one course and some another, the chances that I shall come across two actions which are exactly alike in the relevant respects seem too slim for this to be a constraint at all.

There is also a respect in which a whole moral system may be inconsistent. The set of moral principles that I hold may generate incompatible answers to the question: What should I do in this particular case? I may, for example, have adopted the principle that I ought to keep my word. I may also hold that I ought never to divulge a confidence. Suppose my business partner and I have promised each other that we shall not keep from each other any information that might be relevant to the running of the firm. One of our employees approaches me with what he claims is a personal problem which he wishes to discuss in confidence. It emerges, however, that the information he has given to me does, in fact, have a bearing on the work of the company. What am I to do? One of my principles lays down that I should tell my partner and the other that I should not. Clearly, something has to give. I cannot go on holding both principles to be exceptionless without inconsistency. I must modify one or the other by allowing exceptions, or admit that one of them can override the other. Which one I modify is, of course, up to me.

Once again the burden of consistency appears to be a light one. For all we have said so far there might be an indefinite number of consistent moral systems, with no method of determining which of them is correct, or even whether any one is better than any other. The requirement of consistency seems to fall short of providing a complete theory of justification in ethics. Some writers, such as Hare, have claimed that more mileage can be got from the notion of consistency than I have here allowed. Hare's argument will be examined in chapter 11 but, to anticipate the conclusions there, other constraints have to be added to consistency to get the results Hare wants.

Can even this limited internal constraint on moral systems be justified? A sceptic about the possibility of moral justification might claim that even this little is too much. No reason has been given, he may complain, to justify the claim that our moral attitudes must be consistent. Beliefs, he will admit, have to be consistent because, if they are not, there is no chance that they can all be true. But what is wrong with inconsistent attitudes? Why is inconsistency a vice in this case?

The non-cognitivist explains the need for consistency by appealing, yet again, to the connection between moral attitudes and action. If moral attitudes are to guide actions, whether one's own or other people's, then we must know how to apply them when we come across new cases. Advice that is not consistent is no help at all in telling one what to do. If my consumer magazine offers guidelines for choosing a car which turn out to conflict then it is no use to me when I go to the car saleroom. This is just as true of moral advice.

It is worth repeating that the requirement that we be consistent does not mean that we cannot change our minds. We can, over time, change the content of our principles. When we do so, however, we must revise all our judgements, including ones that we might now make about earlier actions of ours, if we are to avoid the charge of inconsistency.

2.7 OBSERVATION

Just as the non-cognitivist theory appears to leave no room for the notion of moral truth, for there is nothing for my moral responses to be true of, so it seems to rule out the observation of moral properties for there are no such properties to observe. There is a strand in non-cognitivist thought that has seen this conclusion as obvious. Hume, who is the classical source of much non-cognitivist thought, puts the case starkly (1978, pp. 468–9):

Take any action allowed to be vicious; wilful murder, for instance. Examine it in all lights and see if you can find that matter of fact . . . which you call *vice*. In whichever way you take it, you only find certain passions, motives, volitions and thoughts. . . . The vice entirely escapes you, as long as you consider the object. You can never find it till you turn your reflection into your own breast, and find a sentiment of disapprobation, which arises in you, towards that action.

It is true that Hume is asking us to *imagine* a case of wilful murder but it is clear that he would deny that an eyewitness could observe the wrongness of such an act. In this respect, he may claim to avoid a problem which besets the moral realist. For the realist, who does believe that moral properties form part of the fabric of the world, will have to explain how we detect them. But, the non-cognitivist suggests, if they do exist they cannot be detected by any of the normal methods of observation. They cannot be seen or touched or smelt. The non-cognitivist challenges the realist to tell us by what means we do detect evaluative properties, if it is not by sense-observation. Will he not have to resort to some utterly mysterious faculty of moral intuition?

2.8 REALITY AND APPEARANCE

The non-cognitivist is committed to the view that a complete description of what there is in the world would not mention any evaluative property. A proper understanding of what value is shows that it is not the sort of thing that could form part of the fabric of the world. We cannot, however, fully evaluate any claim that only certain things and properties would feature in a complete account of reality unless we have a way of determining what falls on which side of the divide between appearance and reality. The non-cognitivist should provide some principled account of what would figure in a complete account of the nature of reality and what would be excluded.

Scientific method has provided a spectacularly successful tool for uncovering the nature of the world in which we live. By careful observation, experiment and measurement the physical sciences have revealed more and more about the nature of matter and the laws which govern its behaviour. It is natural, at least in our day, to take science to be the proper method for discovering the nature of reality. If we think in that way we shall suppose that only those entities and properties which figure in the scientific account of the world really exist. So not every aspect of experience will be thought of as experience of the real. Experience will be thought of as a combination of elements contributed by the world and elements contributed by us, the beings who are having the experience. So, if experience appears to reveal to us properties other than properties that figure in scientific theories, then those properties must be consigned to the status of mere appearance. They are aspects of the way we experience the world, not parts of that world itself.

While science claims to discover many strange entities and properties, such as sub-atomic particles which have 'charm' or 'colour', evaluative properties, such as beauty and goodness, do not figure in a scientific account of the world. If what science does not tell us about is not really there, then it follows that goodness and beauty are not properties of the world. The evaluative features of our experience are contributed by us.

The fact that science has been so successful in investigating the nature of the physical universe is not, in itself, sufficient reason for claiming that only the entities and properties mentioned by science really exist. To think that this is so without further justification is to fall into the error of *scientism*, the uncritical acceptance of scientific investigation as the only legitimate method of finding out the nature of reality. There may be other aspects of the world, such as value, which are not sensibly investigated by the quantitative experimental techniques of natural science, but which are not, on that account, any less real. An appeal to the scientific world outlook will only support the claim that there is no moral reality if we can provide a conception of what it is to be real that validates the claim of science to give an exhaustive account of what there is. Such a conception of reality is available and I shall discuss it in chapter 4.

2.9 CONCLUSION

We saw in 2.2 that non-cognitivism faced four challenges. The first three all complained that non-cognitivism undermined beliefs that we have about morality. It seemed to deny that there is room for moral truth, for the justification of our moral views, or for moral observation. In all three cases the non-cognitivist response was primarily one of staunch defiance, supplemented by explanations of how the objector might come to be mistaken about these matters. While we may properly talk of moral truth we must not be misled by that into thinking that a substantial theory of truth, of the kind available in science, is appropriate in ethics. While the constraint of internal consistency places some limits on what moral positions may justifiably be held, there is no method that gives rationally acceptable grounds for preferring any one consistent moral system to any other. We cannot observe moral properties because there are none there to observe.

In taking this stance the non-cognitivist is, in effect, adopting an *error theory* of morality. To accept non-cognitivism, on this view, is to recognize that our current moral practice is infected with error and stands in need of revision. At present, moral thought and discourse incorporates realist assumptions: that moral properties are part of the fabric of the world and that our job is to discover which is the correct answer to various moral problems. To accept non-cognitivism will not, if the error theory is correct, leave our current moral thought entirely unchanged. For example, in our present moral thought it makes sense to wonder whether my moral views are mistaken. There is room for such a thought because we distinguish between what I think or feel about a moral quesion and the truth of the matter. It appears that, if we were to accept non-cognitivism, that thought would no longer be available to us.

Much of our moral thought appears to be realist in character. To adopt moral realism would, therefore, not require any significant alteration in our present moral practice. Might this fact not itself constitute a reason for preferring moral realism to non-cognitivism?

FURTHER READING

The simplest version of non-cognitivism is found in Ayer (1946, ch. 6). It was developed by Stevenson (1937, 1938, 1948) and Hare (1952, 1963). Its roots are in Hume's *A Treatise of Human Nature* (1978), especially Book III,

Part I, and in his *Enquiry Concerning the Principles of Morals* (1975). Urmson (1968) is a clear critical study of the emotivism of Ayer and Stevenson.

On 2.3   The classical source of the belief–desire theory is Hume's *Treatise*, Book II, Part III, section iii (1978, pp. 413–8). For its irrealist implications in ethics see Hume's *Enquiry*, Appendix I (1975, pp. 285–94) and Blackburn (1984, pp. 187–9). An incisive account of the debate about internalism is found in Nagel (1978, chs 2–3). The close connection between moral commitment and action is the cornerstone of Hare's prescriptivism (Hare, 1952, 1963).

On 2.4   Stevenson (1963, ch. 2) distinguishes cognitive from emotive meaning. Hare (1952; 1963, esp. ch. 2) distinguishes descriptive from evaluative or prescriptive meaning. For a critical history of the fact–value gap see Prior (1949). For a non-cognitivist account of the gap and its importance see Hare (1952, esp. chs 5–7).

On 2.5   Stevenson (1963, pp. 214–20) attempts to reinstate moral truth after earlier denying its possibility.

On 2.9   Questions about consistency in ethics are raised by Williams (1965, 1966). The main defender of the error theory is Mackie (1977, ch. 1). Note that Mackie confusingly equates moral scepticism with what I have called moral irrealism.

3

Moral Realism – an Outline

3.1 THE PRESUMPTION OF REALISM

The moral realist denies the existence of that sharp and significant division between fact and value which is the hallmark of his opponent's position. In the realist's view, moral opinions are beliefs which, like other beliefs, are determined true or false by the way things are in the world. It follows that moral questions are as much questions of fact as any other. In rejecting the divide between facts and values the realist rejects the other distinctions which stem from that basic contrast, such as that between beliefs and attitudes, or between descriptive and evaluative meaning. Where the non-cognitivist sees division, the realist finds unity.

The realist maintains that the structure of our ordinary moral thought supports his case. Moral utterances appear to be perfectly ordinary statements which are capable of being true or false in just the way that other statements are. We believe that some moral views are correct and others incorrect and that in morality, as in other areas of life, we can be mistaken about which is which. Moreover, our experience of the world seems to include experience of value; we can see the beauty of a summer landscape or the goodness in some-one's face. The main realist charge against non-cognitivism is that it gives a seriously distorted account of the nature of morality; if non-cognitivism were correct then many of our present moral practices and our beliefs about the structure of moral thought would have to be revised or abandoned.

The realist can concede that there are aspects of our moral experi-ence which, at first sight, may seem to support the non-cognitivist case, but he will claim that they too are best understood in a realist context. He can well admit, for example, that morality is an area of human debate in which we find a marked degree of disagreement about many issues (although he would deplore the tendency of some non-cognitivists to play down the extent of underlying agreement on many other moral matters). He insists, however, that the existence of widespread disagreement is not in itself evidence that morality is an area in which we cannot expect there to be right and wrong answers. On the contrary, there can only be controversy and argument where the disputants believe there to be the possibility of truth.

We saw in 1.1 that the non-cognitivist also makes great play of the fact that we often regard moral decisions as personal ones which should be made by the person concerned without interference from others. Once more, the realist can accept this point, while again deploring the tendency to exaggerate it. There are, after all, many occasions on which we think it right to interfere when the action that someone proposes to take will seriously damage the well-being or interests of another. What he denies is that we need to see tolerance, where it is appropriate, as springing from a belief that there are no right answers in such cases. Tolerance is better seen as itself the morally right reaction in some cases – a recognition of the other person's autonomy, of his right to run his own life. Realism and tolerance are not incompatible.

The realist maintains that we should take the nature of our moral experience seriously. In seeking to discover what the world is like we have to start with the way our experience represents the world as being – where else could we start? The realist insists on an obvious, but crucial, methodological point: there is a presumption that things are the way we experience them as being – a presumption that can only be overthrown if weighty reasons can be brought to show that our experience is untrustworthy or misleading. Moral value is presented to us as something independent of our beliefs or feelings about it; something which may require careful thought or attention to be discovered. There is a presumption, therefore, that there is a moral reality to which we can be genuinely sensitive.

Realist strategy

Even if the realist can provide detailed evidence to make good his claim that non-cognitivism seriously distorts the nature of our moral thought this will not be enough to prove his case. The appeal to the nature of our moral experience, to what we might call the *moral phenomenology*, represents the starting point for an argument, not a conclusion. Only a presumption in favour of realism would have been established and presumptions can be defeated. Nevertheless, the starting point of the realist argument influences its shape. Just as, in a criminal trial, the presumption that the defendant is innocent until he is proved guilty places the burden of proof on the prosecution so, the realist claims, the burden of proof in this debate rests with the non-cognitivist. The realist's contention is that he has only to rebut the arguments designed to persuade us that moral realism is philosophically untenable in order to have made out his case. His strategy is thus initially defensive; he seeks to show that his opponent's arguments are, at best, not decisive.

Because of the defensive nature of this first realist response it sometimes appears as if the non-cognitivist is the only one who is making innovative or interesting philosophical moves; the realist is merely appealing to common sense and popular opinion. This impression is misleading, since the moral realist does have a positive philosophical contribution to make, and one that has repercussions elsewhere in philosophy.

The non-cognitivist supports his case by painting a plausible and attractive picture of the world in which realism about values turns out to be untenable. In filling out that picture he draws argumentative support from well-respected positions in related areas of philosophy. Given the force of that case the realist cannot be content to remain on the defensive but must take the positive step of developing an alternative account of the way the world is – an account in which realism about moral values has a proper place. Since theories in areas of philosophy other than ethics are relevant to the debate a complete defence of his position will necessarily involve forays into other parts of the subject. Any theory of ethics is, in the end, only as plausible as the complete picture of the world of which it forms a part. Nevertheless, the realist will claim, the presumption in favour of realism remains. If it turns out that there are no decisive argumentative grounds for rejecting one of these rival pictures of the world and embracing the other then we will have good reason to prefer the moral realist's account, because it accords better with the nature of our moral experience.

3.2 MORAL REALITY

The realist is committed, as I expressed it at the beginning of the chapter, to the claim that 'moral opinions are beliefs which, like other beliefs, are determined true or false by the way things are in the world.' This way of putting it, true so far as it goes, serves to distinguish moral realism from non-cognitivism, but it does not adequately capture what is distinctive about the realist position. To understand what more needs to be added we must examine the debate between realists and irrealists, since non-cognitivism is not the only form of moral irrealism.

Debates between realists and irrealists are by no means confined to ethics but occur in virtually all areas of philosophy. The realist affirms that some particular kind of thing or property exists; the irrealist denies it. As so often in philosophy, we can become clearer about just what the realist is affirming by finding out what it would be to deny it; that is, by looking more closely at irrealism in general.

Debates about whether some entity or property exists are common in the history of human thought, and they are sometimes settled on the side of irrealism. There is a large range of things in whose existence we have ceased to believe: fairies, witches, phlogiston, the ether, the four humours of the body. In denying the existence of such entities we have typically rejected all talk of such things as false. We have looked at the world and found that it contains no fairies. If there are no fairies at the bottom of anybody's garden then there can be no facts about them and no true stories in which they figure. Any tendency to talk as if there really were such beings must be rejected as the product of delusion or fancy.

Philosophers are notoriously given to claiming that certain sorts of thing or property do not exist. From within some particular philosophical perspective certain kinds of fact can appear utterly mysterious; it may seem that the world could not contain any such things. Indeed, there is almost nothing whose existence has not been denied by some philosopher – physical objects, conscious states, numbers and, of course, values. As with the refusal to allow fairies into one's scheme of things, it is possible for a philosopher who denies the existence of something to hold that all claims about such things are simply false. Or, even more drastically, he can declare all statements about the offending entities to be unintelligible or meaningless.

Such a stark rejection of some large area of human thought and discourse would, however, raise serious questions about what we have all been doing when we talked or thought in the rejected manner. The realization, as I grow up, that there are no fairies and no Santa Claus only requires a small adjustment to my view of the world, one which I can easily accommodate. But how could it be that all of us were quite mistaken in supposing there to be physical objects, such as tables, chairs and other people; or what sense can we make of the thought that, in using moral language, we have all been in error, or even speaking nonsense? These beliefs and practices are too deeply rooted in our experience and lives to be simply rejected as mistaken or meaningless. The irrealist must try another tack. He must show that we can continue to talk in the way in question without implying that there are entities of the objectionable kind.

There are various strategies that philosophers have employed which enable them to be irrealist about some area of thought without requiring that we give up talking and thinking in that way. One such strategy, with which we are already familiar in ethics, is non-cognitivism. Moral non-cognitivism encourages us to go on using moral language but claims that we should see such utterances, not as attempting to state truths about the moral facts, but as having some other, but quite legitimate, purpose. These tactics can be employed elsewhere. It has been suggested that in wondering whether your action was voluntary, I am not enquiring about some puzzling, inaccessible fact concerning the freedom of your will. Rather, I am undecided about what attitude to take towards your action; am I willing to praise or blame you for acting in that way? Similarly, it has been maintained that the statement 'Every event has a cause' expresses not a belief that all events in nature are subject to physical law but a determination not to give up looking for causal explanations. In such a case what appears at first to be the expression of a belief about the facts turns out, on philosophical inspection, to be the expression of an attitude.

Reduction

Not all irrealist positions lend themselves happily to non-cognitivist treatment. An alternative strategy for dealing with claims that seem to commit us to the existence of dubious entities is provided by *reductionism*. The reductionist, finding some area of our discourse problematic, seeks some other way of expressing those thoughts which does not have the same unacceptable implications. His goal is to provide a translation of the exceptionable remarks which both captures the meaning of the original and yet does not carry those contentious implications. The hope is that once we understand the original remarks in the way suggested by the translation we can continue to talk in the old way, which may be shorter, or more convenient in other respects, with a philosophically good conscience. A small example, which I owe to Simon Blackburn, shows how an apparent commitment to the existence of a strange kind of entity can be avoided in this manner (1984, p. 153):

Suppose I tell you that Henry's prestige is enormous. Suppose that you are attached to an ontological doctrine (a theory about what kinds of things exist) – roughly that everything which exists has a place in space and time, and has scientifically measurable properties of weight, charge, velocity etc. Then Henry's prestige seems an odd kind of object: you cannot put it into a bucket or weigh it or measure it – what kind of *thing* is it? Your problem is removed by analyzing the original remark so as to remove reference to this mysterious thing: it means nothing different from this remark: other people admire Henry enormously. If your world-view allows for this kind of fact, then there is nothing further to jib at in talking of prestige.

We saw in 2.8 that someone with the ontological view that Blackburn describes might well find moral properties as puzzling as Henry's prestige. His irrealist tendencies about morality might lead him not to non-cognitivism but to a reductionist analysis of moral utterances along the lines on which Henry's prestige was reduced to manageable proportions. He might suggest, for example, that 'x is wrong' should be translated as 'most people disapprove of x'. On this proposed translation moral remarks do turn out to have a truth value and one which is determined by the way things are in the world. The question 'What is the correct view about this moral issue?' amounts to the question 'What do the majority currently think about this moral issue?' Moral disputes could thus be settled by normal methods of factual investigation, such as conducting an opinion poll.

While such a reductionist account ensures that moral views are true or false in virtue of facts which are independent of the speaker's opinion on the matter, it is nevertheless an irrealist position. For it does not allow that there are *distinctive* moral facts which are independent of our current opinions, waiting to be discovered by our moral enquiries. Moral facts are reduced to facts about people's psychological states. Realism insists that there are moral facts, over and above people's psychological states, including their moral beliefs, in virtue of which those beliefs are true or false; this particular reductionist account denies this.

The realist's claim that there is a distinctive range of moral facts, which are not reducible to other kinds of fact, enables him to distinguish his position from other reductive analyses in ethics which do not attempt to reduce moral facts to some function of people's moral beliefs. It might, for example, be suggested that 'x is right' means the same as 'x is the action which would produce more happiness than any alternative action.' Such a translation makes no reference to anyone's evaluative beliefs and it also ensures that moral judgements have a truth value. But this is also clearly not a realist position. The purpose of the reduction is to show that we can rephrase our moral remarks in such a way that they carry no implication that there is a distinctive range of moral facts – the only facts that we need to refer to are familiar and uncontroversial empirical ones about what makes people happy.

Although reductionism allows us to go on talking in the old way it claims that our moral vocabulary could be dispensed with; everything that we now say by using it could be said, perhaps more long-windedly, in other ways. Both non-cognitivism and realism, by contrast, regard moral language as ineliminable, though for different reasons. For the realist, moral language is needed to describe the moral facts; we cannot do without moral language because we need it to describe an important part of our experience of the world. For the non-cognitivist, moral discourse is not reducible to fact-stating language because we use it not only to describe but also, and more importantly, to evaluate. It is this use of moral language that gets lost in the translation.

Difficulties in reductionism

There is a tension within reductionism between its claim to have provided a successful translation of the old, puzzling, discourse and its claim that the new improved way of putting the matter does not raise the same philosophical perplexity. If the new way of putting things is identical in meaning with the old then any substantive problem would survive translation into the new language. In so far as the new fails to capture what was puzzling in the old it looks as if something must have got lost in the translation. The reductionist reply must be that the problem that prompted the reduction was only apparent. Once we have understood the true content of the old, by putting it in the new way, we see that the original puzzles disappear; they are revealed as mere confusion. But this reply in turn raises the question: What right has anyone to claim to have separated out the true reduced content of the old if the problems raised by the old way of speaking suggested that we did, after all, mean something more than the reductionist will allow?

This problem explains why many reductionist accounts that start off by claiming merely to clarify what we now think end up by being revisionary, suggesting that there is something wrong with our ordinary thought and that it ought to be purged of its errors. As in Orwell's *1984* it turns out, after all, that there are things that could be said in Oldspeak that cannot be said in Newspeak. The standard objection to reductionism in ethics is that none of the proposed reductions looks the least bit plausible as an account of the meaning of our original moral utterances. If they are instead put forward as *substitutes* for our present moral language then it needs first to be shown that there are good reasons for giving up our present way of speaking and thinking.

It would be misleading to suggest that it is possible to determine just what the commitments of our present thought and practice are in such a way that we can always decide whether some proposed translation adequately captures the content of our original thought or offers instead a revision of it. Reflection can raise questions about our current thought which are not determinately settled one way or another by our largely unreflective linguistic practices. This indeterminacy in our thought not only makes it difficult to decide on the merits of some reductive analysis but also clouds the dispute between non-cognitivism and realism. For realist strategy, as we saw in 3.1, rests in large part on the claim that non-cognitivism significantly and unnecessarily distorts our moral thought. In so far as there is doubt about what the commitments of our moral thought are, there must be doubts about the force of these criticisms. It would be just as misleading, however, to overestimate these difficulties in the way of deciding just what our moral utterances mean. We can only allow that we do not always know precisely what we mean against a general background of agreement about the broad purport of our remarks. If this were not so then we would have no idea if we were even discussing the same topic.

Because reductionism, like realism, treats moral utterances as descriptive statements with a truth-value it faces all the objections that the non-cognitivist can bring against realism while having extra problems of its own. In particular both moral realism and moral reductionism face a similar challenge in explaining moral motivation. In 2.3 we saw that any theory that supposes that moral opinions are purely cognitive will have difficulty in accounting for the action-guiding nature of moral thought. The realist needs to meet this challenge if he is to make any headway.

3.3 MORAL MOTIVATION

We saw in 2.3 that one of the strongest arguments for moral non-cognitivism was its success in explaining the close connection between moral commitment and action. The realist was presented with a challenge in the form of an inconsistent triad:

1 The belief–desire theory of action explanation is valid.
2 A moral opinion, when combined with appropriate beliefs of the agent, can motivate the agent by providing him with reason to act. (Internalism)
3 Moral opinions are purely cognitive.

Since the realist accepts 3 he must reject either 1 or 2. Not surprisingly, realists divide into two camps, depending on which proposition they reject.

One camp rejects internalism. They maintain that people's moral beliefs are true or false in virtue of moral facts which are independent of those beliefs but they deny that the recognition that an action is morally right is in itself sufficient to motivate the agent to do it. Moral considerations weigh only with those who care about them, those who have the right sort of desires. Thus an externalist moral realist might conceive of morality as a complex system of rules for promoting human welfare. He could then contend that the question of what is good for people and promotes their well-being is a factual one which can be settled by the study of human beings and societies. On this view, both those in whose lives moral considerations play an important role and those who are unmoved by moral constraints will be in an equally good position to find out what actions are morally required or forbidden, but only the former will see the results of any moral deliberation as having a bearing on how they should live. Since many of us do have some concern that things should go better for our fellow man we naturally give moral reasons weight when we are deciding what to do. The externalist thus has no difficulty in explaining why many people are in fact motivated to act morally. But it is perfectly possible that someone might lack the relevant desires and thus be quite unmoved by moral considerations.

The other camp retains internalism and is thus led to the more radical step of rejecting the belief–desire theory of reasons for action. Since the realist holds that moral opinions are purely cognitive the internalist realist must hold that an agent can be motivated to act by a cognitive state alone. His moral belief is sufficient, maybe in conjunction with other beliefs of his, to provide him with reason to act.

The decision between the rival camps must rest on the relative plausibility of internalism and the belief–desire theory. We saw in 2.3 that the main support for internalism comes from the nature of our moral thought. We do find something very odd in the suggestion that someone might conclude that an action was morally required of him but maintain that he had no reason to do it. We think of an agent's moral commitments as motivating states which can explain why he acted. I shall return to this important debate between internalism and externalism in chapter 9.

Consistently with his general strategy, the main argument the internalist realist deploys against the belief–desire theory is also an argument from moral phenomenology, from the nature of our moral experience. Reflection on what it is like to realize that one is morally required to act in a certain way will, he claims, support his contention that a moral belief can be sufficient to motivate an agent.

The authority of moral demands

It is a striking feature of our moral experience (to which I have already drawn attention in 1.5 and 1.6) that situations in which we find ourselves make moral demands on us; we recognize that we are morally required to act in a certain way. Once we are aware of such a requirement our choice of action seems to be constrained by that recognition. Our response is seen as something demanded by the circumstances in which we are making our choice. In particular, the claims that morality makes on us appear to be quite independent of our desires – they may even conflict with what we want.

On the belief–desire theory no sense can be made of this conception of a moral demand. Moral (or any other) considerations can only provide an agent with reason to act if he has appropriate desires. In the absence of such desires moral constraints will carry no weight with him, nor will we be able to supply any reason why he should conform to them unless we can appeal to some desire that he already possesses.

Since both externalist moral realism and non-cognitivism espouse the belief–desire theory, both appear to distort the nature of our experience of moral requirements. They differ in that non-cognitivism builds the desire to act into a moral attitude whereas externalist realism holds that a moral belief can exist without any desire to act in accordance with it. But both deny the authority of moral demands on which the internalist realist insists. A moral demand is experienced as something to which we must conform and it cannot itself depend on our wants and desires for its authority.

Non-cognitivism, in maintaining that value is the product of the agent's desire, reverses the relation between desirability and desire which we find in moral experience. We take it that we desire certain things because we see them to be desirable; non-cognitivism insists that they are only desirable because we desire them. If an agent has no desire to act in a certain way then he will not hold that course of action to be the right one, for to take up a moral attitude is to be disposed to act in the appropriate way. Externalist realism, by contrast, allows that the question of what courses of action are morally desirable does not depend on what desires the agent may have. Someone who has no concern for human welfare may still recognize that inflicting unnecessary suffering on others is morally wrong. But that recognition is held not to be in itself sufficient to give him a reason to desist from causing such suffering. If he lacks the appropriate desires then he has no reason to act in accordance with moral requirements – they are not seen as authoritative.

We can make the point in another way. The belief–desire theory distinguishes sharply between cognitive states, which do not themselves move the agent towards action, and essentially motivational states, such as desires or preferences. The question then arises: On which side of the fence do moral commitments fall? Are they to be thought of as primarily desires or as beliefs? Here non-cognitivism and externalist realism divide. Because non-cognitivism places them on the desire side of the fence it has no difficulty in regarding them as states that can motivate action, but it distances them from the factual in the doctrine of the fact–value gap (2.4). Externalist realism is happy to view moral questions as factual ones, but distances them from motivation in its claim that moral commitments do not, in themselves, provide the agent with reason to act. Although they disagree about where in this picture to put moral convictions they agree about the picture. In particular, they contend that mere awareness of the facts, of how things are in the world, can never on its own be sufficient to provide the agent with reason to act. Neither party, therefore, can allow room in that picture for an agent's being motivated by a purely cognitive state, by his recognition that that is how the moral facts are. Thus both sides must claim that the apparent authority of moral demands is an illusion.

The internalist realist rejects the terms within which his opponents are conducting the debate. He denies that cognitive states are incapable of moving an agent to act. He can therefore allow that the belief that he is morally required to act is sufficient to move the agent to act, without assistance from a quite different kind of state, a desire. Since he is not saddled with a picture of the mind in which there is drawn a sharp distinction between passive, cognitive states and active, motivating desires, the internalist realist sensibly bypasses the dispute between non-cognitivists and externalist realists as to the side of that fence on which moral commitments are to fall.

The claim that an agent can be motivated by a cognitive state is, as we have seen, in tune with the moral phenomenology; the agent is moved to act by his recognition of a moral requirement, a requirement whose nature and existence are not conditional on any desire that he may happen to have. That it chimes with our moral experience provides a presumption in favour of internalist realism compared with its two rivals. Whether or not that presumption can be developed into a convincing case depends on what turns out to be the most satisfying theory of action-explanation – an issue I take up in chapters 7 to 9. Until then, whenever the two versions of realism diverge, it will be the internalist conception that I discuss.

One possible misconception needs to be removed at this stage. It may be objected that, in rejecting the belief–desire thesis, the internalist realist is committed to the uncomfortable claim that the virtuous person has no desire to act in the way that he does, when he acts in virtue of his belief that a certain course of action is morally required. This view, though it may have appealed to Kant, is excessively austere and surely implausible. It is one of the marks of the truly virtuous person that he does what is right willingly, and perhaps even with pleasure. It would be silly to deny that such a person is doing what he wants to do.

The realist need not deny this. He may quite properly hold that we can attribute to the agent a desire to do the right thing. He can make this concession without jeopardizing his claim that a purely cognitive state can motivate. It is his account of what is involved in ascribing such a desire to the agent that differs markedly from the non-cognitivist's. Having rejected the view that cognitive states are passive, and incapable of motivating the agent, the realist should also reject the view that a desire is necessarily a non-cognitive state. In chapter 7 we shall see how he can develop a theory in which (some) desires can be seen as cognitive states.

Given that theory, the realist can claim that the agent who was motivated by his moral belief did have a desire to act in that way. According to the realist, to ascribe such a desire to the agent, after he has acted, is merely to acknowledge that his moral belief was here sufficient to motivate him. He does not think of the desire as a state separate from the belief. The model provided by the belief–desire thesis is quite different. On that account we are to picture the desire in question as a psychologically distinct and separable element which has to be *added* to the beliefs if the agent is to be motivated. The desire is thought of as a distinct necessary condition of action; in its absence no action would occur, even if the agent's beliefs were to remain unchanged. It is this conception of desire that the internalist realist rejects.

3.4 TRUTH AND MEANING

The argument of the last section is crucial. The claim of non-cognitivism that realism cannot explain the action-guiding nature of moral convictions is a major support for its contention that there is a sharp division between factual beliefs and moral attitudes. The internalist realist's response is two-fold. First, he tries to show that a purely cognitive state, such as a moral belief, can motivate action. Second, he attempts to turn the tables on the non-cognitivist by arguing that it is he, and not the realist, who cannot explain our experience of the way in which our moral commitments guide our actions because he cannot take account of the authority of moral judgements.

If the realist has been successful in disposing of one of the main props supporting the fact–value gap then he can continue to insist that moral convictions are beliefs. His approach to moral language and to truth then emerges naturally and straightforwardly. The elimination of the distinction between factual beliefs and moral attitudes in turn brings with it the collapse of the associated distinction between descriptive and evaluative meaning. Whatever account of meaning we adopt should apply equally well to moral utterances as to other statements. Similarly, moral beliefs will be true or false in just the way that other beliefs are.

Truth

To deny that there are moral truths runs counter to our normal thought and speech. The non-cognitivist sought to avoid that conclusion by reminding us that describing someone else's remark as true or false is a way of endorsing or rejecting the opinion he expressed. Since we can endorse and reject attitudes as well as beliefs, moral utterances can appropriately be thought of as true or false. To the realist, the non-cognitivist's reinstatement of the conception of moral truth appears merely cosmetic. Such a thin account of moral truth, precisely because it does not carry any metaphysical implications of the sort that the non-cognitivist would disown, is unlikely to lay to rest the kinds of worry that were raised by the original suggestion that there was no room in moral thought for the notion of truth. We are still left, for example, with the possibility, first raised in 1.2, that there might be an indefinite number of internally consistent but incompatible moral systems.

The realist can push home this attack by pointing out that the non-cognitivist's attenuated concept of moral truth leaves us without the resources to express, or even think, quite commonplace thoughts. To see this, we need to look at our normal conception of truth which, the realist maintains, is far richer and more substantial than that provided by the thin account. In particular, we think of truth as something independent of the views of any individual. On this richer conception there can be a mismatch between my beliefs and the truth of the matter.

All of us, unless we are unusually arrogant, will admit that we are fallible, that some of our opinions may be, indeed no doubt are, in error.

The non-cognitivist account leaves no room, however, for the thought that I am morally fallible, that some of my moral convictions may be mistaken. I cannot express this thought by supposing that some of them might be false, for that would imply a standard of truth and falsity which was independent of my individual opinion. Nor, obviously, can I suppose that my attitudes may not fit the moral facts, for there are no moral facts for them to fit. The only way that I might express the thought that I am fallible about moral questions is to admit that I may come, at some later stage, to have some different attitudes from the ones that I now have. But this is not what we were looking for. The thought that I might now be in error is not equivalent to the thought that I might come to have some different views later. To admit that my views might change over time is not in itself to express any opinion about whether or not my current views may be mistaken.

Nor can we make sense of the notion of moral perplexity. If there is no truth of the matter, what are we puzzled about? Not about choosing the correct attitude but, presumably, about choosing an attitude which we are prepared to act on. Once again, this is not what we were looking for. To worry about which of two courses of action is the right one is not the same as to worry about which of two choices I can live with.

The realist charge is that non-cognitivism seriously distorts our conception of morality and denies that we can make sense of thoughts that appear perfectly intelligible. By adopting the thin account of truth the non-cognitivist may have disguised the degree to which his understanding of moral thought differs from the normal one but, as the arguments of the last two paragraphs show, differences will still emerge. Even if we allow to the non-cognitivist that there is a sense in which moral attitudes can be said to have a truth-value it is not the same sense as that in which factual beliefs can be true or false. And that is the realist complaint.

Meaning

Since moral utterances are, for the realist, perfectly standard statements expressing the speaker's moral beliefs there is no call for there to be two distinct kinds of meaning to go with the alleged difference between describing how things are and evaluating them. Here, as elsewhere, the realist tears down that fundamental divide between fact and value which determines the structure of non-cognitivist thought.

The non-cognitivist, in explaining the supposed difference between descriptive and evaluative meaning, makes much of the fact that moral utterances are used to evaluate, to offer advice, or to commend. The realist can happily accept that, in making a moral statement, a speaker may also be evaluating some object or advising someone on a course of action. What he denies is that this fact lends support to the doctrine that there are two sorts of meaning. It is indeed possible for a speaker to put almost any remark to more than one use; one utterance may involve the performance of more than one speech act. In telling my fellow-picnickers that there is a bull in the field I may not only be making a statement but also, in that context, warning them and advising them to take evasive action. This does nothing to show that the sentence 'There is a bull in the field' has a special kind of meaning.

The realist can accept that moral remarks are often, though by no means always, used to advise or commend without conceding that any special doctrine of evaluative meaning must be invoked to explain this fact. Given the nature of much moral discussion, it is scarcely surprising that such remarks often occur in a context in which one person is advising another or seeking to choose between alternatives. What the realist denies is that these truths show that words, such as 'good' or 'right', that figure prominently in moral discourse differ in meaning from other sorts of words.

The fact–value gap and moral reasoning

The non-cognitivist makes great play with the supposed gap between facts and values; no set of factual statements, it is claimed, can entail an evaluative conclusion. The realist can agree that, generally speaking, no set of non-moral statements can entail a moral conclusion, but he rejects the non-cognitivist's explanation of why this is so and denies that the gap has the importance the non-cognitivist ascribes to it.

The non-cognitivist believes that the existence of such a gap is to be explained by reference to the distinction between descriptive and evaluative meaning. The realist has a more mundane explanation which does not require the construction of an elaborately bifurcated theory of meaning. We saw in 2.4 that one statement entails another in view of a relation between their meanings. The entailed statement is either equivalent in meaning to the one that entails it, or else it captures some part of the meaning of the other. In rejecting reductionism the realist has rejected the view that moral statements can be translated into remarks that contain no specifically moral terms but which capture the meaning of the originals. If such translation were possible then statements about the non-moral features of actions and agents would entail conclusions about their moral properties. If we reject reductionism then we must not expect to find relations of entailment between the non-moral and the moral.

This is not to deny that there are other important relations between non-moral and moral properties. The realist thinks of the non-moral properties of an action as fixing or determining its moral properties. It is in virtue of various non-moral facts about what happens if someone induces heroin addiction in his children that such a deed would be abhorrent. We all appeal to such non-moral facts as reasons in support of the conclusion that such behaviour would be wrong.

The non-cognitivist may remind us that, since there are no relations of entailment between the non-moral and the moral, anyone can accept the evidence that we produce to support our moral stance and yet reject the conclusion without contradicting himself. The short realist reply to this remark is that it is true but unexciting. It does not show that any moral position is as reasonable or as justified as any other. In justifying any belief one is likely to appeal to other beliefs which support the first belief, but it is comparatively unusual for those other beliefs actually to entail the conclusion he is trying to support. Justifying a belief does not usually involve appealing to entailment relations; in this respect, as in most others, the realist does not think of moral beliefs as any different from other beliefs. It is unreasonable for the non-cognitivist to single out moral reasoning as labouring under a special handicap when it shares this feature with nearly all other reasoning.

The realist may plausibly claim that the undue importance which the non-cognitivist attaches to the fact–value gap stems from his over-demanding view of the nature of moral justification. He supposes that we can only show an opposing moral view to be mistaken by demonstrating that to hold it is irrational in the strong sense that it is actually self-contradictory to do so. This leads him to the claim that any internally consistent (that is, non-self-contradictory) set of moral principles is as well justified as any other. But why, the realist enquires, should we adopt this narrow view of justification in ethics when we do not adopt it elsewhere? It is the non-cognitivist's irrealism that drives him to this restricted conception of moral reasoning. Since there is nothing external to a moral system that can provide evidential support for it, the only criterion of rationality that remains is internal consistency. In rejecting his irrealism the realist can also reject the non-cognitivist's impoverished picture of moral reasoning.

3.5 OBSERVATION

There is one method which we often use to support our assertions which, as 'we have just seen, the non-cognitivist believes to be unavailable in ethics. In many cases, if someone doubts the truth of what I say I can simply ask him to go and look for himself. Sometimes, of course, making the appropriate observation can be difficult and interpretation may be required, but that is not an objection to the method as such. By denying that we can observe moral properties – because there are no moral properties to observe – the non-cognitivist attempts to block this move in the area of morality. If, however, there is a moral reality then we can allow for the possibility of moral observation.

As we saw in 2.7, Hume thought that our ordinary moral experience supported his claim that we cannot observe the wrongness of an action. Since the non-cognitivist's irrealism about moral properties stems from a wider irrealism about all evaluative properties he must, in consistency, take the same line about other forms of value experience, including aesthetic experience. To his credit, Hume is clear about this (1975, pp. 291–2):

Euclid has fully explained all the qualities of the circle; but has not, in any proposition, said a word of its beauty. The reason is evident. The beauty is not a quality of the circle . . . It is only the effect, which that figure produces upon the mind, whose peculiar fabric or structure renders it susceptible of such sentiments. In vain would you look for it in the circle, or seek it, either by your senses or by mathematical reasonings, in all the properties of that figure.

Hume's confident assertions about the unobservability of beauty are breathtakingly counter-intuitive. We see the beauty of a sunset; we hear the melodiousness of a tune; we taste and smell the delicate nuances of a vintage wine. Hume's denial that we can detect beauty by the senses flies in the face of common experience. The very derivation of the term 'aesthetic' tells against him – it originally meant 'relating to perception by the senses'.

Hume's account of beauty in this paragraph is uncharacteristically crude. He appears to envisage our awareness of value as a two-stage process. First, there is genuine sense-observation of the properties of the object, among which we would not find beauty or any evaluative property. Second, this observation causes a feeling of pleasure in us and that feeling *is* the beauty ('It is only the effect, which that figure produces upon the mind . . .'). Beauty is not so much in the eye as in the mind of the beholder.

This two-stage story cannot be made to square with the phenomenology. It just does not accurately describe what it is like to see, say, a beautiful sunset. I do not see an expanse of coloured cloud, which is not itself seen as beautiful, and then experience a thrill of pleasure to which I give the name of beauty. The beauty of the sunset is woven into the fabric of my experience of it. I see the sunset *as* beautiful.

An account such as Hume's might be made more plausible if, instead of identifying the beauty of the sunset with the pleasure that an observer gets from seeing it, it were suggested that it is because he gets pleasure from it that he regards it as beautiful. The two elements, the observation of the object's properties and our affective response to them, are so closely and frequently connected that we may not notice their separation in our unreflective moments. This would explain why we are initially inclined to suppose that beauty is observable. Reflection reveals, however, that it is strictly a mistake to talk of seeing beauty.

The realist will admit that I may indeed feel a thrill of pleasure when I see the sunset but will insist that, once again, the non-cognitivist reverses the relation between the observer's evaluative judgement and his affective response. I am thrilled by the sunset because I see it to be beautiful; I do not take it to be beautiful because I, and others, are thrilled by it.

Reflection on the aesthetic case can serve to make us less certain of Hume's claim in the moral case. If I see several children throwing stones at an injured animal I may claim that I can just see that what they are doing is cruel. Similarly, the insolence of a drunken guest's behaviour seems no less observable than the cut of his suit. If this is correct then moral observation could play a role in justifying our moral beliefs.

Non-cognitivists have often retorted that, although the realist tries to allow a place for moral observation in his system, how that observation is supposed to occur is quite opaque. What are the perceptual mechanisms by which moral reality can be revealed to us? It is frequently claimed that the realist must construe moral observation as requiring the use of some mysterious and suspicious faculty of moral intuition – a faculty for whose existence we have, and could have, no conceivable evidence.

The realist must reply that moral observation is not to be thought of as in a special category of its own, quite unlike any other kinds of observation. The belief that moral properties cannot be detected by ordinary methods of observation may, perhaps, be traced to an unduly restrictive view of what can be observed. We might suppose that the only properties that can be observed are the 'proper objects' of the five senses: sight can detect colours and shapes; touch, shape and texture; hearing, sound; and so on. If we adopt this austere account of what can be perceived it is clear that not only moral properties but a great many of the things we normally take ourselves to perceive will be, strictly speaking, unobservable. If, on the other hand, we are prepared to allow that I can see that this cliff is dangerous, that Smith is worried or that one thing is further away than another, then there seems no reason to be squeamish about letting in moral observation. Working out a more generous theory of perception would take us beyond the scope of this chapter but, here as elsewhere, the realist sees no difference in kind between the moral case and others. And if moral properties are observable then we may appeal to such observation in justifying our moral opinions.

3.6 JUSTIFICATION

A realism that held that there were moral truths but that no human being could find out what they were would have little to offer. Any worthwhile realism will have to explain by what method we can get at moral truth, and this will involve showing how our moral beliefs can be justified. It would be absurd for the realist to claim that it is easy to find out the truth about all moral questions or to deny that there is considerable disagreement, not only about what is right or wrong, but also about how we go about finding out what is right or wrong. The difficulty of establishing the truth does not, however, impugn the existence of truth. There are many areas of human enquiry where we suppose that truth is available but find considerable disagreement about what it is. Philosophers, in view of the perennial disputes in their own subject, should be especially chary of asserting that where there are many conflicting views there can be no correct answer.

For the non-cognitivist the only role that observation can have in supporting a moral view is the indirect one of establishing the non-moral facts. Deciding what attitudes to take to the facts is always a further step in which observation can play no part. The realist's counter-claim that moral properties are observable provides the most striking difference between his account of justification and the non-cognitivist's and it is worth spelling the implications out in a little more detail.

What the realist needs is an account which makes it plausible to suppose that, in moral experience, we can be genuinely sensitive to what is there independently of us, but which also explains how moral disagreement is possible. To accommodate this last point the realist needs an account which allows for misperception and even for a complete failure to see what is there. For a promising model he turns again to aesthetic awareness. Someone can fail to notice on first encounter aspects of a painting or a piece of music which, perhaps after repeated study, later become apparent. The natural and almost irresistible conclusion is that he has developed a fuller and livelier appreciation of the work by coming to see or hear more clearly what was always there, waiting to be noticed.

On this observational model of aesthetic appreciation, how would you go about trying to justify your view of the work to someone who disagrees? By bringing him to see or hear it the way you do. That would involve getting him to pay more careful attention to the work by pointing out salient features and giving him hints as to how to approach it. This may be the work of a moment. The other person may only have failed to notice something that he recognizes as soon as it is pointed out. It is more likely, however, that the process will take time, and success may come only after a long period of training. Suppose a newcomer to jazz finds nothing of value in it. To him it is just a muddled confusion of noise. It may be quite hopeless to begin with the complex piece of music to which he has been listening. The connoisseur may need to expose the novice to simpler tunes and arrangements first, and gradually work up to the piece with which he started. Nor is success guaranteed; for one reason or another some people are untrainable. They may simply lack the capacity to enter into an appreciation of things that others find valuable.

The realist claims that this provides an illuminating analogy for moral justification. Two aspects of this analogy are particularly significant. Firstly, the result of successful training in the aesthetic case is a change in perception. Once you have begun to understand jazz you hear it in a quite different way. You now have the conceptual resources to detect complex patterns and harmonies within what was formerly merely an unstructured welter of sound. Training has improved your recognitional capacities in music, your ability to discriminate what was there in the music all along. With that increased capacity goes an increasing appreciation of what you hear, an awareness of what is of value in the music. The change in your evaluation is the result of a cognitive change, an improvement in your ability to hear the music properly and to form correct beliefs about its nature.

Analogously, a change in someone's moral views may be brought about by someone getting him to see the situation in a new light, either by enabling him to appreciate more fully some feature of the situation whose significance he had overlooked, or by revealing an overall shape or pattern which was hidden. Techniques for achieving this goal are similar to those in the aesthetic case: pointing to certain features and showing how they relate to others; starting with examples where the person you are trying to persuade can see what is at issue more clearly and then returning to the disputed case in the hope that what he has grasped in the other cases will illuminate this one. A good example of such a procedure can be found in the story of King David and Uriah the Hittite in the Old Testament. David lusts after Uriah's beautiful wife, Bathsheba, and arranges for Uriah to be sent to the front line of battle, with orders that he should be abandoned by his fellow soldiers. Uriah is duly killed and David marries Bathsheba. The prophet Nathan goes to David and tells him the story of two men, one rich and one poor (2 Samuel, ch. 12, vv. 2–7):

'The rich man had exceeding many flocks and herds. But the poor man had nothing, save one little ewe lamb, which he had bought and nourished up: and it grew up together with him, and with his children; it did eat of his own meat, and drink of his own cup, and lay in his bosom, and was unto him as a daughter. And there came a traveller unto the rich man, and he spared to take of his own flock and of his own herd to dress for the wayfaring man that was come unto him; but took the poor man's lamb, and dressed it for the man that was come to him.' And David's anger was greatly kindled against the man; and he said to Nathan . . . 'the man that hath done this thing shall surely die . . . because he had no pity.' And Nathan said to David, 'Thou art the man.'

The point of Nathan's story is to get David to see his own behaviour for what it really is – not a smart piece of one-upmanship, but an act of mean injustice by a powerful and wealthy man against someone powerless to defend himself against royal authority. David's feelings about himself are indeed changed, but that change is a result of a *cognitive* change, a change in how he understands his action.

The second feature of the analogy which should be stressed is that failure to appreciate a piece of music or a painting is not in any way a failure of *reason*. The person who does not hear the structure of the music is not irrational. According to the realist, this feature carries over to the moral case. We saw at the end of 3.4 that many philosophers have held that you can only show a rival moral view to be wrong if you can prove that it would be irrational to hold it. This is too strong. As in the aesthetic case, you may go on maintaining that you can justify your view, in the face of continued disagreement, without holding that the failure of your opponent to agree is a symptom of his irrationality. To be insensitive is not the same as to be irrational. Yet insensitivity can blind someone to a correct view and cause him to fail to see the very thing which does justify your position.

This account avoids two common objections to perceptual models of moral justification. The first is that such accounts preclude moral discussion – all I can do to settle a dispute is to ask my opponent to look and see. If he sees as I do, fine; if not, there is nothing more to be said. This objection fails to recognize that bringing someone to see something may involve a good deal of discussion, and much else besides. The second is that such a model encourages dogmatism. Those who fail to see things the way I do will, it is suggested, be stigmatized as morally blind and there will be no reason for me to take their disagreement seriously or to allow my confidence to be in the least shaken by it. There is nothing in the realist position that requires, or even encourages, this unattractive approach. Moral truth is not easily attainable. Mistakes are common and there is ample scope for passion and prejudice to cloud moral vision. The realist should therefore have a proper sense of his own fallibility and acknowledge the possibility that his opponent may be in the right. Improving our moral perception should be the result of dialogue and co-operative effort. No party in ethics has a monopoly on dogmatism; the existence of dogmatic realists is not the fault of realism.

Consistency

For the non-cognitivist, consistency is not just *a* virtue of a moral system – it is *the* virtue. Consistency is a virtue with which a philosopher finds it hard to quarrel. What the realist who adopts the perceptual account of justification which I have just sketched does reject, however, is the particular account of moral consistency offered by the non-cognitivist. In rejecting that account the realist relegates consistency to a position of much less importance in his account of moral justification.

We can best see this point by looking at their competing accounts of what it is for a group, or an individual, to have a moral practice or a moral outlook. On the non-cognitivist account, a group can only be seen as having a unified moral system, rather than a heap of disconnected affective responses, if its members consistently pick out the same non-evaluative features of the world for favourable or unfavourable evaluation. Their practice may be quite complex, but an observer should be able, in principle, to discover a pattern in their evaluative responses and thus successfully predict what they would say about new cases. This would be true even if the person or society under observation had a set of values quite alien to those of the observer. If no regularities, at the non-evaluative level, could be found then the conclusion would have to be that what is being observed is not a consistent set of evaluative reactions and so not a moral practice at all, but simply a set of purely capricious responses.

The realist (such as McDowell, 1981) who adopts a perceptual model of moral awareness can reject this account of what it is for a set of responses to constitute a moral practice. He can be sceptical about the claim that an outsider could always understand the moral practice of any alien group to the extent of being able to predict their responses to new situations. There is room in his theory for the thought that the practice of a group may exhibit a genuine sensitivity to some evaluative properties without its being the case that there is any recognizable pattern, at the non-evaluative level, in the things, people and situations to which they respond. It may be that only someone who shares, or at least sympathizes, with the evaluative stance of those he is observing can find any discernible pattern in what they are doing. Only someone who could see the point of their value system would find it intelligible and only such a person could detect its structure. But we have already seen that someone may, through lack of training or an incapacity to develop the appropriate sensitivities, be quite unable to observe what is there to be appreciated. Such an outsider would find their responses impenetrable.

How is it that the realist leaves himself room for the possibility of a moral practice that is opaque to those who do not possess the sensitivities of the insider? The answer lies, as we might expect, in his belief that we can observe moral properties. Both he and the non-cognitivist agree that, if an evaluative term is to be used intelligibly, its use must be guided by the way things are. For the non-cognitivist there is nothing in the world for users to be sensitive to except non-evaluative features. So, for an evaluative term to have any clear sense its use must be guided by the presence of certain non-evaluative features. The presence or absence of those features will be observable, irrespective of the evaluative stance of the observer. The realist, having a richer conception of what is there in the world to be observed, can allow that a person's use of an evaluative term can be genuinely guided by the world, by the way things are evaluatively, without supposing that there must be some set of non-evaluative features that all the things that possess that evaluative feature have in common.

The realist does not deny that it is the non-evaluative features of an object, action or person which determine its evaluative properties. What he does deny is that a particular non-moral property must always and everywhere be morally relevant in the same way and to the same degree.

This realist line of thought has the most startling consequences for our conception of moral reasoning. One of the most radical of these, further explored in the last chapter, is scepticism about the role of moral principles. We traditionally think of moral teaching as the inculcation of moral principles in the young. It is natural to understand a moral principle as a rule which enables the child or adult to go on to make correct moral judgements in each new case that he meets. Such a rule is thought of as singling out some non-moral feature that an action might possess and saying that any action which possesses that feature has a certain moral property. For example, the principle that one should not tell lies says that any action which is the intentional telling of an untruth is morally wrong. And it might reasonably be thought that whether someone was or was not deliberately telling an untruth was a factual matter which could be established by anyone, even if he did not accept the principle. We might then think of all the moral principles that forbid actions of one kind or another as together providing a check-list of those non-moral features that make an action wrong. If an action does not possess any of those features then it is permissible.

If however, as this realist line of thought suggests, there is nothing that all wrong actions have in common, except that they are all wrong, then this account of the utility of moral principles must be mistaken. The only method of arriving at correct moral conclusions in new cases will be to develop a sensitivity in moral matters which enables one to see each particular case aright. Moral principles appear to drop out as, at best, redundant and, at worst, as a hindrance to moral vision. If the realist adopts *moral particularism* (as I shall refer to it) he will, of course, be left with the task of explaining what role, if any, moral principles should play in our life.

3.7 SCIENCE AND REALITY

We live in a physical world, a world of physical objects. Many philosophers have argued that there are only physical things, that there are no mental or spiritual beings, such as souls or a God. This assertion is hotly contested, but the success of science in explaining, in purely physical terms, the way the world works gives the claim some weight.

Suppose, for the sake of argument, that it is correct. Would the adoption of a *physicalist* world view rule out moral realism? Not necessarily. From the fact that all the objects in the world are physical objects it does not follow that all the properties of these objects are physical properties, if by that we mean the sorts of properties that figure in physics. Only if it is held that science gives an exhaustive account of all the properties that exist is there a threat to realism about properties, such as evaluative properties, which do not figure in the scientific story. But there are reasons for resisting a thoroughgoing physicalism, one that allows no room for non-physical properties, states or processes.

The existence of states of consciousness provides a well-known difficulty for extreme physicalism. To feel a pain, to hear a sound, to smell an odour, are quite distinctive conscious experiences which would surely have to figure in any complete account of what it is to be a human being. Yet they seem to be excluded from the extreme physicalist picture of the world. What is going on physically when I am in pain is, presumably, such things as certain receptors in my skin being excited and electrical signals being sent along nerve fibres to my brain. But if the physical story exhausts all that is really happening in the world then there is no room, in a complete account of reality, for what it is like to be in pain, for the way I experience these events on the inside.

A more modest physicalism would allow the existence of what are often called *emergent* non-physical properties. Thus, for example, when the brain and central nervous system of an organism reach a sufficient complexity there emerge conscious states of awareness, such as feeling pain. A full description of the organism and its properties would have to include the fact that it was in pain. Being in pain is not a physical property, nor is it reducible to a physical property. Talk about consciousness is ineliminable; no purely physical description of the organism, remarks about what brain fibres are firing and so on, would convey the same information as the inside story of what it was like to have those experiences. A purely physical account would always leave something out.

Modest physicalism, which leaves room for emergent non-physical properties in a complete account of what there is in the world, is still a form of physicalism for two reasons. First, the only things that exist are held to be physical things. Every object must have physical properties, whether or not it has non-physical properties as well; there are no entities which just have non-physical properties. Second, the non-physical properties of things are fixed or determined by their physical properties. Thus, to take our example of the relation between the brain and consciousness, I am in the particular state of consciousness that I am in virtue of physical states of the world – in particular, the state of my brain and central nervous system.

Modest physicalism can encompass moral realism. Moral properties would then be seen as non-physical properties which emerged from complex interrelationships between flesh and blood physical objects, namely human beings. It certainly seems plausible, as we saw in 3.4, to suppose that the moral properties of an agent or action are fixed by its non-moral properties. For example, it is in virtue of the non-moral facts about heroin addiction and my relation to my children that it would be wrong for me to introduce them to the drug. There may well be a hierarchy of emergent properties; the non-moral ones, from which the moral ones emerge, may themselves emerge from more basic properties. The modest physicalist will insist that there is some point in the chain of emergence below which we only find physical properties.

Modest physicalism does not sell science short. It admits that we live in a physical world and that science is the method by which we explore its physical nature. But it resists any pretension that science might have to give a complete and exhaustive account of every aspect of the world and of the way we experience it. It leaves room for the existence of properties that are not quantifiable and measurable but which are none the less real. Within such a framework, the moral realist may reasonably argue that moral properties should be allowed their proper place in the world.

3.8 CONCLUSION

It has already emerged that in judging between our rival ethical theories we need to take into account two things: first, their degree of cohesion with plausible theories in other areas of philosophy; second, the extent to which they fit the moral phenomenology. On the first count both theories establish a reasonable prima facie case. A final decision will have to await more detailed examination of those areas, such as the explanation of action and the relation between science and reality, which have a crucial bearing on ethics. On the second count, however, the realist has strong grounds for claiming that his theory is in much better accord with our moral experience and practice than the non-cognitivist's. While this advantage is not decisive it is important. As we saw in 3.1, there is a presumption in favour of the theory that best accords with our experience. Non-cognitivism could overcome that presumption if it could prove that there were serious flaws in the realist position which it alone was able to avoid, and if it were able to give a convincing explanation of how and why our moral experience is so radically misleading. But this would be an uphill task. Faced with the kinds of objections which the realist has pressed in this chapter more sophisticated versions of non-cognitivism have been developed which, while preserving the basic tenets of the theory, try to show that it is much less removed from our present moral thought than has so far appeared. One of the most interesting versions was originally put forward by the eighteenth-century Scottish philosopher, David Hume. In the next chapter I develop that approach in a modern context.

FURTHER READING

Clear introductory statements of contemporary moral realism are hard to find, but there is an excellent defence of the kind of realism popular in the early part of this century in Ewing (1962). Murdoch (1970) is a pioneering work in contemporary moral realism. Finnis (1983, chs 1–3) weaves realist themes in with other concerns. Platts (1979, ch. 10) and Lovibond (1983) lay out the main features, but in the context of theories of language with which the reader may be unfamiliar. Nagel (1986, ch. 8) is accessible. A central figure in all discussions of moral realism is McDowell. None of his articles are easy, but McDowell (1978) is a place to start.

On 3.1 On the burden of proof in this debate see Nagel (1986, p. 143). On the general principle that we should take our experience at face value unless there is reason to think it misleading, see Swinburne (1979, pp. 254–76). Dancy (1986) gives the history of the phenomenology argument.

On 3.2 I am much indebted to Blackburn (1984, ch. 5) here.

On 3.3 On the authority of moral demands see McDowell (1978) who tries to explain that authority, and Mackie (1977, ch. 1) who tries to explain it *away*. Kant's notion of the categorical imperative is a classic expression of the claim that moral demands have special authority (Kant, 1972).

On 3.4 For a sustained attack on the fact–value gap see Putnam (1981, chs 6 and 9). (You can skip parts of his account which rely too heavily on points made elsewhere in his book.)

On 3.6 This attack on the non-cognitivist model of justification derives from McDowell (1981) who is himself influenced by Wittgenstein's thoughts on what it is to follow a rule (discussed by Dancy (1985, pp. 73–82)). McDowell's arguments are criticized by Blackburn (1981) and Williams (1985, ch. 8).

On 3.7 Campbell (1970) provides a clear introduction to physicalism.

4

Non-Cognitivism – Further Developments

4.1 A PERCEPTUAL ANALOGY

The non-cognitivist account of morality is far removed from our ordinary thought in three areas. First, if it leaves any room at all for the idea of moral truth it is only in the thin sense that, as a way of expressing the fact that you happen to agree with me in attitude, you may properly say that my moral views are true. Second, it leaves little room for the rational discussion of moral disagreement because the only ground for criticizing a moral outlook is its internal inconsistency. Third, it denies that we can ever observe that an act or a person is, say, courageous or rude. The only properties we can be aware of are non-evaluative ones, since those are the only ones there are.

Is there a way in which the non-cognitivist can preserve his irrealist stance towards evaluative properties and yet develop a theory that fits better with our moral practice? In an attempt to give a positive answer to this question, some non-cognitivists have turned to a common conception of what are traditionally called *secondary qualities* (or properties) – colour, sound, smell, and taste – to find a suitable model for ethics. On that conception, colours, sounds etc. could be thought of as not being real properties of objects. Crudely, when we see grass as green we are not to think of that experience as providing us with an accurate picture of one of the properties of grass. Rather, experiencing colour is the characteristic way in which human beings with normal eyesight respond to something that is real, namely the presence of certain kinds of light waves.

For someone who is trying to articulate a more sophisticated non-cognitivism, secondary qualities supply an attractive model for evaluative properties because there seems to be no difficulty in finding room in their case for the notions of truth, justification and observation. Questions about the correct colour of an object have an answer and there are agreed procedures for establishing what it is. And, if anything is observable, surely colours are.

Primary and secondary qualities

Before we can develop and test this suggested analogy we need to be clearer about the reasons for claiming that certain observed properties of objects, such as their colour or smell, are denied the status of real properties while the primary qualities of objects, such as shape, size and solidity, are thought of as real properties of things. What then are the differences between primary and secondary qualities which might ground this alleged difference in their ontological status? A pivotal difference emerges when we see what is involved in giving a more detailed account of the nature of any property. In the case of secondary qualities it seems impossible to explain their nature without mentioning the way they appear to human beings, whereas no such reference to characteristic human perceptual experience need appear in an account of the nature of a primary quality.

Take a typical secondary quality, such as redness, and a typical primary quality, such as squareness. Something is red if it looks red to a normal human observer in standard lighting conditions. Notice that, on this analysis, you cannot grasp what it is for something to *be* red unless you know what it is for something to *look* red. So blind people, or creatures who lack our sort of eyesight, have no idea of what redness is. This consequence looks right. There may be something else that all red objects have in common – such as their absorbing lightwaves of some lengths and reflecting those of other lengths – which underlies their appearing red to humans. But even if a blind person could find out, perhaps by means of some sort of light meter which he could read tactually, that a surface had the absorbing and reflecting properties characteristic of red things this would not give him an insight into what it is to be red – for that you need to be sighted.

Square things, of course, do look square to normal human observers in standard viewing conditions; but we can give a perfectly adequate account of what it is to *be* square – in terms of being a figure with four straight sides of equal length whose internal angles are all right angles – without mentioning how square things characteristically *look*. Since we can give an account of what it is to be square that does not mention the characteristic visual responses of humans to square things, a being who lacks vision can nevertheless have a perfectly good idea of what it is for something to be square. Possession of one particular sensory capacity, such as sight, is not necessary for an understanding of the nature of a primary quality.

Any creature which can find its way round in our world must be able to detect the primary qualities, such as size and shape, of objects in it, although the form that his experience of size and shape takes may vary greatly from creature to creature. Thus blind humans, and creatures who lack vision, can detect the shapes and sizes of objects by touch. Since we share this kind of experience with them we know how size and shape appear to them. But there are creatures which can detect size and shape by means of sensory apparatus that we do not possess. Thus a bat, which emits high-pitched squeaks and uses echo-location to perceive the world, must be aware of the size and shape of things, otherwise it could not avoid bumping into them. Lacking, however, this kind of sensory capacity we have no conception of the characteristic secondary quality experience of the bat. That is, we have no idea of the way the world appears to a bat. We cannot 'picture' the world the way the bat does.

4.2 THE ABSOLUTE CONCEPTION OF REALITY

These differences between primary and secondary qualities are striking, but are they sufficient to support the claim that the primary properties are real and the secondary ones are not? We cannot answer that question until we see how to draw the line between reality and appearance, between the way the world really is and the way it appears to us to be. An attractive line of thought, to which Bernard Williams has drawn our attention (1978, esp. pp. 245–9) leads to a conception of reality which identifies what is real with what is accessible from any point of view. Such an account relegates sound, colour, taste and smell to the side of mere appearance precisely because the nature of such properties cannot be grasped by beings who lack the relevant sense-organs.

This natural progression of thought begins with the now familiar idea of our fallibility. Any particular person's conception of the world is likely to contain error. Another person may be able, because he stands outside the viewpoint of the first, not only to correct those errors but also to explain how, from the first person's point of view, such errors came about. This process is indefinitely repeatable; a third person may correct and explain the errors of the second, and so on. It follows that there can never be any guarantee that we have reached the end of this process; there is always the possibility that a more comprehensive view of things may emerge which reveals that some of our current beliefs are mistaken, distorted by intellectual prejudice or perceptual error.

While the quest for knowledge is thus never ending (for we cannot ever be sure that we have reached our destination) we may hope that we can approach the truth by transcending less adequate points of view, incorporating their insights into our own and rejecting, while at the same time explaining, their errors. A classic example of this process at work in science is the replacement of Newtonian by Einsteinian physics. Einstein's theory does not completely reject Newton's; it explains why its predictions provide a very good approximation to the truth for most practical purposes. But it also transcends Newton's, explaining phenomena which the earlier theory could not cope with.

This line of thought is open to an obvious extension. If a particular person's conception of the world might be mistaken in various ways because of peculiarities in his particular perspective on the world, is it not possible that the human point of view itself might constitute a perspective which gave us an inaccurate picture of the world? The example of our experience of secondary qualities might provide a case in point. It is only from the point of view of creatures with our kind of sense-organs that the world can be experienced as coloured, noisy and smelly. To arrive at an accurate picture of the world might we not have to omit those features of our experience? From an external viewpoint those features could be explained in terms of our particular way of reacting to a world that was not coloured, noisy or smelly.

If we do extend our original line of thought in this way then we need to preserve two features of the original account. The first is that, in seeking to correct the distortions of an individual's point of view, we have to discount any aspects of his experience which are produced by the peculiarities of his particular perspective. So, if we are to attain a conception of the world as it really is, not just as it appears to us to be, we must strip away whatever in human experience is contributed by our peculiar way of perceiving and understanding the world so that we can form a corrected picture of what is there independently of us. The second is that, from our more comprehensive viewpoint, we should be able to explain how error arose in the conception of the world which we are attempting to criticize and to transcend. So we should hope for a conception of the world as it really is which would enable us to understand and explain how it is that the world appears differently to different observers occupying different points of view. Such a conception of the world could truly be called *absolute*, since it both transcends and explains those pictures of the world which are only valid relative to the viewpoint of some particular group or species.

Assuming that we can make sense of the absolute conception of reality, is there any way in which we might seek to attain it? Is there a method by which we can transcend our own parochial point of view, detecting, correcting and explaining its errors? Science appears as the most likely candidate. In scientific investigation we seek to minimize the subjective element and to use conceptual tools, such as mathematics, which might be thought to be accessible to all intelligent beings and not just to humans. Science explains our experience of secondary qualities in terms of our exposure, as organisms with a certain range of sensitivity, to waves and particles which can be fully described in primary quality terms. Both we and the bats share a common world, one which can be described by science, although it no doubt appears very differently to bats than it does to us.

Science has a long way to go. We have not yet achieved the goal of an exhaustive and accurate account of the nature of the universe and perhaps we never will. But at least we have a method which offers the hope of progress to that goal, a method which will enable us to distinguish what is really there in the world from what merely appears, from our particular point of view, to be there. We may wonder, however, whether this is enough to give the non-cognitivist what he wants. If we have not yet attained the absolute conception how can we be sure what properties will or will not figure in it? The non-cognitivist can reply that, however science develops, there is good reason to believe that certain properties will not figure in any final account of reality. Colours, sounds and smells are to be excluded because the nature of our secondary quality experience depends on our possession of certain modes of sense-experience. Just because we cannot form any conception of such properties unless we share that form of sense-experience they are unsuitable candidates to feature in an account of the world as it is in itself, independently of the point of view of any particular kind of observer.

Similar remarks, the non-cognitivist can claim, apply to evaluative properties. Just as we only experience secondary qualities because we possess certain modes of sense-experience so, we might suggest, we only experience things as having value because of our peculiar concerns, interests and tastes. It is absurd to suppose that our particular conception of what is of value would be shared by beings whose emotions and form of life were quite different from our own. For example, a being who lacked the concept of pain, because it did not have our kind of central nervous system, would not share our concern for the injured. Such concepts, which are tied to a particular mode of experiencing the world, cannot figure in an account of reality that is absolute.

If the absolute conception of reality is the correct conception then the non-cognitivist has supplied a quite general criterion for distinguishing what is really there from what merely appears to be so. On this criterion both values and secondary qualities turn out not to be real properties. That is one point of analogy between them. Are there any others? We saw that an object is red if it would look red to a normal human observer in standard lighting conditions. Can we give a similar account of what it is for an action to be right?

4.3 MORAL PROPERTIES AS SECONDARY QUALITIES

According to the simple version of non-cognitivism, which was expounded in chapter 2, someone who says that an action is right is expressing his personal approval of it. He is not claiming that there is any reason to expect that other people will also react to it with approval, though he may wish them to do so and may seek to persuade them to adopt his attitude. When, however, someone judges that some object is red, and not just that it looks red to him, he is committing himself to the claim that it will look red to anyone who has normal colour vision and is seeing the object in suitable viewing conditions. If we take seriously the suggestion that moral properties are analogous to secondary qualities then we will build into our account an expectation that other people will share our moral attitudes, provided that they are in the appropriate state and are making their judgement in suitable circumstances. But why should we take this proposed analogy seriously? And what content can we give to such notions as 'appropriate state' and 'suitable circumstances' in this context? To answer these questions we need to reflect on the purpose of morality and moral language; why have human societies developed these tools?

The moral point of view

One plausible sketch, which we owe to Hume, is as follows. It is not only desirable but essential that members of a society should live in some degree of harmony with each other. If a society is to survive it needs to find some way of resolving disputes about how that society is going to be organized that is generally acceptable to most of its members. If each person looks at any dispute solely from his own position in that society, thinking only of what he wants for himself, his family and friends, then reasoned discussion, let alone agreement, is impossible. What is required is that each of us adopts a point of view which is shared with others and which provides a mutually acceptable framework within which discussion can take place. People can, however, only be encouraged to adopt a more social and less self-centred point of view if it is one that is natural and attractive to them.

Human beings are social animals who care about the welfare of other humans. In cases where our own special interests are not threatened and we can be relatively detached, most of us normally prefer that things should go better for other people rather than worse. When we hear of some disaster, such as an earthquake, in distant parts, we sympathize with the suffering of those affected; when we hear of some kind, brave or generous act we are warmed by the news, even though the people involved are totally unknown to us. Our natural sympathy with other human beings as such gives us access to a viewpoint which transcends any individual's self-centred perspective and which all of us can share simply in virtue of being human. From this point of view the welfare of any one person is no more important than that of any other and conflicts are to be resolved by determining which course of action will produce the most benefit for the most people.

It is natural to identify this detached perspective on human affairs with the moral point of view. In order to avoid confusion we need to know whether someone is claiming to speak for his own interests or from the moral viewpoint. We have thus developed a specialized moral vocabulary that enables us to signal when we are adopting that perspective. As Hume elegantly puts it (1975, p. 272):

When a man denominates another his *enemy*, his *rival*, his *antagonist*, his *adversary*, he is understood to speak the language of self-love, and to express sentiments, peculiar to himself, and arising from his particular circumstances and situation. But when he bestows on any man the epithets of *vicious* or *odious* or *depraved*, he then speaks another language, and expresses sentiments, in which, he expects, all his audience are to concur with him. He must here, therefore, depart from his private and particular situation, and must choose a point of view, common to him with others: He must move some universal principle of the human frame, and touch a string, to which all mankind have an accord and symphony. If he means, therefore, to express, that this man possesses qualities whose tendency is pernicious to society, he has chosen this common point of view, and has touched the principle of humanity, in which every man, in some degree, concurs.

To adopt the moral point of view is, on this account, to consider the desires and interests of each person impartially, giving no more weight to one person's claim than to another's. A speaker who employs moral language implies that he is taking that stance, though he may, of course, be deceiving others, and even himself, in making that claim. While the moral point of view provides a common framework for discussion which holds out the hope that our differing moral viewpoints will converge, there is no reason to believe that agreement will be swift or easy. The difficulty of sustaining an impartial perspective and the complexities of determining what will most promote human welfare may stop us ever attaining the ultimate goal of complete agreement.

Rightness and redness

What of the alleged parallel between colours and moral properties? Just as I cannot see colours unless I have the right kind of sensory capacity, so I cannot be sensitive to the moral qualities of people and their actions unless I have the appropriate capacity – a capacity to feel sympathy for the concerns of other humans. Moreover, just as I will only see things in their true colours if I have properly functioning colour vision and am viewing the object under suitable conditions, so my moral feelings are only reliable if I am fully informed about the effects of the action on all the people affected and if my view is not distorted by bias or prejudice. In short, an action is right if it would elicit approval in a fully informed, impartial and sympathetic spectator.

While this account of rightness has obvious parallels with the account of redness already suggested there are also points of dis-analogy. If we contrast the circumstances in which someone will see the correct colours of things with the conditions which would have to obtain for someone always to respond to moral issues with the correct feelings we see that undistorted moral experience must be a great deal rarer than accurate colour vision. Since most of us have good colour-vision and live in daylight which, for most purposes, constitutes ideal lighting conditions, our perception of the colour of things is generally accurate and there is comparatively little dispute about what colour things are. The attainment of the moral point of view seems, by contrast, virtually impossible for mere humans. The notion of the vantage point of a fully informed impartially sympathetic spectator appears to be a description of a God's eye point of view. For that reason the theory is often known as the *ideal spectator* theory. Proponents of this account of moral judgement can, however, claim that this dis-analogy between the case of colours and of moral properties fits our practice. We do hold that questions about the morally correct course are more difficult to answer than questions about the correct colour of things, and that public discussion may help us to move towards the right answer. If moral disagreements were irresoluble then it is unclear why we would bother to go on arguing about them; if they were too easily resoluble then it is unclear why we would need to go on arguing about them.

4.4 THE NEW THEORY AND THE OLD

Simple non-cognitivism developed from the thought that morality is an area in which each individual has complete freedom of choice to select his own moral viewpoint in accordance with his feelings. As a consequence, the moral philosopher was in no better (or worse) position than anyone else to offer moral advice since no amount of critical reflection on the nature of morality could yield a criterion by which we could determine which moral views were justified. The ideal spectator theory is very far removed from this starting point.

It encourages us to think of morality less as a matter of individual choice and more as something which is the creation of human society. Moreover, we are no longer to conceive of moral positions as being chosen, by what may seem an arbitrary and even capricious act of individual will, but as having evolved in response to the specific requirements of communal living. This distinct shift of emphasis may involve no great loss, for the idea that you can sit down and choose what your values are is highly implausible. I do not *choose* to be against cruelty and injustice, in the way in which I might choose to wear the blue sweater today; I *am* against cruelty and injustice. There was, in any case, an unresolved tension in simple non-cognitivism between the thought that moral commitments spring from the will of the individual and the emphasis the theory places on the role of feeling and desire – for our likings are not, in any normal sense, subject to our choice. The picture of the pure individual will, divorced from society and un-affected by desire, simply choosing its moral outlook is a myth – and a myth that the non-cognitivist can profitably abandon.

The ideal spectator theory offers us an example of an *ethical theory* – a theory about what it is to adopt a moral viewpoint – which has implications for *moral theory*; that is, for the method we should use to determine the answer to specific practical moral questions. In giving content to the notion of what it is to be an ideal spectator – he should be impartial and sympathetic – we place restrictions on the range of moral opinion that is acceptable. If, for example, Pius's view that the law should ban trading or professional sport on a Sunday can be shown to be the product of bias in favour of the interests and preferences of his religious faction this would provide a reason for rejecting it. It would not have been formed by the appropriate process of reasoning.

Some philosophers (including, perhaps, Hume) have thought that the ideal spectator theory rules out all moral theories except one – namely, *utilitarianism*. The utilitarian takes it that our moral task is to maximize happiness; the right action is the one that produces more happiness, or less misery, than any alternative action. The argument for this conclusion is that, since he is sympathetic, the ideal spectator will wish for the welfare, rather than the harm, of those under his gaze; since he is impartial between them he will seek to harmonize their desires and interests so that as many of them can be satisfied as possible. He will, in short, seek to make as many of them as possible as happy as possible. The question of whether there is such a close connection between ideal spectator theory and utilitarianism is one to which I will return in chapter 11.

The claim that a direct link can be forged between ethics and moral theory conflicts with a once popular dogma: that moral philosophy is morally neutral and that no substantive moral conclusions can be drawn from its study. This dogma has its roots in the scepticism about the possibility of moral justification which was fostered by the boo-hurrah theory. If the ethical position we adopt commits us to rejecting the possibility of showing any moral view to be more justified than any other then it follows, trivially, that the study of moral philosophy will tell us nothing about how we should live our lives. This tells us nothing, however, about what the relation between ethics and practical moral questions may be *in general*; it merely follows through the consequences of moral scepticism. As the ideal spectator theory shows, the study of moral philosophy may be held to have a bearing on practical issues, even if we are working within a broadly non-cognitivist framework. The extent to which the new theory rejects the sceptical tendencies of the old is a mark of the distance between the two.

4.5 TRUTH

The ideal spectator theory offers us at least the rudiments of a decision procedure in ethics; a way of determining whether some proffered view is justified or not. If it allows room for justification does it also supply the materials for a substantial account of truth in morals of the sort that seems applicable in other areas? If we look at some field, such as chemistry or history, where we think that truth is available, we find that certain features are present which appear to give the notion of truth its grip in that area. We might call these the *marks of truth*. We have already seen that truths must be *consistent*; it must be possible for them all to be true together. We also think that whether or not a belief is true depends on something which is *independent* of itself; typically, on the way the world is. There is just one way the world is so there is a *unique* complete set of true beliefs about the world; there cannot be several consistent sets of beliefs each with equally good claim to constitute the truth. Any individual belief, therefore, must have a *determinate truth-value*; it is either true or false, depending on the way things are in the world.

There is also a connection between truth and justification. In an area where we think that there are true and false answers then we have a justifiable hope that we might be able to resolve disagreement by rational means – a hope that makes it worth continuing the debate. For we should be able to find the correct answers by paying careful attention to the evidence. It may not be easy to find the truth but if we persevere then, as false answers get eliminated, the opinions of rational enquirers should begin to *converge*. It is reasonable to suppose that, in the indefinitely long run, we will all agree, and that what we will all agree on will be the truth. The progress of science gives us a model which we might apply to ethics. Although scientists disagree about many details there is agreement about method and it is on this agreement that the hope that the scientific community will ultimately reach unanimity on scientific questions is founded.

The ideal spectator theory offers at least the rudiments of a non-arbitrary method for eliminating moral disagreement and arriving at a unique set of correct moral views which are consistent with each other. There is thus the prospect that morality will turn out to be a field in which the marks of truth can be found. This does not mean that agreement on moral questions will be easy to attain. As we have seen, the recalcitrance of moral disputes appears to stem from two sources. One is the difficulty, familiar from economic and political debate, of determining what courses of action will in fact most increase the general welfare. The other is the temptation, not restricted to moral thought but prevalent in it because of the way moral decisions vitally affect our lives, to allow bias to creep into one's assessment.

4.6 OBSERVATION

Since the non-cognitivist denies that values are to be found in the world then, as we saw in 2.7, it is tempting for him to claim that value is un-observable. When someone has noticed the observable, non-evaluative, properties of something then his realization that it has value is not a product of further observation, but a matter of his reacting favourably to what he has observed. Yet this picture seems, as the realist argued, to distort the nature of our experience of value, to be untrue to the phenomenology. The beauty of the sunset, or the rudeness of the guest's behaviour, are observable in just the way that other properties are. Our experience of what is of value does not come conveniently divided up into two parts: an awareness of what is genuinely there to be observed and a subsequent affective response to what we have seen.

The analogy with secondary qualities suggests, however, that the non-cognitivist need not deny the phenomenology; he can take on board the claim that values can be observed without abandoning his irrealist account of them. Colours, sounds and smells are paradigm cases of observable properties – if any properties are perceivable then they are. Yet, on the account of them which we adopted in 4.2, colours as we see them and sounds as we hear them would not figure in a comprehensive description of what the world is really like. The case of secondary qualities clearly illustrates that to be unreal is not necessarily to be unobservable; properties which, on the absolute conception, are not real may yet figure in our perceptual experience.

The difficulty of attaining the absolute conception stems from the fact that those elements of our experience that are owed to the peculiarities of the human point of view, and those elements that accurately reflect the way things are in the world, are intertwined. It requires reflection even to realize that the two can be separated and it would require a degree of sophistication that we have not yet achieved to disentangle them completely. On this model, we should not expect that our moral experience will arrive neatly pre-packaged into an evaluatively neutral piece of observation followed by an affective response. Rather, just as we see objects as coloured, even though this part of our experience of them comes from our particular type of visual capacity, so we will experience things as having value, even though it is we who contribute the evaluative element in experience. Value, like colour, is interwoven into the fabric of our experience of the world, but that part of our experience does not accurately represent anything in the world. Colour and value are to be thought of as something we create in perceiving the world. They are modes of our awareness of the world and not properties of the world.

We project, as it were, our valuational response on to the object of our experience so that the response becomes an integral part of that experience. The philosophical task then becomes that of unmasking nature, of stripping away what is contributed by us and revealing reality, naked and unadorned. This vision is sketched with characteristic lucidity by Hume. In Hume's version the creative role is assigned to the faculty of taste, which includes both moral and aesthetic awareness, while reason has the cleansing task of removing the decoration which has been applied to the world by taste (1975, p. 294):

Thus the distinct offices of *reason* and of *taste* are easily ascertained. The former conveys the knowledge of truth and falsehood: the latter gives the sentiment of beauty and deformity, vice and virtue. The one discovers objects, as they really stand in nature, without addition or diminution: the other has a productive faculty, and gilding or staining all natural objects with the colours, borrowed from internal sentiment, raises, in a manner, a new creation.

This improved account which, following Blackburn (1984, ch. 6) we might term *projectivism*, does not fit happily with Hume's earlier insistence that we do not experience objects as having value, a claim that conflicts with the moral phenomenology. The present doctrine incorporates all the points about the phenomenology on which the realist insists but still maintains that we cannot draw any realist conclusions from the nature of our moral experience. Our experience is of a world suffused with value; nevertheless, philosophical reflection shows that value is not a genuine feature of that world. Value is one of the many aspects of our experience that is contributed by us and not by the world.

4.7 IS THE NEW THEORY NON-COGNITIVIST?

Our new theory is irrealist about moral properties. But can it still be construed as a non-cognitivist theory? We saw in 3.2 that there are other strategies open to the irrealist. He could be a reductionist, claiming that moral utterances are indeed true or false but that this does not commit us to the existence of a distinctive range of moral facts. The provision of a suitable translation of moral remarks will remove any apparent and, from the point of view of the irrealist, objectionable commitment to realism about moral properties. On these criteria the theory we have developed in this chapter appears reductionistic. First, it does allow room for moral truth, in a suitably substantial sense. Non-cognitivism, you will recall, saw the point of moral language lying in some other purpose than the expression of truth-claims or beliefs. Second, it proffers what looks suspiciously like a reductionist trans-lation of moral language: what we mean when we say that this course of action is the right one is that a fully informed, impartial sympathetic spectator would approve of it. The apparent reference to the meta-physically suspect property of rightness has disappeared in translation, to be replaced by familiar language about actual and possible psycho-logical states.

The ideal spectator theory *can* indeed be treated as a purely reductionist account of the meaning of moral terms, but it can also be adapted to fit a non-cognitivist approach. On the latter account moral language is not seen, as it is on the reductionist account, as simply a convenient form of shorthand for the rather more long-winded formulation provided by the ideal spectator theory. It is also used to express a commitment, both emotional and practical, to the value of human welfare and happiness. Someone who spoke the language of morality but who had no concern at all for the welfare of human beings would be using moral terms incorrectly, for his way of speaking would imply that he had a range of attitudes to human welfare which, in fact, he did not possess. We can make this point clearer by reverting to the example (in 2.4) of the speaker who did not realize that 'nigger' is a term of abuse. We supposed that he had a complete grasp of the descriptive meaning of the term in that he correctly applied it to blacks, but that he had failed to grasp its evaluative meaning. In using the term he would misleadingly give the impression that he had an attitude of contempt and hostility towards blacks of which, in fact, he was wholly innocent. Similarly, a visitor from another planet (a favourite character in philosophical fantasy) who had no concern for the welfare of humans might nevertheless arrive, as a result of prolonged anthropological observation, at a theory about the purpose of our moral thought and activity rather like the one put forward in 4.4. If he did so he could perfectly well discuss with us whether some action was one of which an impartial sympathetic spectator would approve. But agreement on this question would not constitute agreement in moral attitude, for our postulated alien has no interest in, and cares nothing about, those issues of human well-being which are of such importance to us. If he employed moral language at all it could only be in an uncommitted way, using the terms in an inverted commas sense.

It still remains the case that no amount of evidence about the likely effects of some course of action on the well-being of others can suffice, on its own, to show that an agent has good reason to adopt any particular attitude to that course of action. The agent's attitude will also depend on non-cognitive elements in his make up – what he cares about and what he desires. However, if the agent is committed to those sorts of concerns for human welfare that constitute the moral point of view then there is, as we have seen, an agreed decision procedure for dealing with difficult cases. That is what distinguishes the present theory from its starkly sceptical predecessor and lends legitimacy to the notion of moral truth.

The boo–hurrah theory insisted that we can take up any attitude towards the facts. Since different people may adopt different criteria of value, that theory left no space for an agreed rational method by which disagreement in attitude between those with conflicting value systems might be resolved. The present theory need not deny the claim that there are many attitudes we might rationally take up towards the facts. What it insists on is that to adopt a moral attitude is to take up one particular stance, the moral point of view, which brings with it a set of criteria for determining what is of moral value. That stance is not just one among many, nor are the criteria which it incorporates arbitrary. We can recognize its appeal for human beings and see why so many people adopt it. To adopt it is, nevertheless, to take up an attitude; it is to move beyond trying to understand the world and to commit oneself to changing it.

4.8 MOTIVATION AND THE CORRECTED POINT OF VIEW

Red objects do not always look red; under sodium light, for example, they look brown. There is nothing puzzling about this if we remember that a red object is one that looks red to a normal observer in normal conditions. So long as we are familiar with the effects of sodium light and have seen the object in daylight we shall not be deceived. We will correctly judge that what we are seeing is a red object, even though our visual experience is more like the one we would get if we were looking at a brown object in normal daylight than it is like the one we would have if we were looking at a red object in daylight. This ability to allow for abnormal conditions enables us to reach a large measure of agreement in belief about the colour of objects, even when they are presented to us in an unusual guise.

Sufficient knowledge about the circumstances in which we are making a moral judgement similarly enables us to allow for bias, ignorance and lack of concern in order to arrive at a correct judgement. Making the appropriate allowances is, as we have seen, often much more difficult than in the case of colours, partly because far more complicated factors have to be taken into account in the moral case and partly because some of the distorting factors, such as prejudice and partiality to oneself, are not conducive to clear thinking. Nevertheless, there is room for an analogy with the colour case: I may judge that an action is, say, morally wrong even though it is not producing in me the sort of moral experience, namely a feeling of disapproval, which it would produce in an ideal spectator.

Failure to be moved to indignation when contemplating a wrong act may be due to a variety of factors: that the act happened a long time ago to people of whom I know nothing; that I am depressed and cannot even bring myself to care about my own problems let alone anyone else's; that the person to whom the wrong was done is someone I hate or my enemy. In my moral thinking I can allow for such facts and form the correct judgement even though my feelings are not engaged; I judge that such an action would arouse disapproval in an impartial fully sympathetic spectator.

It may seem that the new theory has severed that close connection between moral conviction and action, which was one of the strengths of non-cognitivism. It looks as if I might judge that I ought to do an action and yet have no desire to do it, because my feelings are not engaged. Given the belief–desire theory, it would follow that, in such a case, I had no reason to do the action. This suggests that our new theory takes an externalist position about moral motivation. Realization that an action is wrong would not, by itself, give the agent reason to act. For the agent to have a reason to act, a desire, conceived of as a state external to the moral conviction, would have to be added.

Can the non-cognitivist avoid this conclusion? He can, for reasons that emerged in the previous section. On the non-cognitivist version of the ideal spectator theory, to judge that an action is right is not just to have a belief that an ideal spectator would approve of it. It is to express a commitment to act as morality requires. Even if my feelings were not initially engaged, my realization that I ought to act will, because of that commitment, provide me with reason to act. We can regard that commitment as a standing desire to do what is right, which can be brought into play whenever I judge that I ought to do something. So the realization that an ideal spectator would disapprove of my failing to act can after all serve to arouse such disapproval in me, by directing that standing desire to an appropriate object. I explore this suggestion a little further in 8.5.

FURTHER READING

On 4.1   The classical source of the primary/secondary quality distinction is Locke (1961, Book II, section viii). McGinn (1983) provides a modern discussion. Nagel (1974) asks 'What is it like to be a bat?'

On 4.2   Williams (1985, ch. 8) draws consequences for ethics of adopting the absolute conception.

On 4.3   Among those who have drawn attention to the disanalogies between secondary and moral qualities are McGinn (1983, pp. 145–55) and Blackburn (1985).

On 4.4   It was Hume's pupil, Adam Smith (1976), who developed the idea of the impartial sympathetic spectator, already implicit in Hume's work. Modern discussions include Firth (1952), Brandt (1954) and Harman (1977, ch. 4).

On 4.5   I owe the idea of marks of truth to Wiggins (1976, p. 357).

On 4.6   Blackburn (1984, ch. 6) develops projectivism, acknowledging his debt to Hume.

5

Realism and Reality

5.1 BARE REALITY

From Plato onwards, distinguishing reality from appearance has been seen as one of the major aims of philosophy. Reality is pictured as difficult to discern and the philosopher's task is portrayed as revelatory; by rending the veil of appearance he can hope to reveal a privileged glimpse of the world as it really is. The non-cognitivist, in appealing to the absolute conception of reality in order to support his irrealism about moral properties, fits firmly into this tradition. By stripping away whatever in our experience is contributed by our peculiar cognitive and sensory make-up it is hoped to reveal 'objects as they stand in nature without addition or diminution'.

We saw in the last chapter that there were powerful reasons for claiming that, on the absolute conception of reality, both secondary qualities and moral properties only figure in an account of the world as it appears to us and not as it really is. What excludes both kinds of property from the real world is that our conception of them is ineliminably subjective. By this I mean that it is impossible to have an understanding of what these properties are like unless you are capable of being in a certain sort of subjective state. Unless you can experience things as coloured you can have no conception of what it is for something to be red or blue. Unless you share human concerns and patterns of feeling it is impossible to understand what it is for an action to be cruel or compassionate. It is because our conception of them is not accessible to those who do not share our form of experience that these properties are debarred from figuring in the absolute conception of reality. The concepts of such subjective properties are inescapably permeated with elements drawn from what is peculiar to the human point of view.

If the moral realist is to counter this argument then two main lines of approach are open to him – the second more radical than the first. He can accept the way of drawing the distinction between appearance and reality that is encapsulated in his opponent's approach but try to show that moral properties are to be placed on the reality and not on the appearance side of the fence. Assuming that colours-as-we-see-them and sounds-as-we-hear-them have no place in an account of the real world, absolutely conceived, then he can do this only by rejecting the secondary quality model for moral properties and arguing that they should be seen as more akin to primary qualities. More radically, the moral realist can reject his opponent's way of drawing the distinction between appearance and reality and insist that the attempt to strip from experience every aspect that is contributed by our peculiar way of viewing the world is fundamentally misguided. If he rejects the claim that what is real is to be equated with what is accessible from any point of view then he opens up the possibility that properties which are subjective, in the sense just explained, may nevertheless be real. On this stronger approach he can accept that our conception of secondary and moral properties contains an irreducibly subjective element without jeopardizing the claim that they are real properties of things. What reasons can he proffer for rejecting the absolute conception of reality?

5.2 ABSOLUTE REALITY

If it is possible, even if only in principle, to give an account of the real world which meets the demands laid down by the absolute conception then we must be able to disentangle, within our experience, those elements that depend on our distinctively human point of view from those that accurately represent things as they really are. Such an enterprise is open to a fundamental objection. It appears to require that we find some point of view from which we can see the world as it really is and that we then compare the real world with our experience of it in order to see where the two correspond and where they do not. As soon as it is spelled out, this demand seems absurd. Where in the world, or rather out of it, would we have to be in order to transcend the human point of view on the world and come to see it as it really is? Archimedes said that if he had a point outside the world which could act as a fulcrum then, with a long enough lever, he would be able to move the world. His task would seem easy in comparison with the search for a philosophical Archimedean point from which we could prise off, within our conception of the world, what is merely contributed by us, in order to reveal the underlying reality.

The difficulty is simply this: any conception that we can form of what the world is like will still be one that uses *our* concepts and draws on *our* experience. So it will still be our conception, and thus cannot meet the demand that we form a picture of the world as it really is, quite apart from the way we conceive it to be. If we remove all the aspects of our conception of the world for which we are responsible then we remove everything. We are not left at the end of such a process with a definite, if austere, account of what is really there but with a completely empty conception of something we know not what.

This objection, though powerful, is not immediately decisive. The proponent of the absolute conception of reality can reasonably reply that he is not committed to the hopeless task of constructing an account of the world which does not use human concepts and which somehow succeeds in transcending the human point of view. The correct response to someone who is alarmed by the unavoidability of using our human conceptual scheme has been memorably given by Hilary Putnam – 'Well, we should use someone else's conceptual system?' (quoted by McDowell, 1983, p. 14). What we need to do in order to formulate the absolute conception is not to abandon using human concepts but to ensure that we only use concepts that are objective – concepts which could be grasped by beings who did not share our particular modes of awareness. Concepts of secondary qualities are, as we have seen, unacceptably subjective. Scientific concepts however, including those of the primary qualities, can be explained without essential reference to the way that such properties are experienced by human beings.

Science as a route to reality

Even if this reply succeeds in quelling doubts about the very coherence of the enterprise there is still considerable room for scepticism as to whether it can be carried out. In particular, following McDowell (1983, pp. 13–16), we may be sceptical about the ability of science, as the chosen means of fleshing out that conception, to deliver the goods. Science, after all, is just as much a product of the human mind as any other area of human thought. Why should it alone be thought to provide us with a peculiarly transparent mode of access to reality? Might not the lens of science itself introduce distortions into our portrait of the world?

The proponent of the absolute conception offers us the following broad picture of scientific progress. In areas of scientific debate we are offered the hope that, as investigation proceeds, competing views will gradually converge and that the point at which they converge will be the truth. What supports this hope is the capacity of science to provide an observational method for eliminating false views of the world. Because our choice of scientific theories is guided by observation of the world we can reasonably suppose that increasing agreement is a result of our getting closer and closer to finding out what the world is really like. If only one theory survives it will have done so because it represents most accurately the way the world actually is.

Sceptics in ethics have often pointed to the alleged divergence of our moral views as a reason for denying that there are any moral facts. The point here, however, is not whether there is a reasonable chance that our moral opinions might converge on one set of answers, but what the explanation of any such convergence would be. The suggestion is that the best explanation of convergence in scientific opinions is that we are getting closer to an accurate account of the world. This explanation of the hoped-for convergence differs, according to the proponent of the absolute conception, from possible explanations of convergence in our moral opinions. Such explanations must appeal, not to the claim that we are getting closer to a description of reality (for moral thought is not seen as depicting the world as it really is), but to underlying similarities in our psychological make-up. We are to think of any convergence in moral opinion not as primarily world-guided but as governed by such cultural and psychological factors as similarity of upbringing and education, and shared interests and concerns.

This contrast depends for its force on the claim that convergence in scientific opinion is not itself to be explained in terms of psychological and cultural factors. We have already seen that a general doubt about this assertion is raised by the reflection that science is itself as much a product of human history and culture as any other activity. Scientific theory has changed, sometimes dramatically, at particular historical junctures, and there is no guarantee that it will not change radically again. Why should a scientific view of the world be thought to be less parochial and historically conditioned than any other view?

The reply must be that in scientific *method* we have a means of developing our *current* scientific knowledge, which may well be historically conditioned, in a way that will progressively eliminate what is unacceptably subjective in our everyday view of the world. Does our present conception of scientific method live up to this claim?

Theory and observation

The picture of scientific advance which has just been sketched presents too simple a picture of the relation between theory and observation. It overstates the role of observation of the world in selecting scientific theories and underplays the place of other factors. It is now generally accepted that all theories, including scientific ones, are *underdetermined* by the data. That is, for any set of data, there are an indefinite number of theories that would explain those data. Astronomy provides an example. Before Copernicus, the observed relative movements of the stars and planets were explained by the theory that the earth was stationary and that the planets and stars moved round it in circles at constant velocity. However, in their observed track across the heavens the planets sometimes went faster, sometimes slower and even appeared to go backwards for short periods. These retrogressions and changes in speed were explained by postulating that, while each planet moved in a basically circular orbit, each also moved in smaller circles (called epi-cycles) within that overall circular orbit. Their motion as seen from the earth was the product of more than one circular motion and this theory thus fitted, and explained, the observational data. After Copernicus the preferred picture had the sun as the fixed point around which the planets, including the earth, moved in elliptical orbits. Since both theories fit what we see when we look at the heavens there is no observational test that will be decisive in determining which of them is correct. Our reasons for preferring the heliocentric theory proposed by Copernicus and others must lie elsewhere.

There are in fact several criteria to which we can appeal in determining which of two theories that fit the observational data offers the best explanation of those data. One theory will be preferred to another if it fits better with our other beliefs and theories; if it gives a more plausible and satisfying explanation of the data; if it is simpler, and if it explains a wider range of phenomena. Both our choice of these criteria and the way we apply them in selecting the favoured theory may, however, be governed by considerations that only appeal to beings with our particular way of organizing experience and understanding the world.

Firstly, we may wonder whether the choice of this particular set of criteria has any authority over and above the fact that we find them natural and attractive. The simplicity of a theory, for example, is taken to be a guide to its truth; but what can we bring forward to support this contention other than the fact that we take the two to be connected? Secondly, even if we accept this particular list of desirable qualities in a theory, they are abstract features which need considerable interpretation before they can be applied to particular choices. What counts as simplicity in a theory will depend on what other beliefs we hold, so that a theory which, against one background, will look simpler than its rival, may look more complicated when viewed in another context. Even where there is agreement about which features are relevant in determining whether a theory is simple there may be no clear method for determining which one is overall the simplest, when different features point in different directions. Thus pre-Copernican astronomy could be held to be simpler than ours in that circular motion is simpler than elliptical motion. Equally, our present view could be held to be simpler in that it does not require the rococo construction of epi-cycles within epi-cycles.

Thirdly, even if we can decide which theory is the simplest, the problem of reaching an overall verdict when there are conflicting indicators re-emerges when we are trying to decide which theory is overall the best. Given that there are several independent criteria of theory selection which can pull in opposite directions there seems to be no completely determinate method of weighing one against the other in such cases and deciding which theory is, on balance, the most successful. At each stage our choice of the preferred theory is not fully determined by the criteria.

In short, the alleged contrast between scientific and moral thought is hard to sustain. We have various grounds which we offer as reasons for preferring one scientific theory to another but, so the objection runs, that we see them as good reasons may depend on factors peculiar to the human point of view – factors which are no less subjective than those which are supposed to debar moral reflection from telling us anything about the world as it really is. This conclusion casts considerable doubt on any claim to have found in science an objective route to an account of the real world, absolutely conceived.

Doubts about the ability of science to attain the absolute conception of reality also undermine the claim that there is a contrast between the scientific and the moral case when it comes to providing the best explanation of convergence of opinion. The collapse of that alleged contrast still leaves us with an unresolved question. If the absolute conception of reality is unattainable are we to think that convergence in both scientific and moral opinion might be explicable by supposing that we are getting closer to an accurate account of the world? Or is neither convergence to be explained in this way? The answer will depend on whether we can find some plausible account of what is real, other than that offered by the absolute conception. I return to this question in 5.5, after we have looked at other difficulties which beset the absolute conception.

5.3 PERCEPTION AND REALITY

Talk of stripping away those features of our experience which do not accurately represent the way the world is suggests that, at the end of the process, a substantial part of that experience will emerge unscathed. But this suggestion may well be misleading. For the account of the world that is given by current physics is apparently so different from our everyday picture that it would be nearer the truth to say that virtually every aspect of our experience will end up being relegated to the status of mere appearance. While physics has room for primary qualities such as extension and solidity in its account, its description of a solid, extended object would be almost nothing like the everyday one. The modest proposal that we remove, from our experience, the staining and gilding with which we have covered the clear face of reality has changed into the more radical suggestion that we may have never beheld its face at all.

This proposal raises obvious difficulties for any account of perception. If what we are aware of when we perceive objects is so different from the picture that science gives us of their nature then a serious question must arise as to whether we ever really observe what is there at all. A person's experience can suffer a small amount of distortion and yet be sufficiently accurate for it to be reasonable to say that he is aware of what is really there, although he misperceives it somewhat. In this case, however, the difference between the scientific account of the world and our usual one is so vast that there seems to be no sense to the thought that we have even a distorted perception of the world as it really is. Moreover, our inability to perceive the world correctly turns out not to be a merely contingent restriction due to the limitations of our sensory powers. Nothing could possibly count as seeing or touching an entity, such as a quark, which has that strange property physicists call 'charm'. The scientific view of the world is not a possible view in the literal sense, but an abstract conception.

The moral realist's insistence that we take the phenomenology seriously now acquires a new urgency. If the twin claims that reality must be conceived absolutely, and that science offers the route to that conception, lead to the conclusion that *nothing* in the world is the way our perceptual experience represents it as being then we shall need very strong reasons for adopting that conception of reality. If we can provide an account of reality which leaves room for the scientific account of the world, but which saves the phenomenology, then that account will be preferable to the one provided by the absolute conception.

For these and similar reasons some philosophers have suggested that we should not think of the everyday and scientific conceptions as being in competition, with the loser being relegated to the realm of appearance. Rather, the two accounts should be seen as complementary descriptions of the world which are drawn from two different points of view. Neither account is better or more accurate than the other; they serve different purposes and have different roles. It is only from within some particular perspective that we can ask what is really there and the answer will be determined by the frame of reference which that particular perspective provides. It is the misguided attempt to elevate one perspective into a dominant position that creates the problems.

An analogous case where we seem to allow two radically different descriptions to coexist without thinking of them as in competition can be found in the world of art. On the one hand we can describe a picture in terms of the depth of the depicted scene, the quality of the light, the motion of the figures, and so on. On the other, we can describe it as a canvas of such and such dimensions on which oil paint containing such and such pigments has been laid to a maximum depth of, say, a quarter of an inch. No part of the canvas or the paint is in motion at all. Both descriptions are equally valid and each could sensibly be offered as an answer, in a particular setting, to the question 'What is the painting like?' In a context, such as an art appreciation class, in which the first would be an appropriate response the second would not be so, and vice versa. Neither need be thought of as a more correct answer to the supposedly perspectiveless question 'What is the painting really like?' For the contrast between appearance and reality only makes sense within a particular perspective. On this account, it would be as absurd to conclude that values were unreal merely because they did not figure in a scientific account of the world as it would be to try to refute the claim that a painting has great depth by measuring the thickness of the pigment.

The proponent of the absolute conception must, of course, reject such a reassuringly pluralist position. For him there is one privileged perspective from which alone we can discern the way things really are. As we have seen, we arrive at that perspective by trying to conceive of the world in a way that excludes any elements whose presence depends on the peculiar psychological make-up of any particular kind of observer – a conception of the world as it is in itself. But what gives this conception its supposed authority?

The aim is to arrive at an account of the world that is accessible to all observers. By excluding any point of view that contains aspects that are not intelligible to those outside it, we raise the hope that agreement on what remains might be achieved. It is not, however, simply the prospect of consensus that justifies the claim that only what can be envisaged from within that conception can be counted as real. We cannot justify demoting everything else to the side of appearance simply on the grounds that we cannot get a group of very different observers to agree on it. To equate what is real with what everyone can agree on would be to ignore the possibility that there may be truths which are available from one perspective but not from another.

What underpins the pretensions of the conception of the world as it is in itself to give an exhaustive description of reality is its alleged ability to embrace and explain the other perspectives. We saw in 4.2 that the drive towards the absolute conception is an extension of the process in which, from within one perspective, it is possible to detect, correct and explain the errors that are contained within some less adequate perspective. The conception of the world as it is in itself can claim to be the absolute conception only if it can explain the existence of rival conceptions in a way that demonstrates its superiority to them. It does so by showing what is misleading or erroneous in other conceptions and explaining, from its own point of view, how that error arose. Every other conception is then shown to be relative to some parochial point of view and it alone is seen as absolute. The claim of the conception of the world as it is in itself to be the privileged perspective from which we can find out what is real depends on the success of this attempt to explain how the other perspectives offer a misleading view of the world.

5.4 EXPLANATION AND PROJECTION

Science offers to explain the physical basis of colour perception in terms of a theory about the nature of light, the way that bodies absorb and reflect light, and the construction of our visual equipment. We might naturally suppose that the task of the science of colour-vision is to explain how objects, which are in fact variously coloured, appear so to us. But what is striking about this explanation, as it is envisaged by the proponent of the absolute conception, is that it is to be seen, not as explaining what it is for something to be coloured, but as explaining it *away*. The thought that something is really coloured will have no place within the absolute conception – 'the scientific picture presents the

reality of which the secondary qualities, as perceived, are appearances'
(Williams, 1978, p. 245). How exactly does this purported explanation
work?

The general strategy is to explain our experience of subjective
properties, including colour, as a projection on to the world of our subjective responses to an objective reality. The first point to note is that
the scientific account can never explain why our colour experience
takes the characteristic form it does. Nothing in the story of light waves
striking the retina and stimulating rods and cones, which in turn send
electrical impulses down the optic nerve, can explain why grass is seen
as green or blood as red. So there is no attempt to explain the nature of
our subjective responses.

Secondly, and perhaps more damagingly, it is unclear how the
purported explanation of our (mis)identification of a subjective
response with a property of the real world is supposed to run. (See
McDowell, 1983, pp. 9–12.) What we are offered is a range of
metaphors: of projecting those responses on to the world, of objectify-
ing them, of 'gilding and staining those objects with colours borrowed
from internal sentiment'. But those metaphors are never cashed. Just
how is a subjective response projected on to the world and then read
off from it as if it were an objective property? What the absolute
conception should offer us, if it is to perform its explanatory role, is a
perspective from which colours, and other subjective properties,
could still be seen as having a place in our experience but now
revealed as not being properties of objects but as purely subjective
responses. But how can it offer such a perspective?

In the case of colours there is a model of perception which appears to
offer the appropriate picture. On this model, the immediate object of
perception is not a physical object but some mental representation of
an object. Most of the time these representations correspond to something in the external world but sometimes, as when someone halluci-
nates, they do not. When things are going well our perceptual states
resemble the way things are. At an unsophisticated level, we take each
aspect of our perceptual states to resemble some property of the object.
The object is represented to us as having shape, size and colour and we
naturally take it that it has all these properties. We project the content
of our perceptual states on to the world and suppose that what is out
there resembles what we perceive. If we think of reality in the terms
suggested by the absolute conception we might come to believe that,
after all, our secondary-quality experience did not resemble anything
in the objects. Our primitive conviction that grass resembles our
perception of it in being green turns out to be understandable but

mistaken. On such an account there really is something which is green, but it turns out that it is a perceptual state and not the grass. There is also an explanation of how we come mistakenly to believe that greenness is also a property of the grass.

Two objections might be raised to this model. First, many philosophers believe that it rests on a mistaken view of perception which interposes perceptual representations between us and the world, rather than allowing us to be in direct perceptual contact with the world. Second, we may wonder how perceptual experience, or any conscious state, can figure in the account of the world as it really is in itself, for that account is only to make use of concepts employed by the physical sciences. (This was the difficulty for extreme physicalism that was raised in 3.7.) We have already seen that creatures who lack our form of colour vision can have no grasp of the concept of greenness. It would seem, therefore, that no mention of something's being green, whether that something is a physical object or a perceptual representation, should appear in an objective account of the world. Once we adopt the absolute conception, therefore, we must be at a loss to understand a projectivist account of how we come to think of objects as coloured. For we are deprived of the materials out of which such an account could be fashioned.

However that may be, when we turn from perception of secondary qualities to experience of value we are not even offered a sketch of a plausible model for projection. We have seen that the non-cognitive element in moral experience is variously taken to be a feeling, emotion or desire. Whichever of these versions is the most plausible, no sense can be attached to the notion that we could suppose a feeling or desire to be a property of an object. Because perceptual states are thought of as representing the way the world is, some content can be given to the thought that one might attribute to a perceived object a property which turned out to be merely a property of the representational state. But desires and feelings, on the non-cognitivist account, are not representational states and it is impossible to imagine how they could be falsely assumed to be so. We are left with no story about how the projection takes place but with the bare assertion that it must do so somehow.

We have already seen that there are strong reasons for rejecting the claim that science provides us with a way of finding out what is real that is entirely uncontaminated by anything that might be thought of as distinctively human. We have now seen that such a conception of the world as it is in itself cannot make good its claim to be the absolute conception because it cannot explain how there can be experience of colours and values in a world which does not in fact contain them. The conclusion must be that the scientific conception has not been shown to be any more than one conception of the world among others, with no special claim to give an exhaustive description of reality.

5.5 MIND-INDEPENDENT REALITY

The moral realist thinks of moral value as something which exists out there in the world, independently of our experience of it, waiting to be encountered. This thought captures, in admittedly rather vague terms, not only what it is to be a realist about moral experience but, more generally, what it is to be a realist about any aspect of our experience. The real world is thought of as what is there anyway, irrespective of what we may happen to believe about it. It sets the independent standard to which our beliefs must conform if they are to be true. What is real is independent of our minds.

How is the moral realist to understand the notion of mind-independence? One obvious proposal is that we should try and conceive of what the world would be like if there were no minds in it. This suggestion is unhelpful on two counts. Firstly, it does not, on its own, offer any clear account of what should be included in this picture and what should not. What you think of as remaining in a world without minds will itself depend on which aspects of experience you think of as revealing what is real. So the suggestion that we form such a picture does not offer us a test of what is real, for the picture cannot be completed unless we already have some means of knowing what is real. Secondly, such a test would be particularly unhelpful in the case of *moral* realism, since it is human agents and actions that are the bearers of moral properties. In imagining a world without minds, and hence without humans, we certainly imagine a world without moral properties. This does not offer us a quick disproof of moral realism, however, since the reason there would be no moral properties is that we have excluded from the world the only things that could have them.

The absolute conception tries to make better sense of the thought that the real is what is mind-independent, not by suggesting that we imagine a world that does not contain human beings, but that we strip away from our experience of the world every element whose presence depends on our peculiar mode of cognition or perception. This gives us a very strong interpretation of the criterion of mind-independence. Any thought or experience that is accessible only to creatures with our cast of mind cannot be a thought or experience of what is real. The difficulties that attach to the absolute conception of reality raise the question whether a less demanding conception of mind-independence might nevertheless leave us with a workable account of what it is to be real – an account that would be congenial to moral realism.

If we reject the absolute conception and allow subjective properties, such as colour, a place in the real world then we need to revise our account of the role that our particular kind of perceptual awareness plays in colour perception. In the picture offered by the absolute conception, colours are thought of as the *product* of our peculiar mode of perception. An alternative view, which is now open to us, is that our mode of perception does not create colours but makes us able to see them. They are to be thought of as real properties, but properties which can only be perceived, or indeed conceived, by beings who have a certain kind of perceptual experience.

Similarly, moral properties are not to be thought of as created by our feelings, but as real properties which can only be experienced by beings who share a whole network of emotional response with us. The non-cognitivist, on this view, was right to stress that the affective side of our nature has a crucial role to play in moral experience, but he mis-described that role. Possessing an appropriate range of emotional responses is indeed a precondition of having any moral experience, or even making sense of it. But that does not make our awareness of moral properties any the less cognitive. We can allow that in moral experience we may be genuinely sensitive to a moral reality while conceding, indeed insisting, that such a sensitivity is only present in those who share with us a pattern of concerns. Thus we may recognize, for example, that a father's over-protective attitude to his teenage son is undesirable because it is demeaning and undermines the son's self-respect. But someone who did not share a range of emotional experi-ence with us would be unable to appreciate the son's feelings, and so unable to recognize the wrongness of such behaviour, or even have any understanding of how it could be wrong.

What conception of mind-independence remains to the moral realist? We can still think of objects and their properties as existing independently of our awareness of them. A real object or property does not have to be perceived or recognized in order to exist. There may be occasions when no one is looking at some particular object but we think of it as existing, with its properties, whether someone is looking at it or not. Having an hallucination or an after-image is not thought of as an experience of anything real precisely because we think that the content of the experience does not exist independently of the

experience. By this criterion, secondary as well as primary qualities
come out as real. We think of the leaves of a tree as retaining their
colour whether or not someone is seeing it; a tree that falls on an
uninhabited island makes a noise. Similarly, the moral realist has
argued, value is presented to us as something out there waiting to be
encountered; the moral quality of the action does not depend on
anyone's recognition of it. If we come to realize that an action was
wrong then we do not think of its wrongness as existing only in virtue of
our response. On this account of what is real, the moral realist can
accept the analogy between secondary qualities and moral properties
but be a realist about both.

Even if it is only from the human point of view that we can speak of
what is real it is still open to us to explain convergence in the opinions
of enquirers, whether on questions of science or morality, by supposing
that they are getting closer to the way things really are. Of course, not all
convergence of opinion needs to be explained in this way; where we
think some group of enquirers has been led away from the truth we may
give a sociological or psychological account of their agreement. But
nothing in the account of reality offered here casts doubt on the hope
that there is one common human world and that our investigations can
reveal its nature.

To sum up. Are we to think of reality as mind-independent? The
answer to that question depends on what it is for something to exist
independently of the mind. If we reject the account of reality given by
the absolute conception then we might say that reality is to be thought
of as *perception-independent* but not as *conception-independent*. That
is, what is real is thought of as there in the world, whether or not we are
experiencing it, waiting to be encountered. But we need not think of
what is real as being independent of our particular way of conceiving of
the world. Our conception of real properties may be drawn from
elements which are only available to creatures with our kind of
experience. By adopting a weaker account of the mind-independence
of the real than that which we were offered by the absolute conception
we can find room, within our conception of reality, for moral value.

FURTHER READING

McDowell (1983) is a crucial, but difficult, paper on which I have relied
heavily in this chapter. He criticizes Mackie (1977, ch. 1), who denies that
there are objective values, for employing a notion of objectivity which derives
from the absolute conception of reality.

On 5.2   Williams (1985, ch. 8) agues that any convergence of opinion in morality would not be world-guided in the way that convergence in science is.
On 5.3   Strawson (1979) argues that the everyday and scientific accounts of the world are compatible and that neither has special claim to be the correct account. Dancy (1985, chs 10 and 11) sets out the main theories of perception.
On 5.5   The idea that what is real need not be independent of our way of conceiving the world comes from Kant. Putnam (1981, ch. 3) gives an excellent short introduction to this difficult area. I examine the question of whether there can be a plurality of ways of conceiving the world in chapter 10.

McDowell (1985) argues that the realist can accept that redness and rightness are analogous, in that both are real properties, whose concepts are, nevertheless, subjective. McDowell's position is criticized by Dancy (1986) as being insufficiently realist and by Blackburn (1985) as being too realist.

6

The State of the Debate – an Interim Report

6.1 QUASI-REALISM AND THE ERROR THEORY

The debate between realists and non-cognitivists about the status of moral properties is essentially an argument as to which account provides the best explanation of our moral thought and experience. In chapter 2, I posed four initial challenges to non-cognitivism, four issues it needed to tackle if it were to make a plausible case for itself. The first three concerned features of the theory which appeared to conflict with our everyday moral thought. Non-cognitivism apparently denied the possibility of moral truth, of moral justification and of moral observation.

The initial response to these challenges was to adopt an error theory of morality; that is, to admit that philosophical reflection undermines much of our normal practice, showing it to be based on mistaken realist assumptions. An error theory would not offer an analysis of our current moral thought, but proffer a sanitized substitute for a way of talking that had turned out not to be well-grounded. For we talk and think as if there were moral properties which we could describe, reason about, know about or be mistaken about. If there is no moral reality must we not give up talking and thinking as if there were? An error theory is thus revisionary rather than descriptive.

An error theory should only be adopted as a measure of last resort. The realist exploited this point in chapter 3, claiming that only his theory could explain our present moral practice. To concede that it is only in terms of realism about moral properties that we can make sense of moral justification and truth is thus to play into the hands of the moral realist. For it leaves the non-cognitivist with the unappetizing task of explaining how our moral thought came to be so riddled with error.

A more promising line for the non-cognitivist is to show that he can find room for these concepts within his theory. Simon Blackburn

(1984, chs 5–6) has recently called such attempts to show how the features of our moral thought that apparently support realism can be explained on a non-cognitivist basis, the project of *quasi-realism*. According to the quasi-realist our present moral thought is not infected with error. Non-cognitivism does indeed unmask an error, but it is not in our moral thought but in the philosophical conclusions we are tempted to draw from it. For we falsely suppose that only a realist ontology can support our present moral practice. The ideal spectator theory can be seen as, in effect, an example of a quasi-realist attempt to construct a version of non-cognitivism which makes sense of those implications of our moral thought that have tempted people to realism.

When the debate started, it looked as if whether one was a realist or a non-cognitivist made an enormous difference to how one thought about morality. If the project of quasi-realism turns out to be entirely successful it will make no difference to one's approach to morality which theory one supports. The theories will have got so close to each other that a serious question would arise as to whether there is any longer a real difference of any sort between them. Would there be any content left to the question of whether there is a moral reality if nothing about the nature of our moral experience hangs on the answer? Before we have to answer that difficult question we need to be persuaded that quasi-realism can deliver the goods. I return to the issue in chapter 12.

6.2 IRREALISM ABOUT MORAL PROPERTIES

The fourth challenge to non-cognitivism asked it to provide a general account of the distinction between appearance and reality, which would justify the relegation of moral properties to the appearance side of the fence. The absolute conception attempted to supply such an overarching explanatory framework, within which irrealism about moral properties would find its place in a more general irrealism about subjective properties. The apparent failure of this ambitious scheme is a severe blow to non-cognitivism but it does not necessarily mean that moral realism runs out the automatic winner. Even if the non-cognitivist has no general account of how to draw the distinction between appearance and reality he may still be able to argue that moral properties should not be included in our picture of the world. Gilbert Harman (1977, ch. 1) has produced an elegant argument intended to show that moral facts and moral properties are explanatorily redundant – we do not need to posit them in order to explain our moral experience.

We saw that simple non-cognitivism denied the possibility of moral observation, there being no moral properties in the world to observe. Harman agrees with the realist that this claim does not match our experience. Given that there is moral observation the question remains: Do we have to posit the existence of moral properties or moral facts in order to explain such observations? It is Harman's contention that we do not. He contrasts two cases of observation: in the first, a scientist, in seeing a vapour trail in a cloud chamber, takes himself to have seen a proton; in the second, I see a gang of kids pouring gasoline over a cat, and setting it on fire, and I take myself to be seeing a wrong action. In the first case, Harman maintains, we can best explain the scientist's observation by supposing that there really was a proton passing through the cloud chamber but in the second case we need not posit the existence of a property of wrongness in the action in order to explain the observation.

What is the difference between the two cases? It is not just that the second observer will only see the kids' action as morally wrong if he approaches the situation with a whole set of assumptions about what is morally acceptable and what is not. For the same is true of the scientist. He will not see the vapour trail a⸜ the passing of a proton unless he approaches the cloud chamber with a whole set of assumptions about nuclear physics. All observation is theory-laden; there is no such thing as 'pure' perception, unsullied by interpretation. The difference is this. In explaining why the scientist saw the proton we not only have to refer to the theories which influence his observation, we also have to suppose that a proton really passed through the cloud chamber. But in explaining the moral observation we only have to posit the existence of the non-moral facts (about what the kids have done to the cat) and the observer's moral theory, the psychological set which he brought to the observation. We do not need to posit the existence of moral properties or moral facts.

Harman's argument does not rely on an appeal to the absolute conception to draw the distinction between appearance and reality. So far as his argument goes, he could admit that the theories which we bring to all observation may reflect peculiarities of the human way of understanding the world. His contention is simply that the best explanation of moral observation does not require the positing of moral facts. Harman does not tell us much about the way in which this explanation of moral observation in terms of psychological set will work but we can assume that it will be similar to those proffered by non-cognitivist theories. Each observer will carry round within him a moral theory which will dispose him to behave in certain ways when certain non-moral facts are judged to be present. In the case of the cat, for example, his moral theory will dispose him to experience feelings of disapproval, to make remarks to the effect that this behaviour is wrong and to assent to such remarks made by others and, perhaps, to take steps to intervene to stop what is being done.

This alleged asymmetry between moral and scientific observation grounds the claim that, while the observation of a vapour trail in a cloud chamber can provide confirmatory evidence for a particular theory in quantum physics, the observation that what the kids did is morally wrong provides no evidence to support the moral views of the observer. The scientist's observation supports his theory because, in explaining why he made that observation, it is reasonable to bring in not only facts about his psychological set *but also* a scientific fact, namely that a proton really did pass through. Whereas, in explaining the moral observation it is only necessary to mention the psychological set of the observer and his awareness of certain *non-moral* facts – for example, that the kids were setting fire to the cat. Moral observations, therefore, provide no support for the moral theories which underpin them.

A realist response

The realist will reply that there are aspects of moral observation which Harman's account cannot explain and which moral realism – the view that the observation is best explained as awareness of the moral facts – can explain. Firstly, as we saw in 5.4, while an explanation in terms of psychological set might account for the observer's tendency to have certain feelings, act in certain ways and make certain remarks it cannot explain the way the experience strikes him. Nothing in an account like Harman's explains why he takes his subjective reaction to be experience of a property out there in the world. Since, for the realist, the world just is as his experience represents it as being, realism does better on this score. Secondly, as we saw in 3.3, such an explanation must regard the authority of moral claims as illusory. There is no room in Harman's model for the thought that recognition of a moral requirement makes a demand on our compliance, because the observation is explained by the agent's moral opinions and so cannot confer any validity on them.

Thirdly, Harman's model is committed to the success of the project to disentangle awareness of the non-moral facts from affective reactions to those facts. To comprehend someone's moral practice, on a model like Harman's, is to grasp which non-moral facts elicit favourable moral reactions from him, and which unfavourable ones. As we saw in 3.6 there is room for considerable scepticism about this conception of what it is to understand a moral practice. If that scepticism is well-founded then Harman's account cannot explain the complexity of our moral reactions. The fourth area in which Harman's account appears inadequate raises an issue that has already been hinted at but which now requires fuller discussion.

Conversion

There is no place in Harman's scheme of things for moral conversion as a result of observation. What I have in mind is this. Someone may be committed to a moral theory which dictates that a certain course of action is right (or wrong). However, as a result of his experience of such a situation, he comes to believe that his original moral judgement was mistaken and so revises his moral theory in the light of experience. Since, on Harman's scheme, no moral observation can confirm or disconfirm the moral views of an agent (for the observation is itself merely the product of those views) such conversions must be impossible. But they seem to be rather common, as two examples may illustrate. Suppose Pius is convinced of the wrongness of extra-marital sexual relations. As a result he condemns all cases of two people who are not married to each other living together. Now suppose that a couple come to live next door to him whom he gets to know and greatly admire. After he has known them for some time it transpires that they are not married because one of them cannot obtain a divorce from a previous unhappy marriage. It may be that Pius finds himself unable to view their relationship as morally unacceptable and so rejects his previous blanket censoriousness about extra-marital relationships. Lest it be suspected that such cases occur only in the imaginations of moral philosophers, my second example is taken from George Orwell's graphic description of a hanging in Burma (1961, p. 11):

At each step his muscles slid neatly into place, the lock of hair on his scalp lanced up and down, his feet printed themselves on the wet gravel. And once, in spite of the men who gripped him by each shoulder, he stepped slightly aside to avoid a puddle on the path. It is curious, but till that moment I had never realized what it means to destroy a healthy, conscious man. When I saw the prisoner step aside to avoid the puddle I saw the mystery, the unspeakable wrongness, of cutting a life short when it is in full tide. This man was not dying, he was alive just as we were alive. All the organs of his body were working – bowels digesting food, skin renewing itself, nails growing, tissues forming – all toiling away in solemn foolery. His nails would still be growing when he stood on the drop, when he was falling through the air with a tenth-of-a-second to live. His eyes saw the yellow gravel and the grey walls, and his brain still remembered, foresaw, reasoned – even about puddles. He and we were a party of men walking together, seeing, hearing, feeling, understanding, the same world; and in two minutes, with a sudden snap, one of us would be gone – one mind less, one world less.

Harman could attempt to explain such experiences in one of two ways, depending on the type of case in question. Firstly, he could maintain that, until the agent actually witnessed the event he had not realized the presence of non-moral facts which, once he knew of them, caused him to make a different moral judgement from the one he had previously made. In other words, if he had been fully informed, in the beginning, of all the non-moral facts he would have originally made the moral judgement about the particular case that he in fact ended up making. Secondly, he could suppose that there was some hidden inconsistency or tension in the moral theory with which the agent approached the situation, so that his original moral judgement only reflected a part of his moral views. Once he was faced with a concrete case the suppressed part of his moral theory came to the fore. In that case, the moral observation could still be entirely explained by his observation of the non-moral facts and his existing psychological set.

While it might be the case that all such experiences could be explained in one of these two ways, it seems unlikely. There is, I believe, an air of ad hoc adjustment to save the theory in insisting that all examples can be squeezed into these two categories. The moral realist offers us a third possibility: that such an experience can reveal the moral quality of the action, so that the agent comes to revise his moral theory in the light of his moral observation. On this view moral theories resemble scientific theories in that they can be tested in the light of experience, and altered if found wanting. This model, unlike Harman's, makes perfectly good sense of the common belief that the moral judgement of someone who has very limited experience, and a narrow life-style, is less worthy of serious consideration than that of someone who has had a wide and challenging life.

6.3 CHOICE OF ETHICAL THEORY

Despite the narrowing of the gap between the two theories, the discussion of the last section has shown that there are still important differences between realism and non-cognitivism in their understanding of the nature of moral experience. Which of them is in the best position?

Earlier in this chapter we saw that there are various criteria by which we choose between competing theories. One theory is to be preferred to another if: it has more explanatory power, explaining things its rival cannot; it is explanatorily more comprehensive, explaining a wider range of phenomena than its rival; it is more conservative, preserving as many of our present beliefs in the field as possible, as well as fitting better with our beliefs in other fields; it is simpler, not needing to invoke ad hoc adjustments or posit unnecessary extra entities.

Moral realism claims to be a better theory about morality than non-cognitivism on the following grounds. First, as has been frequently stressed, it accords well with the phenomenology and thus does better on the criterion of conservatism. Non-cognitivism undermines our belief in the authority of moral demands, and in the possibility of certain kinds of moral conversion, whereas moral realism can accommodate them.

Second, where non-cognitivism conflicts with one of our beliefs about morality it needs to explain how we came to have that false belief. Moral realism claims that in the case of conversion, and of our observation of moral properties, those explanations are not very convincing. In the case of the authority of moral demands, non-cognitivist explanations tend to appeal to Freudian theories about the formation of the super-ego by internalization of parental demands (for instance, Harman, 1977, pp. 60–2). There is an obvious difficulty with such an explanation. Given his commitment to the belief–desire theory the non-cognitivist ought to hold that it is inconceivable that moral demands should have the authority we ascribe to them. So the appeal to Freud will have to explain how we come to have a belief that is not only false, but incoherent. This is a tall order.

Third, realism about values can claim to be a simpler theory in that it adopts one unified approach to our experience. Moral awareness, like other aspects of our experience of the world, is seen as cognitive, as revealing what the world is like. Moral non-cognitivism is divisive, claiming that we need two different models for interpreting experience, a cognitive model for dealing with experience of the factual, and a non-cognitive model for dealing with experience of value. This bifurcation of models also leads to·a linguistic theory with two radically different kinds of meaning, whereas the realist can offer a unitary theory of meaning.

Non-cognitivism's claim to greater explanatory power comes primarily in the area of action. Realism, it claims, precisely because it takes them to be purely cognitive, cannot account for the motivational role of moral commitments. Non-cognitivism can also claim to be a simpler theory by the test known as Occam's Razor, which states that one should not multiply entities beyond necessity. In refusing to countenance evaluative properties or evaluative facts, non-cognitivism presents us with a slightly less cluttered world. This claim would not be very strong if we thought of evaluative properties as being similar in kind to others. After all, Occam's principle only tells us not to postulate unnecessary entities; if we need to postulate a wide variety of properties to encompass the richness of our experience, why stop at evaluative properties – isn't it necessary to postulate them also? If, however, we think of moral properties as being very extraordinary ones, quite unlike anything else in our experience, then we may have good reason to adopt a theory which does not require us to postulate their existence.

This brings us back to the motivational force of moral commitments. The moral realist who adopts an internalist account of moral motivation is apparently committed to the existence of properties whose nature is such that merely becoming aware of them will supply the observer with reason to act. Surely, the non-cognitivist contends, a theory which does not include such very odd, indeed unintelligible, properties must be preferable to one that insists on them. The important, and unresolved, issue of moral motivation is pursued in the next three chapters.

FURTHER READING

On 6.2 Werner (1983) provides a perceptive and accessible criticism of Harman's argument against moral realism.

7

Moral Motivation

7.1 A DEFENCE OF THE BELIEF–DESIRE THEORY

We saw in 2.3 and 3.3 that the non-cognitivist embraces the belief–desire theory of action explanation and that the realist rejects it, at least when it comes to explaining moral motivation. The issue between the two is: Can an action be explained by appeal to a cognitive state alone or must the explanation always include a non-cognitive element, a desire? In taking the former view the realist is adopting a cognitivist view of motivation. I shall leave open for the time being the question of whether a cognitivist in the theory of motivation is claiming that his account is to be preferred in the explanation of only some types of action or of all.

The belief–desire theory has often appeared almost self-evident to its supporters. Once it is challenged, however, reasons for holding it are a little hard to come by. The first argument in defence of the belief–desire thesis suggests that whenever someone acts intentionally he must, in some sense, want or desire to do what he does. Intentional action requires the presence of an appropriate desire in the agent. This claim is contentious and everything hangs on the sense of 'want' being appealed to here. Fortunately, we do not need to discuss this tricky question because we have already established, in 3.3, that the realist can happily concede that an agent who was motivated to act by a purely cognitive state may properly be said to have wanted to do what he did. To ascribe such a desire to him is merely to acknowledge that he was motivated to act by his conception of the situation.

In making this response, the supporter of a cognitive theory of motivation is, in effect, offering us a cognitive account of desire. More accurately, if the opponent of the belief–desire theory believes that a cognitive account of motivation fits all cases of action then he will offer us a global cognitive account of desire. If he does not extend the cognitivist account of motivation to all cases then he will be running two accounts of desire in tandem. Sometimes when we ascribe a desire to an agent we shall be crediting him with a particular conception of the situation, which was sufficient to motivate him. Sometimes, however, in saying that he has a desire we shall be thinking of it, in the manner of the belief–desire theorist, as a non-cognitive state.

What all opponents of the belief–desire theory find objectionable is not the claim that motivation requires desire, but the claim that a desire must always be a non-cognitive state. On a cognitivist account of desire, we need not see desire as a non-cognitive state which needs to be added to the agent's conception of the situation in order for him to be motivated. Rather, if the agent's conception of the situation is such that it is sufficient to motivate him to act, then to have that conception *is* to have a desire.

A second defence of the belief–desire thesis fares no better. Beliefs, it may be thought, are motivationally inert; they are merely passive responses to the way the world is. Desires are active; directed as they are towards obtaining something, they are intrinsically 'pushy'. This, however, is not an argument but just a colourful way of putting the claim that beliefs alone cannot cause action. The realist merely denies the unsupported characterization of beliefs as inert and desires as ert (if I may be allowed this coinage) that his opponent offers.

However, this failed argument contains the seeds of a third and better one, which has recently been put forward by Michael Smith (1987). What is required is an explanation of why beliefs should be thought of as active and desires as passive. That explanation is supplied by the thought that beliefs are responsive to the way things are whereas desires are directed towards changing them. The point is usually made by saying that beliefs and desires have different 'directions of fit' to the world. Beliefs aim at the truth; desires aim at their own satisfaction. Beliefs are true if they fit the world; desires are satisfied if the world fits them. As Mark Platts has succinctly put it (1979, pp 256–7; quoted by Smith, 1987, p. 51):

Falsity is a decisive failing in a belief, and false beliefs should be discarded; false beliefs should be changed to fit with the world and not vice versa. Desires aim at realization, and their realization is the world fitting with them; the fact that the ... content of a desire is not realized in the world is not yet a failing *in the desire*, and not yet any reason to discard the desire; the world, crudely, should be changed to fit with our desires, not vice versa.

The third argument makes use of the concept of direction of fit in two ways. Firstly, it appeals to the fact that beliefs and desires have different directions of fit as providing support for the claim that they are quite different kinds of state. Secondly, its objection to the cognitivist theory of action explanation is that it does not ascribe a state to the agent which has the right direction of fit to explain his action. We can only explain someone's action if we ascribe some aim or goal to him, if we see him as trying to bring about some change in the world. We can only do that if we ascribe to him some state whose satisfaction will consist in the world being altered to fit it. Only desires have a direction of fit that runs that way.

What the cognitivist offers as an explanation of the agent's action is a belief; but the direction of fit of a belief will not do the job. Ascribing to the agent a state which has to fit the world cannot explain why the agent acted so as to change the world. Only a state that seeks its realization in a change in the world can do that. Only a desire can explain why the agent acted in the way he did, rather than acting in some other way, or not acting at all. Desires are active, in a way in which beliefs are not, in that they seek satisfaction in changing the world to suit them.

We might put the point this way. Beliefs are like maps – they reflect the way things are on the ground. If ascribing beliefs to an agent is rather like picturing him as having a map of where things are in his head, then it is clear that simply thinking of him as having a map of where things are would not, on its own, explain why he chose to go one way rather than another. Maps usually depict how things are at the time they are drawn, but we can imagine maps of how things might be if certain changes took place. We can thus add to the agent's mental furniture maps of how things might look if he acted in certain ways. These internal maps will be accurate if they fit the world – not the world as it currently is, but the world as it would be if he chose various courses of action. We now have an idea of what alternatives he envisages, what changes he thinks could be achieved. But we are no nearer explaining his decision to implement one change rather than another. There is nothing in our picture of his mind that could explain why he would select one alternative rather than another. We need to add to our picture something quite unlike a map; we need to add a preference for one alternative way the world might be – that is a state that would only be satisfied when the world was changed to fit it. Beliefs alone cannot explain action; we need to add desires, conceived of as non-cognitive states.

The realist reply

This is a powerful argument. It challenges the realist to show how ascribing a cognitive state to an agent can explain why he acted as he did, and it offers reasons to suppose that the task is impossible. There are two lines of defence that the realist can adopt if he wishes to preserve his cognitive account of motivation. One is to reject the notion of opposing directions of fit as unhelpful. The other is to accept it, but to maintain that at least some cognitive states can be seen as having, as it were, directions of fit running both ways. I shall explore the latter strategy, partly because the notion of direction of fit does seem to me a valid one, and partly because, if the realist can defeat his opponent, having allowed him his choice of weapons, then his position is a strong one.

To be aware of a moral requirement is, according to the realist, to have a conception of the situation as demanding a response. Yet to conceive of a situation as demanding a response, as requiring one to do something, is to be in a state whose direction of fit is: the world must fit this state. The requirement will only be satisfied if the agent changes the world to fit it. But the realist also wishes to insist that the agent's conception of the situation is purely cognitive. That is, the agent has a *belief* that he is morally required to act and so his state must have the direction of fit: this state must fit the world. For his belief will only be correct if it fits the world, if it accurately reflects the way things are. If he becomes convinced that things are not, morally speaking, as he believes them to be, then he must give up his moral belief. He is committed, therefore, to the claim that the awareness of a moral requirement is a state which must be thought of, Janus-like, as having directions of fit facing both ways. The agent's conception reveals to him both that the world is a certain way and that he must change it.

The non-cognitivist will reply that a state cannot have more than one direction of fit, and that the way the fit runs provides a criterion for distinguishing beliefs from desires. His challenge to the realist is, therefore, two-fold. First, he attacks the realist's claim that we should think of the agent who takes himself to be under a moral requirement as being in a *single* mental state with directions of fit running in both directions. The presence of the two directions of fit just shows, he claims, that there are two separable states, a belief and a desire. Second, even if it were conceded that such a strange hybrid state could exist, on what grounds does the realist claim that we should classify it as a belief? We have lost our grip on our only criterion for determining that a state should be thought of as a belief.

The non-cognitivist has a theory which neatly dovetails considerations about direction of fit with the belief–desire theory of action. Since the realist, as I am portraying him, rejects the latter but thinks the former has a role to play it will be helpful to see what parts of the non-cognitivist account of directions of fit he thinks should be retained. First, he will keep the connection between a state's being a belief and its having the direction of fit: this state must fit the world. It is sufficient reason for abandoning a belief that it does not fit the way things are. No state that lacked that direction of fit could be thought of as a belief. Second, he will keep the connection between explaining an intentional action and ascribing to the agent a state whose direction of fit is: the world must fit this state. No state that lacked that direction of fit could, on its own, explain what the agent was doing, for we need to ascribe to him a state that enables us to see him as having an aim. We need to know what change in the world would constitute a satisfactory outcome to his action.

The realist does not claim that all beliefs have both directions of fit; he can divide beliefs into those that are motivational and those that are not. In the case of the latter, all that needs to be said about their direction of fit will be exhausted by the claim: this state must fit the world. In the case of motivational beliefs, whose existence is in dispute, the realist claims that these beliefs also involve the recognition that some action is required of the agent, or that some action is desirable. That state of recognition is one whose satisfaction would consist in a change in the world, in the agent's doing something.

Can the realist meet the non-cognitivist's two-fold challenge? His first objection is one with which we are already familiar. It is simply the demand that we disentangle the cognitive and the affective elements in our moral experience. The realist reply is also by now familiar. It insists on the indivisibility of our experience of value and on the distortion of that experience which results from the attempt to construe it in the way that the non-cognitivist claims it should be construed. We cannot separate out, as non-cognitivism requires, the way the agent conceives the situation to be, from his taking it that he is required to act in a certain way. In meeting the second objection the realist needs to show that the single state in question can be plausibly held to be a belief, even though it has both directions of fit. His answer must be that it is a sufficient condition of a state being a belief that it has the direction of fit: this state must fit the world. It does not lose the status of a belief if it happens to have another direction of fit as well.

7.2 A COGNITIVIST ACCOUNT OF DESIRE

One of the most striking consequences of the non-cognitivist doctrine that beliefs and desires are separate and distinct states is the claim that it is logically possible, though perhaps psychologically unusual, to desire any state of affairs. If the agent's beliefs about the desired state of affairs, his way of conceiving of what he desires, is quite independent of his desiring it then he can consistently desire anything, no matter how he conceives of it. There is no limit to the combinations of beliefs and desires that are possible. At first sight, this view seems to find empirical support in the wide variety of things that people do desire. One phenomenon that is often cited in this case is masochism. The masochist appears to desire pain, something that most of us would do a good deal to avoid. On an account which sees desire as a non-cognitive state this is entirely intelligible. While most of us happen not to like pain some people desire it; this is no more surprising than the fact that some people like cold rice pudding.

Closer examination, however, shows that this account of desire is not very successful in explaining action. Indeed, it can be argued that a cognitivist account of desire does much better in getting us to understand certain actions. It has often been pointed out that there are some desires which appear unintelligible – the desire for a saucer of mud, for example. If we cannot make sense of that desire then we cannot make sense of an action explanation which appeals to that desire. Ascribing such a desire to the agent does indeed tell us what he is aiming at, what would constitute the satisfaction of the desire. But that is not enough to explain his action fully. The difficulty is that we have no insight into why being in the desired state should bring satisfaction. We cannot see the light in which the agent finds that state of affairs attractive. It is here that the realist can make his point. What is missing, he claims, is an account of the way the agent conceives of the desired state of affairs. Only when we have supplied that will we have a complete explanation of why the agent acted.

The way to come to understand how someone can desire, and enjoy, an activity which holds no attractions for you is to come to appreciate how he sees things. Take the case of rock climbing. Since I suffer from fear of heights I find it difficult to see why on earth anyone should want to go in for this sport. Suppose a devotee wishes to get me to understand. He thinks of the danger as part of the appeal. So long as I suppose that the rock climber's appreciation of the danger is just like mine – completely numbing and stomach-churning – then I shall, of course, fail to see how that can be a factor which motivates someone to climb. What the devotee needs to do is to remind me of other activities where the presence of danger, even of a mild sort, adds spice to the experience. He has to get me to understand it from the inside, as it were. I need not, perhaps cannot, come to share his view of the activity, but I do need sympathetically and imaginatively to enter into it. If I fully shared his appreciation then, presumably, I would also be motivated to climb.

Similar remarks apply to the case of masochism, which at first seemed to support the belief–desire theory. People do find masochism puzzling; they cannot understand how anyone can enjoy severe pain. So long as we think that the masochist is experiencing just what we would when we were, say, being mercilessly flogged then the puzzlement is well-placed. How could anyone enjoy *that*? Yet, on the belief–desire theory, we are wrong to be puzzled. According to that thesis we have fully explained someone's choosing to be flogged when we have explained that he believes it will cause him great pain and that is what he desires. This is surely mistaken; more is required to have fully explained his action. The realist theory tells us what that more is. We need to appreciate the masochist's view of the whipping, to discover the light in which it can be seen as attractive. There are many ways into this; we may, for example, point out that some things that are normally experienced as mildly painful can be enjoyable when we are sexually excited, or that punishment can have the pleasurable effect of relieving guilt. One philosopher who had a masochistic friend asked her to explain its attractions and she said 'You know how you always want to ride the wildest looking horse.' Since, as a matter of fact, he didn't, the explanation was not a success! Her approach, however, was right. What all such strategies have in common is to make the outsider see the experience in a fresh light. Just as the jazz devotee does not hear the music the way the novice does – it sounds different – so the masochist does not experience the pain in just the way that other people would.

The realist claims that understanding comes from appreciating, though not necessarily sharing, the experience of the person whose action he is trying to explain from the inside. The role of the agent's conception of the world, of how things are, is not limited, as we saw in 2.3 that Hume supposed it was, to providing information enabling the agent to channel any desire he may happen to have in the right direction. The agent's conception of the situation has the more important role of making his desire intelligible. It is only in the light of his conception that we can make sense of his desire.

The radical upshot of this line of thought is that, at least in the sorts of case we have been considering, the desire, as an independent element in action explanation, drops out as redundant. Once we have understood the attractiveness of the desired object, as the agent conceives it, we already understand why he is motivated to act the way he does. Nothing needs to be added to his conception to complete the explanation. If we entirely shared his conception we would be motivated in the same way.

This is a crucial point in the debate. If the realist has established that an account of desire as a cognitive state is superior to one which sees it as a non-cognitive state then the case for a non-cognitivist account of morality has collapsed. Moral attitudes, it was argued, are not solely cognitive states because they are motivating states and thus contain a desire as an element – and a desire is a non-cognitive state. If, however, desire is not, or not always, to be thought of as a non-cognitive state then the whole basis for the distinction between attitudes and beliefs has been undermined, and with it the case for moral non-cognitivism.

7.3 COGNITIVISM AND CARING

No one can live a virtuous life unless he cares about the things with which morality is concerned. It is built into non-cognitivism that we care about evaluative issues. To adopt an attitude *is* to care; the addition of feeling and desire to a cognitive state are what distinguishes an evaluative attitude from a belief. Where does the notion of caring fit into the realist picture, given that the realist adopts a cognitive account of moral motivation? Realism might seem to offer us the chilling, and implausible, picture of the virtuous person as someone completely cold and uncaring who simply sees what is right and does it without emotion or concern. Feeling or passion would have no place, except as incidental accompaniments to the entirely unemotional process of recognizing the moral facts.

We can now see that this austere portrait is based on a misconception which springs from the false opposition between belief and desire which the cognitivist account of desire seeks to transcend. The crucial mistake, on the cognitivist view, is to fail to realize that a way of seeing a situation may itself be a way of caring or feeling. Again the analogy with aesthetics is helpful here. It is impossible to separate out the musical person's way of hearing Mozart's music from his appreciation of its beauty, and to appreciate its beauty is to care about it. Yet that response is to a quality of the music that, on the realist conception, is there to be experienced in the music.

If the beauty of Mozart's music is a genuine feature of the music, to which one can be sensitive, does not this commit the realist, the objector might continue, to the view that any creature, even one without our tastes, might come to be aware of it? For, if some property is genuinely in the world, then it ought to be accessible, at least in principle, to all observers. Yet, if the outsider did not share our tastes, he would not find it beautiful, which contradicts our original supposition. The realist response to this objection is, as we saw in 3.6, to claim that *only someone who shares our human tastes and sensibilities* can be aware of things in the way that we are. Far from thinking of moral cognition as an essentially passionless matter it is quite compatible with his position to claim that there may be some evaluative features that can only be seen by someone who cares very deeply.

7.4 THE AUTHORITY OF MORAL REQUIREMENTS

In 3.3, I argued that both non-cognitivism and externalist moral realism, because of their adherence to the belief–desire theory, could not account for the authority of moral requirements. Moral requirements are thought of as being independent of desire, in that neither their existence, nor their claim to provide us with reason to act, depends on what the agent happens to desire but, rather, on his conception of the situation. Only a cognitive account of moral motivation can accommodate this understanding of a moral requirement. The agent's belief that some course of action is morally required is sufficient to supply him with reason to do it.

In 7.1 I said that I would leave open for a while the question of whether a cognitivist account of motivation is preferable in all types of action explanation or only in some. If the line of argument just advanced is acceptable then the scope of the cognitivist explanation of action will be wider rather than narrower. It will certainly include, as we have seen, actions whose motivation is nothing to do with morality. This might seem to raise a difficulty for the present account of the authority of morality. Moral requirements are often held to have a special authority. Yet, so far as the present account goes, any reason for action which is supplied by the agent's conception of the situation will carry similar authority, in that its claim on the agent will not be conditional on the presence of a desire. We have not yet isolated what is special about the authority of moral requirements. Our account requires supplementation.

It is not just that the recognition of a moral requirement provides the agent with some reason to act in accordance with it, for that would be compatible with his finding more reason to act in some other way. What is distinctive of moral requirements is that they are thought of as providing a reason to act which outweighs or overrides any reason the agent may have to act in some other way. Moral requirements are thus seen as independent of desire in the further sense that they have a claim on our obedience that is not conditional on there being nothing else which we want more. In other words, once an agent has formed a conception of the situation in which he takes it that morality requires an action, then the thought that there might be some other action which he has more reason to do is no longer available to him.

The view that moral *requirements* provide reasons for acting which override other kinds of reason must be distinguished from the view that moral *considerations* always override other reasons for acting. The latter view would commit us to saying that any moral reason, however weak, always outweighs any other reason, however strong. But there are situations where, although there are moral reasons in favour of a certain action they are not decisive; they do not constitute a *requirement* that one acts in that way. Suppose I have promised to mark a student's essay by first thing tomorrow. That certainly gives me a moral reason to read it. Nothing of great importance to the student hangs, however, on my completing the task by the promised deadline. It is late and I am extremely tired. I decide that considerations of personal comfort are more important than keeping my promise and go to bed.

In such a case I am surely justified in allowing non-moral considerations to override moral ones. It would be unduly rigorous to claim that, in the situation I have described, morality requires that I mark the essay at whatever personal cost. The only way we could save the thesis that moral considerations are overriding would be by claiming that my duty to keep my promise was outweighed by some other moral duty – the duty, say, to keep myself in good mental and physical shape. But this construal of the matter is desperately implausible. It seems both simpler and more accurate to allow that there really are cases where moral considerations can be outweighed by other considerations.

7.5 MORAL VIRTUE

So far the realist has suggested that when a morally admirable person sees a situation as being one in which morality requires an action his conception is such that all other reasons are overridden by his perception of the moral requirement and he is motivated to do that action. On this account, whatever reasons there may be for acting in a way that is incompatible with the constraints of morality do not cease to weigh with him; it is just that the demands of morality weigh more. He still sees reason to do what is wrong; but he sees more reason to do what is right. He is attracted to the bad; but he is more attracted to the good.

I think we may reasonably follow McDowell (1978, pp. 26–9) in doubting whether this account matches our picture of the completely virtuous person. While there may be much to admire in such a person he seems to fall well short of the moral ideal. He is a good person, but that is all. The truly virtuous person, we might think, is not attracted to the bad. Once she is aware that a certain course of action is required of her then she acts willingly, and without effort. Immoral action holds no charms for her. The good person weighs the reasons in favour of the morally right course against those which favour the wrong one and concludes that, on balance, there is more reason to do what is right. By contrast, once the virtuous person has seen that one action is morally right then the reasons in favour of other courses fall away; they are silenced by her appreciation of what is required.

We are not to think of the virtuous person as an ascetic, as someone whose appetite for all worldly things is so meagre and weak, whether by training or natural inclination, that it cannot compete for her attention with the demands of virtue. Where the dictates of morality do not forbid it, the virtuous person can pursue pleasure with as much zest as anyone. Where, however, she sees that morality requires a certain action then considerations which would, in other circumstances, count as reasons for her to pursue an alternative action simply do not weigh with her at all. Her perception of what is morally required silences them. The virtuous person does not decide that, on balance, the path of virtue is to be preferred to that of vice. Vice has nothing to put into the balance which could weigh against virtue.

There is something superhuman about such virtue and we may doubt whether we can attain it. It represents, however, the natural conclusion of the realist account. What distinguishes the virtuous person from others is her distinctive way of seeing situations which enables her to have a clear perception of the demands of morality. The clearer her perception of a moral requirement the less she will be distracted by other ways of looking at the situation, by considerations of what would be to her advantage or would satisfy some craving. Once she has fully attained the correct conception, once she has perceived what morality requires, she will be unmoved by competing attractions because she will not even see them as attractions.

If we conceive of virtue in this way we seem to cut ourselves off from any understanding of the phenomenon of moral weakness. It seems clear that people often know that morality requires an action of them, and yet are tempted and fail to do it. How could this be if they had a clear conception of what was morally required? For the wrong action would hold no attraction for them. It looks as if there cannot be a full-blown case of moral weakness where the agent clearly sees the right but does the wrong. Her doing the wrong must be a result of the unclarity of her moral vision.

FURTHER READING

On 7.1   M. Smith (1987) defends the belief–desire theory along the lines suggested here.
On 7.2   Hare (1964) offers the kind of explanation of masochism which I am arguing against.
On 7.3   McDowell has explored the realist's account of why we care about moral matters in many of his papers. McDowell (1979) is directly relevant, but difficult.
On 7.5   McDowell's conception of the virtuous person comes, in part, from Aristotle (1972, esp. Books 1–7).

8

Moral Weakness

8.1 MORAL WEAKNESS

So far we have been scrutinizing our rival accounts of morality to see how well they can explain moral motivation. A theory that cannot give a satisfying account of how our moral convictions find their expression in action must be rejected. But our conviction that morality is action-guiding must be balanced against the common observation that people can fail to be motivated by moral considerations. An acceptable theory must explain not only how awareness of a moral demand can move an agent to act, but also how it can fail to do so. Not surprisingly, theories that are designed to be good at one of these tasks may do less well on the other.

People are often morally weak; they fail to do what they firmly believe they are morally obliged to do. As St Paul (*Romans*, ch. 7, v. 19) memorably and succinctly put it: 'For the good that I would I do not: but the evil which I would not, that I do.' Even the most conscientious person has lapses of this kind. He may be strongly attracted towards some course of action which he knows to be morally wrong and give in to that temptation. He may be depressed or worn down by personal problems and fail to respond to some moral demand which requires time or effort. He may be the victim of his own high moral standards; he may have such exalted ideals that, although he strives hard to live up to them, it is a foregone conclusion that he will not entirely succeed. The morally weak person takes seriously the moral demand on which he fails to act; he sees it as giving him good reason to act. The result of his failure to act is likely to be the familiar one of feelings of guilt and self-reproach coupled with resolutions to do better next time.

An agent exhibits moral weakness when he acts in a way that he takes to be incompatible with what morality requires. At the end of the last chapter we saw that there are occasions on which moral considerations can be overridden or outweighed by other kinds of reason. As my example of the teacher who decides not to keep his promise to the student illustrates, an agent may recognize that moral considerations favour one course of action and yet fail to take that course without exhibiting moral weakness. In such a case the agent does not believe himself to be in breach of a moral requirement, takes himself to have acted properly, and feels, or should feel, no remorse. In the case of morally weak action the agent judges that, whatever attractions other courses of action may hold, some particular action is morally required of him – and then acts contrary to that judgement.

Both our theories appear to have difficulty in accommodating moral weakness, for both adopt an internalist account of moral motivation. The internalist believes that moral convictions can and do motivate their possessors to act without the assistance of some further motivating state. If that is so, how can a state that motivates in some cases fail to motivate in others? If the presence of a moral conviction is sufficient to motivate must it not always motivate?

A quick way with moral weakness?

Some internalists have succumbed to this line of thought and have accepted the startling conclusion that no one ever fails to act as he believes morality requires. They contend that the test of whether someone is sincere in his claim that he accepts a certain moral principle is whether he acts on it. Failure to match word and deed is a sure sign of hypocrisy. The person who acts contrary to his professed moral principles, unless he is compelled to act as he does, is exposed as merely paying lip-service to them; they do not represent his real convictions which are revealed in his actions.

This simple but stark view may have an appeal to the rigorous puritan but it flies in the face of common experience. There is indeed always the possibility that the man who says one thing and does another may, despite his protestations, not have the moral convictions that he says he does. But the proposed test for this condition and the account of its nature offered here are both too simple. A single failure to act on one's professed moral view is clearly insufficient evidence on which to convict a man of insincerity. A whole range of considerations need to be taken into account – the circumstances in which he failed to act; whether there have been other similar failures; whether he felt remorse afterwards and tried to make amends. Moreover, even if we are convinced that his moral convictions are not what he says they are, hypocrisy is not the only possible verdict; there is plenty of room for self-deception about these matters. The fact that it may sometimes be difficult to distinguish between a genuine example of moral weakness and a case of hypocrisy or self-deception does not show that there is no distinction between them.

8.2 WEAKNESS OF WILL

The phenomenon of moral weakness threatens to undermine our understanding of what it is to explain an intentional human action. We saw (in 2.3) that it is generally agreed that we explain why someone acted as he did, what motivated him to act, by appeal to his reasons. But in a case of moral weakness the agent fails to act in accordance with his reasoned assessment of the situation. He has looked at the various courses of action open to him and concluded that the correct course of action, the one that he has the best reasons to choose, is the one that morality requires him to take. How can he fail to do what he judges he has most reason to do, and how can we explain his acting in that way? This problem, the problem of irrational action, is not confined to cases of moral reasoning. It is a general problem about the relation between practical reasoning and action. Practical reasoning, reasoning about what one should do, is not confined to moral questions. We can reason about many topics: what career to pursue, where to go for our holidays, how best to lose weight. In each case, it is possible that we may come to a conclusion and yet fail to act on it. Nor are guilt, remorse and resolutions to do better confined to cases of moral lapse, as would-be dieters, or those trying to give up smoking, can testify.

The problem of moral weakness is thus merely a specific instance of the larger difficulty traditionally known as the problem of weakness of will. It can be simply stated: How can an agent act freely and intention-ally in defiance of his own considered judgement as to what would be his best course of action? An example, which I owe to Davidson (in *Feinberg*, 1969, pp. 101–2) will serve both to reveal the difficulties and, incidentally, to illustrate the claim that not all cases of weakness of will are cases of moral weakness. Suppose that I am lying in bed when I suddenly realize that I have not yet cleaned my teeth. I am just about to drift into unconsciousness and I know, from past experience, that if I do get up at this stage I may not sleep at all. I also accept that the increased risk of dental decay from postponing my teeth cleaning for one night is so minimal as to be negligible. I judge that, on balance, it would be best not to clean my teeth but to stay in bed. Old habits die hard, however, and up I get and seize my toothbrush. On my return to bed I spend a sleepless night cursing myself for not having acted in accordance with my own best judgement. Why does the existence of such examples pose a problem for action theory?

For ease of exposition I shall concentrate on the case where an agent's choice, as in the example above, is between two courses of action, a and b. How are we to characterize his judgement so as to reveal the difficulty? It is not puzzling that he can judge that a is better than b in some respect or other and then do b, for he may judge that there are other respects in which b is better than a. What is puzzling is that he should judge that, all things considered, a is better than b and yet still do b. Here the agent has weighed all the reasons that he can think of which bear on the matter and concluded that he has more reason to do a than to do b yet he does b freely and intentionally. This description raises three related problems. There are reasons for claiming that the agent's action must be inexplicable, irrational and unfree. In which case he cannot have acted freely and intentionally.

We have seen that it is common ground between a cognitivist account of motivation and the belief–desire theory that we explain an agent's intentional action by setting out his reasons for doing what he did. In the case we are considering it appears that we cannot explain the agent's doing b by appealing to his reasons, for his reasons point towards his doing a. This way of putting the matter is misleading, however, for it might be thought to imply that the agent has no reasons for doing b. The agent clearly does have some reasons for doing b. (In our example I do have reasons for cleaning my teeth since I wish to avoid dental decay.) What is inexplicable by appeal to his reasons is not his doing b but his doing b rather than a. Since intentional action is explained by appeal to the agent's reasons, an action that cannot be so explained cannot be intentional.

Weak-willed action is irrational. The agent takes himself to have more reason to do a than to do b yet does not act in accordance with his reasons. It is natural, in such cases, to say that the agent was overcome by temptation. A whole range of metaphors has been used to illustrate this point: the good self being temporarily over-mastered by the bad self; passion taking over the reins from reason. These pictures may be misleading and themselves encapsulate unsatisfactory theories about weakness of will. But what they all suggest is that the agent's will was not entirely under his control. How could a totally free and unfettered agent choose what he believed to be the worse course?

The problem of weakness of will is a classic example of a philosophical paradox. The phenomenon appears to be only too common, yet reflection on what it involves makes it difficult to see how it can occur. As always, there are two strategies in such a case. One is to accept that the phenomenon occurs and to insist that there must be some error in the philosophical assumptions that appear to show that it is incoherent. The other takes the philosophical considerations to have shown that there can be no such thing; the task then is to show how we could all be deceived into thinking it did occur. The second position is highly counter-intuitive and we need to have explored and rejected all possible versions of the first approach before accepting it.

I am one of those who believe that weakness of will is possible, but to argue the case in detail would take us far beyond the scope of this book. What I shall do, therefore, is to indicate a general condition which must be met by any satisfactory account of how weakness of will is possible. We can then use that condition to test the adequacy of theories of motivation in two ways that will have a bearing on the debate between moral non-cognitivism and moral realism. We have been offered two accounts of what it is for an agent to have a reason for action: the belief–desire theory and the cognitive theory. First, therefore, we need to check whether each of them can meet the condition. Since each theory of motivation is tied to one of our rival ethical theories a failure by either general account of motivation to meet the condition would reflect back on the adequacy of its associated ethical theory. Second, we need to assess the specific account of moral motivation which each ethical theory gives to see if this imposes any special difficulty in allowing room for moral weakness.

8.3 A CONDITION FOR AN ADEQUATE ACCOUNT OF WEAKNESS OF WILL

Any satisfactory account of how weakness of will is possible must explain how an agent can behave in a way that is contrary to his own better judgement. But there are many ways of doing so which would not meet the objections to the possibility of weakness of will which were laid out in the last section. What those arguments sought to show is not that the agent cannot act against his own best judgement, but that he cannot freely and intentionally do so. It is not denied that an agent may find himself, perhaps driven by unconscious forces, acting in ways that he does not wish to act. In such cases, however, both we and the agent are likely to view his behaviour as something that happened to him, not as something he did and chose to do. The central thrust of these arguments is that it is not possible to combine the claim that the agent acted against his own best judgement with a continued assurance that he was, in this particular case, an *agent* – someone who acted and can be held accountable for that action.

When we explain an ordinary action by appeal to the agent's reasons we are explaining what he did from his point of view as an agent. We are trying to explain his action from the inside; to show the process of thought by which he arrived at his decision. We might, of course, also be in a position to offer various external explanations of why he acted as he did, in terms of, say, an unresolved Oedipal complex, or his biological drives. Such external explanations do not, however, offer a picture of him as an agent, as someone who is acting intentionally and with a purpose that he himself recognizes and endorses (which is not to say that the applicability of such external accounts is incompatible with his being an agent). What is needed, if we are to retain our sense of the weak-willed man as an agent, is an account which shows how the action which he judged worse could appear sufficiently attractive to the agent for him to choose it, contrary to his own best judgement. No solution to the problem of weakness of will can be satisfactory unless it explains the agent's action from the inside, unless it enables us to understand how, given his view of the situation, he came to act in the way he did.

The concepts of weakness of will and strength of will belong together. We can only understand an agent's choosing the action he judges the worse if we can see how that action could appear more attractive to him than the one that he judged the better. Equally, we can only see someone as exercising strength of will if he is strongly attracted to the action he judges worse and yet resists the temptation. I do not exhibit strength of will in acting in accordance with my best judgement if the alternative holds no attraction for me.

8.4 WEAKNESS AND THE BELIEF–DESIRE THEORY

The belief–desire theory claims that for the agent to have a reason to act he must have a desire as well as some appropriate beliefs. Before we can see how it can cope with weakness of will we need to ask the prior question: How can the agent determine, on this account, which action he has most reason to do? The obvious, but unilluminating, reply is: by finding out which one he most strongly desires to do. This simply raises the further question: What, on this view, is it to desire one thing more strongly than another? We need to recall that this theory, in its original Humean form, envisages desires as being radically different sorts of state from beliefs. Desires are not passive cognitive states but active motivational ones. This difference is one that is revealed in consciousness. When we desire something we feel ourselves drawn towards it; we experience it as an urge or pull. It is natural, therefore, to suppose that the action the agent has most reason to do is the one with the greatest felt strength; the one which exercises the most drawing power; the one which it requires most effort to resist.

If we adopt this account can we envisage a case in which the course which the agent judges the worse is also the one which he finds the more attractive? It seems not. For how else can we explain one action being more attractive than another except in terms of felt strength? Given that felt strength is the *only* relevant difference between desires which is discernible from the agent's point of view then the action which the agent judges he has most reason to do will be the one to which he is most strongly attracted. No other course of action can look more attractive than the one he judges best and so he can never be tempted to act contrary to that judgement.

This picture of practical reasoning is absurdly over-simplified. Indeed, it can scarcely be said to be an account of reasoning or judgement at all; the agent simply reacts to whichever of his desires currently has the greatest (felt) strength by acting on it. What is needed is a more sophisticated account of practical reasoning which is yet true to the non-cognitivist insistence that an agent can only have a reason to act if he has a suitable desire. What has so far been omitted from the account is our ability to reflect on our desires and ask ourselves which ones we would like to see satisfied.

The first thing that reflection reveals is that I cannot satisfy all my desires, either because they are directly incompatible or because, given the way the world is organized, the satisfaction of one will, in practice, rule out the satisfaction of another. Desires may conflict in that satisfying one desire may bring about consequences which would frustrate the satisfaction of some other desire. I may have a strong desire to smoke cigarettes but recognize that I run the risk of destroying my health, which is something else that I mind about. What I need to do is to form some fairly stable long-term picture of what I wish to achieve and then be prepared to forgo the satisfaction of those desires that cannot be fitted into this picture. In this way I can form a conception of the person I would like to be. In terms of that conception I have reason to act on some of my desires and not on others. I may even repudiate some of my desires, as ones that I feel ashamed of having, and identify with others, wishing to encourage them.

Through reflection we can form desires about which of our desires should be satisfied and which frustrated. In more technical terms, we form second-order desires about which first-order desires should motivate us. At the level of reflection we identify with some of our first-order desires and dissociate ourselves from others. The person who is trying to give up smoking does not want his desire for cigarettes to move him to action. His reasons include, perhaps, his wish to remain healthy, and a desire not to be the sort of person who is in the grip of a craving. Desires, however, do not come and go at our behest. They are not under the direct control of the will. As many who have tried to give up smoking can testify, first-order desires do not vanish merely because we have decided not to satisfy them. They may not only remain, but be very powerful, continuing to exercise a strong drawing power.

This account of a two-level structure of desire stands in need of further complication and refinement, but we can already see that it satisfies the condition that we should be able to make sense of the agent being more attracted by what he judges worse. It is perfectly possible that I decide, on reflection, that there are very good reasons why I should not do the action for which I have the strongest desire. My second-order evaluation of the weight I should give to my various desires will almost certainly not reflect their relative (felt) strengths. So we can make good sense of my not finding the action which I judge to be best the most attractive one, if we measure attractiveness in terms of strength of desire. Because we can now make sense of the agent choosing the action that he judges to be the worse we have left room for weakness of will. By the same token we have made space for strength of will; for only where someone is attracted to the worse course of action can he exercise strength of will in resisting temptation. The connection between having a reason to act and having a desire is not severed because my having a reason not to act on my strongest first-order desire is grounded in my second-order desires as to which first-order desires I want to see satisfied.

The scope for conflict within the agent, because of a discrepancy between the strength of a desire and the weight he assigns to it when he is deciding what to do, can be quite radical. It is not just that some desires may be found to have a strength, relative to others, which is not in line with the weight the agent gives them in evaluation. It is possible that an agent will completely discount, in evaluation, a desire which has considerable strength. The would-be non-smoker may not regard his craving for tobacco as giving him *any* reason to smoke. Indeed, an agent may regard a desire which strongly impels him towards some course of action as a reason against doing it. Thus a sexually mal-adjusted but morally sensitive teacher may regard the fact that he will get sadistic pleasure from punishing a child as providing an important reason for not taking up the cane. In such situations it may prove very difficult to exercise strength of will; the strain can become too great.

8.5 NON-COGNITIVISM AND MORAL WEAKNESS

The most basic non-cognitivist theory is virtually silent about what constitutes a moral attitude or what moral approval is, as distinct from other kinds of attitude or other forms of approval. The ideal spectator theory tries to rectify this omission. To adopt the moral point of view is to adopt the viewpoint of the impartial sympathetic spectator. To take that stance, it was claimed, is to have a standard, the utilitarian standard, by which to judge the correctness of any moral view. To take that stance is not just, as I argued in 4.8, to adopt a method whereby we can hope to find out which actions are right and which wrong. On the non-cognitivist version of the theory, it is also to embrace a commitment to be concerned about human welfare.

I suggest that we view that commitment to morality as a second-order or reflective desire. From the utilitarian point of view, the agent will want to be motivated by some of his desires and not by others. Roughly, he will want to be motivated by desires whose satisfaction will promote general well-being and he will not want to be motivated by desires whose realization will have the opposite effect. The reasons why someone should form such a second-order desire are complex, but we can see how reflection on the problems of living together in a society might incline someone to approve of those desires which promote harmonious social life and to disapprove of those that are in conflict with it. That commitment can be strengthened by education and by the encouragement and approval of those around him.

Seeing the commitment to morality as a second-order desire enables the non-cognitivist to explain how an agent can be motivated to do what is right, even when he has a strong desire to do something else. We have a natural, first-order, concern for the welfare of other humans, which can often motivate us to do what is right. It is, however, both weak and variable, and there will inevitably be occasions when the agent has other first-order desires which conflict with it, and which have greater felt strength. Suppose that an agent, who is committed to the moral point of view, judges that it would be right to visit his sick grandmother, yet very much wants to spend the day at home in his garden. His sympathy for the old lady is not that strong, and his passion for leek-growing is prodigious. How can the recognition that an ideal spectator would approve of his visiting his grandmother motivate him to abandon his gardening, when that is what he most wants to do? The realization that he ought to visit his grandmother can motivate him, even in these circumstances, because he is committed to moral ends. That commitment takes the form of a firm second-order desire to act out of certain first-order concerns, such as a desire to help the sick and aged.

This model also allows for the possibility of moral weakness. The strength of his passion for leek-growing may tempt him from the path of duty. For there is a perfectly good sense in which his visit to his grandmother, which he sees as his duty, is the less attractive of his options.

8.6 COGNITIVE THEORIES OF MOTIVATION AND MORAL WEAKNESS

The realist offered us, in the last chapter, two conceptions of the virtuous person and thus two conceptions of what it is to be aware of a moral requirement. In the weaker version the agent's perception that morality required a particular action always outweighed any reasons that favoured other courses of action. In the stronger version that perception silenced all reasons in favour of other courses of action so that, in that situation, they did not count as reasons at all. From now on, I shall distinguish these versions thus: the weaker conception of what a moral requirement is, is the one a good person would possess; the stronger I shall continue to refer to as the conception of the (truly) virtuous person. In tackling the question of whether the realist theory can accommodate the phenomenon of moral weakness I shall take each version in turn, beginning with that of the good person. The more general question of weakness of will will be dealt with as we go.

We saw in the last chapter that those who give a cognitivist account of moral motivation differ on how far the cognitive theory extends. One camp takes a global view, extending the cognitive theory of motivation to cover all cases. They deny the need to posit desires, thought of as non-cognitive urges, to explain any action. In a mixed account, by contrast, it is only claimed that some actions can be fully explained by reference to purely cognitive states of the agent; in other cases we may also need to appeal to a desire, conceived of as a non-cognitive state.

The mixed account makes available an explanation of moral weakness which, as was the case with non-cognitivism, appeals to the felt strength of desires to explain the attractiveness of the competing, but morally unacceptable, courses of action. In virtue of his conception of the situation the good agent may decide that a particular action is morally required, and yet he may have desires of great strength – conceived of as non-cognitive urges not under the control of that conception – which tempt him towards another course. The degree of attraction that these competing desires exert can explain his failure to act on his best judgement.

On this picture, the motivation to do what is morally right is of quite a different kind from the motivational forces that lead us into temptation. Accounts of this kind have been popular with many philosophers in explaining the difficulties of the moral life, and the possibility of moral weakness. On the one side we have the agent's judgement, usually taken to be the voice of reason, declaring that some course of action is morally required. Ranged against this are various desires, conceived of as sensuous urges or pulls, which tempt him away from the path of virtue. The outcome of this conflict between two quite different sources of motivation will lie with the agent and his moral worth depends on how he makes that choice.

If we do adopt such an account of moral weakness then we may not be able to use it as a model to explain weakness of will in general. For moral weakness is here seen as a special case, where the motivating forces on each side are of different kinds; this might not be true of every case where the agent acted against his better judgement.

What we have so far offered is a model to explain how, on the mixed account, the person who sees moral requirements as outweighing other considerations might sometimes be tempted away from the right. This model is not available in the case of the conception of a moral requirement possessed by the truly virtuous person. For her, awareness of what is morally required is such that it silences all other considerations. The thought that some other course of action might offer her pleasure does not engage her inclinations at all. Since she does not find that other course of action in the least attractive, she clearly cannot find it more attractive than the one that is morally required.

How then could a virtuous person fail to act as virtue requires? The answer is that she cannot, so long as she retains her clear perception of what is required. I follow McDowell (1978, p. 28) in maintaining that the agent who fails to do what virtue demands cannot have that clear conception of the situation which is the hallmark of the virtuous person. His moral vision must be clouded by desire.

I stated at the beginning of the chapter that one way of putting the problem of moral weakness to the internalist was to ask: How can a state that is sufficient to motivate the agent to act in one case fail to motivate elsewhere? The answer, in the case of the virtuous person's state of moral awareness, is that it cannot fail to motivate. Does this show that weakness of will is impossible, on this strong conception of what it is to be aware of a moral requirement?

The difficulty is this. An agent is morally weak if he acts contrary to his judgement that an action is morally required. But, the objection runs, how can this be? If an agent shares the virtuous person's conception of a situation in which he is morally required to act, then he acts. If he does not act then he cannot have seen that the action is morally required. So moral weakness is impossible.

There are two reasonably plausible solutions to this objection. Firstly, we might claim that, in order to see that something is morally required, one does not have to see the situation in just the way that the virtuous person does. The morally weak person may share enough of the virtuous person's conception of the situation to allow us to say that he recognizes the moral requirement, even if his vision is not sufficiently clear to silence the call of competing attractions. He can grasp that it would be wrong to take another course without, perhaps, grasping completely, and in vivid detail, everything that the virtuous person grasps.

The second solution admits that the agent could only have grasped that he was morally required to act if he shared, at some time, the virtuous person's conception. But that need not mean that, at the time he failed to act on that knowledge, the agent still had that clear conception. His vision may have subsequently been clouded by desire. (It is one thing to see the wrongness of adultery when there is no prospect of it, and quite another to keep a grip on that conception when the occasion presents itself.)

To the second solution it might be objected that, since the weak-willed agent did not have a clear conception of the requirement at the time he acted, he did not *then* believe that what he was doing was wrong. If he has lost the conception of the situation which grounded his belief has he not lost the belief as well?

This objection can be met. The agent can still be convinced, at the time he acts, of the truth of the moral judgement that he made when his perception of the situation was unclouded. He does not need to be able to recreate that perception; it is enough that he once had it. Another analogy from aesthetics may help here. Suppose I have heard a piece of music on a couple of occasions when I was in a suitably receptive mood. I was impressed by its simplicity and its haunting tenderness. I listen to it again when I am fretful and preoccupied, hoping it will have a calming effect. On the contrary, it sounds banal, unimaginative and trite. Must I conclude that I was mistaken in supposing it contained the admirable qualities I detected on first hearing? No. I may conclude that the fault lies in me, not in the music.

The global cognitive theory

The attempt to explain temptation and moral weakness in terms of a battle between the opposed forces of reason and desire has exerted a fascination on western philosophers from the very beginning. But there is always something unsatisfying about a mixed theory; considerations of simplicity lead one to prefer a system where all motivation is of the same kind. Once a cognitivist account of motivation has been accepted in some range of cases there is a drive towards extending that account to cover the whole field. If that extension is made then the conflict that can lead to moral weakness cannot be represented as one between two different kinds of motivation – a cognitive state and competing desires. A move to the pure theory seems to leave the possibility of moral weakness problematic once again. If the agent's conception of the situation points to or even demands one course of action, and if there is no room in the picture for competing non-cognitive sources of motivation, how can some course of action, other than the one he judges best, seem more attractive to the agent?

The solution, on the global theory, to the problem of moral weakness in particular, and weakness of will in general, lies in the possibility of competing conceptions. We have already seen that, in a typical case of weakness of will, there is something to be said in favour of both courses of action. Viewed from one standpoint one action may seem better than the other; seen from another position the reverse may hold. From one point of view certain features of the situation spring into prominence and others recede into the background; from a different point of view that configuration will change. Looked at from the point of view of economic advantage it may seem best to build a motorway in this beautiful and remote valley; looked at from the point of view of quality of life it may not. On the cognitivist approach the aim of practical reasoning is to organize these competing conceptions into an overall picture in which the various considerations find their proper place.

Although the competing and more limited conceptions are taken up into the overall one, they are still available to the agent. Even after he has formed a judgement as to what is best, it may still be possible to view the situation from just one point of view, ignoring the aspects that would have to be fitted into a rounded picture. A particular way of looking at things may be one to which the agent is specially susceptible.

When he looks at the situation from that point of view the course of action which he judges to be overall the best may look less attractive than some alternative action. The harder he finds it to maintain the overall conception, and the more prone he is to fall back into the more limited conception, the more attracted he will be to a course he judges to be the worse.

We may wonder why it should be hard to maintain the overall conception; if I have reached a view in which all the things to be said for and against a course of action have found their proper place, how can I then fall back into a more partial view? We need to remind ourselves that the ability to see the world as the virtuous person sees it is not one that is easily attained; it requires training and practice. Few people manage to see the world in that way consistently; in trying circumstances it is all too easy to fall back on less demanding conceptions.

An example may make this clearer. Suppose that I, a naturally somewhat cowardly person, am put in the position where I can help my friends by some deed of bravery. There are various lights in which I can view such an action. From the point of view of my own personal safety such action is profoundly unattractive. From other points of view there is much in its favour. I would be responding to the call of friendship and exhibiting courage. Suppose that my overall assessment ranks my personal safety much lower than the other aspects and I judge that I should act bravely. In reaching that conclusion I may be guided by a conception of the kind of person I would like to be: a person loyal to his friends, adventurous and free of fear. Such a conception may, however, be hard to sustain, especially if my previous habits of life and childhood training have encouraged me to assess situations predominantly with a view to avoiding danger. This more limited conception may come to dominate my view of the matter and lead me to find cowardly inaction more attractive than the action which I judge, and continue to judge, to be the better. In short: in order to judge what is best I need to attain a conception of the situation in which various considerations in favour of different courses of action find their proper place; in order to avoid being tempted away from my considered judgement when the time comes to act I need to sustain that conception so that no features of the situation come to have an undue prominence. If I fail to sustain that conception then I may act weakly.

8.7 POSTSCRIPT: FREE, EXPLICABLE BUT IRRATIONAL ACTION

I have shown how different accounts of motivation can satisfy the condition, laid down in 8.3, which needs to be met by any adequate account of weakness of will in general and moral weakness in particular. To show that a particular account can meet that condition is not, however, to show how the objections to the very possibility of weakness of will that were raised in 8.2 can be met. While I do not propose to furnish a complete defence of that possibility here, it is worth indicating how the problem might be solved.

Since weak-willed action is irrational, how can the agent freely and intentionally act contrary to his best judgement? Weak-willed action is irrational, but it is not completely irrational. The agent does have reasons for doing the action he judges worse; it is not as if there is nothing to be said for it. What he does not have reasons for, and so what cannot be explained in terms of his reasons, is his choosing the course he believes to be worse in preference to the better. What other explanation can we offer? The argument of the last section has shown how we may describe the attractions of the worse alternative so that we can understand the agent choosing it. Weak-willed action is irrational, but it is not without rationale. Weakness is not incomprehensible if we can see, from the agent's point of view, the appeal of the course that he chose. If such action is explicable can we construe it as intentional?

I suggest that we should modify our original account of how intentional actions may be explained. Any satisfactory explanation must exhibit, first, what the agent was aiming to achieve and, second, why he wanted to achieve that aim rather than something else. We explain an agent's intentionally acting the way he does if we can show why the act was attractive to him, and why it appeared more attractive to him than alternative actions. We normally provide such an explanation by setting out his reasons for acting. In the case of weak-willed action, however, we have to show how the action could appear more attractive than the alternative, despite his judging that he had more reason to do something else; this we have done.

Weak-willed action is explicable and intentional but how can it be free? How can an agent fail to do the action he sees he has most reason to do unless he was compelled, by the strength of the temptation, to do the worse? If he was compelled to do the worse then he was not free to do the better. This argument asks us to equate an impulse that was not resisted with one that was irresistible. I see no reason for the identification unless we accept, with those who deny free will, that there is no distinction between actions we could have avoided doing and those we could not. If no action can be free, however, then it is no complaint to say that we cannot see how weak-willed action can be free. If we think that some actions are free then there seems no reason why some weak-willed actions should not be free. This is not to deny that there are many cases where we cannot decide whether the agent could have resisted temptation or not. Of course, we could not understand an agent's freely choosing the worse if we could not understand how the worse seemed more attractive, but I hope to have shown how this is possible.

FURTHER READING

Mortimore (1971) supplies a useful introduction to the huge topic of weakness of will, and includes relevant extracts from Plato and Aristotle (see below). Pears (1984) encompasses much recent discussion.

On 8.2 Hare (1963, ch. 5, also in Mortimore, 1971) apparently denies, on internalist grounds, that moral weakness, as I have described it, is possible.

On 8.6 Aristotle (1972, Book 7, chs 1–3) appeals to the idea that desire can cloud perception to explain moral weakness. Plato (1966, 351b–358d) held that no one does wrong willingly, precisely because, if the agent saw clearly what was best, he would do it.

9

Amoralism and Wickedness

9.1 WHY AMORALISM AND WICKEDNESS THREATEN INTERNALISM

We saw in 2.3 that accounts of how moral convictions motivate us to act come in two main varieties: internalist and externalist. According to the internalist, an agent's moral convictions supply him with reason to act, and are thus capable of motivating him to act, without the assistance of some further motivating state. The externalist denies this, claiming that some additional motivating state is required – a desire of some appropriate kind. In the absence of this further state the agent's belief that a particular course of action is morally right will not, on its own, supply him with any reason to do it and so he will not be motivated to do it. We rejected externalism because it failed to account for the authority of moral judgements. In this chapter we shall examine the charge that internalism, in its turn, is unable to make any sense of amoralism and wickedness. Externalist moral realists, such as Brink (1986), claim that these notions are quite intelligible and that it is a strength of externalism that it has no difficulty in accommodating them. If the charge sticks then we shall have to reconsider our rejection of externalism.

There are several different ways in which moral considerations may fail to motivate an agent to act. The morally weak person fails to be motivated by his recognition that an action is morally required of him. But this admission does not undermine the internalist picture. Firstly, the morally weak person acknowledges that the existence of a moral requirement provides him with good reason to act in accordance with it; indeed, that he has more reason to do the action that is morally required than any alternative. Secondly, that the morally weak agent is not, in fact, motivated on this occasion by his recognition of a moral requirement does not show that such a state is not capable, without external assistance, of motivating him to act. It would have done so had it not been that the attractions of a competing course of action proved greater than those of the morally right course, and had he not given in to the temptation.

There appear, however, to be more radical ways in which someone can fail to be moved in an appropriate way by moral considerations. While most of us are swayed, to some degree, by the dictates of morality, and suffer from the prickings of conscience when we fail to follow them, it seems possible that there are people who are entirely indifferent to moral considerations. In traditional philosophical literature, and perhaps also in real life, we meet the *amoralist* – the person who scorns the curbs of morality and sees no reason to act in accordance with moral demands, except when it happens to suit his book. Such a person will be motivated by considerations other than moral ones. These might be considerations of self-interest, but they need not be. He may have some ideal of how life should be lived which is not a moral ideal. Such an attitude is perhaps exemplified by those who place the value of art above that of human life, like the aesthete who did not care that thousands died to build the pyramids because the result was so glorious. Unlike the morally weak person he need suffer no internal conflict – he is not torn between the requirements of morality and the temptations that are luring him away. Since he gives moral considerations no weight in deciding how to live, he will feel no guilt when his actions breach moral constraints.

We may also need to find a niche in our scheme of things for the *wicked person*. Philosophers have, with some justice, been accused of ignoring the important concept of wickedness and we might be in some doubt as to how we are to characterize such a state. Perhaps the greatest wickedness imaginable would be to do evil for its own sake. The wicked person, we are supposing, is not indifferent to moral considerations; they motivate him but in the opposite direction, so to speak, to that in which they motivate the virtuous person. The wicked person delights in doing evil things for their own sake. He is attracted not to the good, but to the bad. By contrast, the bad person may, in prosecuting his designs, be prepared to cause unjustifiable suffering or injustice to others, but it is not the injustice or cruelty of what he is doing that motivates him. What is so frightening and repellent about this conception of wickedness is the thought of someone who takes a disinterested delight in the ills that befall others and even, perhaps, in his own depravity. He would be attracted to a course of action *because* it was cruel, unjust, sordid or obscene. He is the mirror image of the virtuous person – like Milton's Satan his motto is: 'Evil, be thou my good.'

The existence, or even the possibility, of amoral or wicked people raises a direct challenge to internalism. In the amoral person we find someone who gives no weight to moral considerations in his practical reasoning; he is completely unmoved by them and does not believe that, in themselves, they provide him with any reason to act. Internalism denies this possibility; no one can recognize a moral demand and see no reason to act on it. The wicked person does see moral considerations as giving him reason to act, but not in a way that is congenial to internalism. He thinks the fact that a course of action is evil is a reason in favour of, not against, doing it.

9.2 A NON-COGNITIVIST RESPONSE

Many non-cognitivists have been prepared to argue that amoralism and wickedness are inconceivable. Indeed, this conclusion is built into their account of the meaning of moral terms. I outlined in 2.4 the non-cognitivist claim that it would demonstrate a failure of linguistic grasp if a speaker did not realize that some moral terms, such as 'good' or 'right', are standardly used by speakers to express favourable evaluations, and others, such as 'wicked' or 'evil', to express unfavourable ones. On this view someone who said that the fact that a course of action was evil was no reason for not doing it, or even a reason in favour of doing it, would simply demonstrate that he meant something different by the word from the rest of us. Although such a person may say he believes such a course to be evil he cannot really think it is evil in the sense in which we use the term. For to hold that some action is evil just is to disapprove of it and to be disposed not to do it.

If such a person is not using terms such as 'evil' with their normal evaluative meaning then he must be using them in an 'off-colour' or 'inverted commas' sense. In his mouth these words no longer have their standard evaluative meaning, but only their descriptive meaning. Using the distinction between the normal and the 'inverted commas' sense of a term, the non-cognitivist can now make sense of such apparently paradoxical remarks as the one ascribed to Satan by Milton: 'Evil, be thou my good.' The term 'evil' is not being used evaluatively but only to describe the kind of action which most people consider to be evil. Satan, on this view, does not himself hold his actions to be evil, but only to be what most people call 'evil'. The word 'good', by contrast, is being used in the normal evaluative way so that Satan is to be understood as saying that he will approve of just those actions which the rest of us condemn. If he really thought they were evil, he would not be able to approve of them.

In building the inconceivability of wickedness and amoralism into his account of the meaning of moral terms the non-cognitivist appears to have won a cheap victory. He has defined his terms in such a way that we cannot have a substantive discussion as to whether amoralism or wickedness can exist since he declares the question to be incoherent from the start. He also runs a considerable risk. If we think there might be amoral or even wicked people and that the question is meaningful, then we will have to reject the non-cognitivist distinction between description and evaluation, thus undermining a central pillar of the theory.

9.3 AN INTERNALIST REALIST RESPONSE

The internalist realist will have to go along with the non-cognitivist in rejecting amoralism and wickedness, as they have so far been described, as inconceivable. His reasons for doing so will, however, differ from those of the non-cognitivist, because his account of how motivation is built into moral convictions is different. The internalist moral realist conceives of a moral belief as a purely cognitive state, a way of understanding the situation, which can motivate the virtuous person to act. It can do so because, on both the stronger and weaker accounts of virtue, her conception does not leave open the question of which course of action is the one to take. Her awareness of a moral demand already supplies her with sufficient reason to act. It follows that no one else could be in the same cognitive state that she is in and fail to see that the situation requires that particular action. If someone cannot see that there is good reason to act in that particular way, that can only be because his conception is markedly different from hers.

Thus we cannot, on this view, make sense of the amoralist, if we are required to think of him as recognizing the existence of some moral requirement and yet seeing no reason to act on it. For that to be the case the amoralist would have both to share and yet not to share the virtuous person's conception of the situation. Since he is thought of as recognizing the moral requirement he must share the virtuous person's conception; since he does not see that requirement as giving him any reason to act he cannot share that conception – his cognitive state must be different in a way that explains his remaining unmoved by that recognition.

9.4 AN EXTERNALIST RESPONSE

The externalist has no difficulty in conceiving of amoralism or even wickedness. According to him, believing that some action is right is one thing, being motivated to do it another. He does not deny that many of us are motivated to act by moral considerations; what he does deny is that moral beliefs alone are sufficient to motivate us. We can provide a partial explanation of why an agent did a certain action by pointing out that he believed that action to be morally right, but that explanation needs supplementation if it is to be a complete one. We need to supplement it by showing how acting in that way satisfies some desire of his, by explaining how acting morally furthers his ends. He may have a direct or an indirect interest in acting in accordance with the dictates of morality. His interest would be direct if he cared about the ends which morality promotes – human welfare, respect for the rights of others and a fair distribution of goods. His interest would be indirect if, while not caring about those things directly, he believed that acting morally would be a means of getting something else he does care about – for example, personal security, the respect and trust of others, or a place in heaven. The externalist will, no doubt, represent most people who are moved to act by moral demands as being influenced by some combination of these considerations.

It is quite possible, on this account, that someone should see no reason to act as morality requires. Such a person would not find valuable the ends which morality promotes nor would he believe that acting morally will give him something else that he wants. The amoralist is therefore a perfectly conceivable, if somewhat unusual, character. Externalism also seems to make room for the possibility of wickedness; the wicked man would take a direct interest in frustrating the ends at which morality aims. He would see the promotion of injustice and suffering as desirable goals.

The intuitions which bear on the debate between externalism and internalism are conflicting. The internalist can appeal to the fact that there is something odd in the idea that an agent might recognize that he is morally required to do something and yet not believe that he has good reason to do it. The externalist can appeal to the fact that many ordinary people, as well as moral philosophers, have found nothing unintelligible about the idea of amoralism or wickedness. It is on his ability, and his rival's failure, to find a place for such concepts that the externalist bases a great deal of his case. Can the internalist find a way, after all, of making sense of these concepts?

9.5 INTERNALISM AND AMORALISM

The internalist's best strategy is to allow the possibility of amoralism but to reject the description of it that we have so far been offered. We should not think of the amoralist as someone who accepts the existence of moral constraints but sees no reason to act on them, but rather as someone who rejects morality. We may picture him as regarding the whole institution with ironic detachment or even outright scorn. He will normally avoid moral language because it expresses requirements and demands that he does not recognize. The earlier account portrayed him as someone who shared our moral categories but saw them as having no practical importance. On the present account the difference between the amoralist and the good person is more radical. The amoralist rejects the very framework within which the good person assesses actions and agents.

If we adopt this new conception of the amoralist then we can show that there is no real conflict in our intuitions. A great deal of our moral discourse is conducted in what might be called the language of practical necessity; we talk of what is morally required or demanded, of moral constraints and what we are obliged to do. We are right to find something distinctly odd in the suggestion that there could be someone who recognized a moral requirement but saw no reason to act in accordance with it. For in what sense could he be said to recognize it *as* a requirement? He cannot accept the whole panoply of moral concepts and be prepared to use them to express his way of looking at life unless he accepts the implications as to how he should act which are embedded in that way of talking and thinking. Acknowledging the force of that intuition is, however, quite compatible with the possibility of amoralism. For the amoralist is now depicted as rejecting moral thought and language along with moral action. Internalism is a doctrine about the connection between making a moral judgement and acting on it; it does not rule out the possibility of someone refusing to make moral judgements. So internalism, whether of the realist or noncognitivist variety, can make a space for amoralism, properly understood.

To allow for the bare possibility of amoralism is one thing; to show why someone might adopt it, another. If we are to make a convincing case for saying that amoralism is a real possibility we have to show that it is an intelligible position. As I argued in chapter 7, we cannot make sense of a preference unless we can begin to understand the viewpoint from which it is attractive. We cannot make sense of someone rejecting the moral viewpoint unless we can see him as embracing some other perspective from which morality is seen as of no value, or even as a positively undesirable institution. Perhaps the most common charge that those sympathetic to amoralism have levelled against morality is that it exalts weakness and denigrates strength ('blessed are the meek'). It fosters a social system in which the feeble and cowardly band together to frustrate those who are more adventurous and capable than themselves. It is mainly enforced by despicable psychological weapons, by appeal to the meanest and most cramping of human emotions – guilt and fear.

While these charges can, I believe, be answered they are not without force. Their force comes from the fact that they appeal to values, such as strength and self-reliance, which we share with the amoralist. We can begin to appreciate his objections, although we may think them exaggerated or even distorted, only because we have enough in common with his point of view to enter into it, even if we cannot share it.

Two things follow. First, the simple characterization of the amoralist as someone who rejects moral values leaves amoralism totally mysterious. It is only when some suitable explanation is provided that we can begin to make this position intelligible. Second, it is very unlikely that the amoralist will utterly reject every moral value. In rejecting morality he appeals to values that he shares with us. Not all of these need be moral values but it is likely that some will be. He may be opposed to a great part of morality, but it seems probable that what he seeks to replace it with will contain some elements in common with our present moral thought. In other words, he is not hostile to moral values just because they are moral but because, and only in so far as, moral values are incompatible with the values he cherishes.

9.6 INTERNALISM AND WICKEDNESS

The wicked person was earlier described as someone who recognized that what he was doing was evil and for that reason wanted to do it. The internalist can make no sense of this description; how can he see the evil nature of his deed as a reason for doing it? It would, however, be premature to conclude that the internalist can make no room for a position that he ought to be able to include. For we may well wonder whether wickedness, so described, is intelligible. We could not make sense of the amoralist unless we could understand why he rejected morality. Similarly, we cannot make sense of the wicked person unless we can comprehend why he chooses evil. The purported explanation – 'I chose it because it was evil' – is no explanation at all. We must be able to elaborate the motivation of the wicked person in a way that would make his choice intelligible. What I shall argue is that there are various different intelligible positions which are properly described as wicked, but in none of them does the agent choose the morally wrong course *because* it is morally wrong. He has other reasons for his choice, reasons which are intelligible from an internalist perspective. Internalism would only be threatened if the externalist could produce a clear example where we would be forced to say that what motivated the agent was his appreciation of the evil nature of what he was doing. Until he does so the internalist has no reason to revise his position.

There are various stock characters who figure in philosophical discussions of wickedness, but on closer examination none of them seem to fit the picture of the person whose choice of action is determined by a desire to do evil for its own sake. We have already met the first such character – the devil himself; or, rather, Milton's portrayal of him. Satan might be thought of as an example of someone with a disinterested love of the bad. He does not merely desire to do evil things himself; he wants there to be as much evil in the universe as possible and he calls on others to join him in this task.

However, Milton's explanation of Satan's motivation makes it clear that it is not wrongdoing as such that appeals to him. He is depicted as having led an armed rebellion against God to satisfy his ambition and lust for power. Defeated, he and his army plot how they may continue the war and exact their revenge. Their aim must be to frustrate whatever purposes God may have in order to spite him.

> to be weak is miserable
> Doing or Suffering: but of this be sure,
> To do aught good never will be our task,
> But ever to do ill our sole delight,
> As being the contrary to his high will
> Whom we resist. If then his Providence
> Out of our evil seek to bring forth good,
> Our labour must be to pervert that end,
> And out of good still to find means of evil;
> Which oft times may succeed, so as perhaps
> Shall grieve him, if I fail not, and disturb
> His inmost counsels from their destind aim.
> (*Paradise Lost*, Book I, lines 157–68)

Evil is not here seen as attractive in its own right; its attractiveness lies in the fact that the enemy, God and his angels, hate it and wish to eliminate it.

Approaching Eden, where he intends to wreak fresh mischief by perverting Adam and Eve, Satan realizes what he has lost in rejecting goodness and God. He rejects repentance because he scorns submission and knows it is too late to be reconciled to God, his sworn enemy. The path of evil is chosen, not only because it is a means of pursuing the war against heaven, but also because it represents Satan's only remaining hope of power – dominion over an evil empire.

> So farwel Hope, and with Hope farwel Fear,
> Farwel Remorse: all Good to me is lost;
> Evil be thou my Good; by thee at least
> Divided Empire with Heav'ns King I hold,
> By thee, and more then half perhaps will reigne;
> As man ere long, and this new World shall know.
>   (*Paradise Lost*, Book IV, lines 108–13)

If we take Milton's Satan as the model of wickedness personified then it is a picture which poses no problem for the internalist account of moral motivation. Satan still recognizes, at least in solitary moments of reflection, the attractions of the moral life from which he is now cut off. He embraces evil, not for its own sake, but because it is the only way to satisfy his ambition and preserve his pride. These vices can be seen, along internalist realist lines, as distorting his perception of the good and giving him a warped sense of values. Because his view of the world is ego-centred, coloured by his exaggerated sense of self-importance, he fails to see the harm he proposes to do to others as providing him with sufficient reason to desist from his plan.

High in the pantheon of twentieth-century demonology comes the figure of the committed Nazi, prepared to exterminate millions of people – Jews, gypsies, homosexuals and the physically and mentally handicapped – in the name of racial purity. Evil though the Nazis were, it is clear that they do not offer an example of the kind of wickedness that would embarrass the internalist position. They did not think of their aims as evil; what makes them truly horrifying is that they apparently persuaded themselves that they were good. They thought of the people whom they exterminated as dangerous vermin, unworthy of moral consideration. 'Every single child must realize that the Jew is the Absolute Evil in this world and that he must be fought by every means, wherever he appears' wrote Gerda Bormann to her husband Martin.

Top Nazis appear to have been genuinely worried that, in carrying out this morally necessary but distasteful task, decent Germans might become brutalized. Eichmann said after witnessing extermination by gas van: 'It is horrible ... Young men are being made into sadists.' Himmler addressed his SS generals thus: 'Most of *you* know what it means when 100 corpses are lying side by side, or 500 or 1,000. To have stuck it out and at the same time ... to have remained decent fellows, that is what has made us hard.' Himmler's concern that he and his generals remain 'decent fellows' is obscene, but his is not the language of the disinterested lover of evil for its own sake. We may, of course, suspect that there is a strong element of self-deception and even hypocrisy in the Nazis' attempts to persuade themselves and others that their motives were morally pure. But even if these professions were merely a cloak for greed and the lust for power we still do not have a case of people pursuing evil for its own sake.

The quotation from Eichmann reminds us of another great evil – sadism. For the sadist the suffering of his victim is wanted for its own sake rather than as a means to some further goal, such as the defeat of God or the destruction of non-Aryans. This looks closer to wickedness as we originally conceived it. One of the main aims of morality is the relief of suffering, yet here is a person who takes delight in inflicting it. Yet we can hardly describe the sadist as taking a disinterested delight in the increase of evil as such. His concerns are too limited for that. First, he is not interested in the promotion of all kinds of morally unacceptable behaviour, such as injustice, deception and so on, but only in one particular kind, namely cruelty. Second, he is, one imagines, not interested in increasing the total amount of cruelty in the world, wherever it may be, but only in the infliction of pain from which he can get pleasure either as a torturer or as an observer. In both respects his interest in increasing the sum of evil in the world is much less universal than Satan's; the latter, in his battle with God, will rejoice whenever any human being inflicts any moral wrong on another.

Does the existence of sadism pose an insuperable problem for the internalist? I am not sure we understand the phenomenon of sadism clearly, but I don't believe it does. Sadism appears to stem from a perversion of the common human desire for domination over others; the infliction of pain is also frequently a source of intense sexual pleasure to the sadist. In some cases the sadist recognizes the wrongness of what he is doing but does not always succeed in resisting the strength of his sexual desires. The internalist has already allowed for such cases of moral weakness. In others the sadist does not appear to care about the moral rights and wrongs of the case; he is only concerned with his own sexual gratification. Internalism has also made space for an amoral attitude of this kind. We do not have to suppose that it is the moral wrongness of what he is doing that is actually part of the attraction.

We have examined various kinds of human (and non-human) vileness but we have not found a case of the kind of wickedness whose possibility would cast doubt on internalism and thus support the externalist cause. My overall conclusion is that internalism can perfectly well make sense of both amoralism and various kinds of wickedness, provided these are properly described and understood. It is in good shape to meet the externalist challenge.

9.7 THE BAD PERSON

We have been trying to show that our two theories can make space for amoralism and wickedness. These are rather exotic categories of moral renegade – most of us, like the inhabitants of Dylan Thomas's Llaregyb, fall into the more mundane category of those who are 'not wholly bad or good'. Can our theories also accommodate the person who is, at least sometimes, morally bad? It is a mistake to think that there is only one way of being bad, so the question lacks focus at present. I take it that the person who is occasionally bad will not, like the amoralist, be unmoved by the demands of morality. Nor, like the weak person, does he acknowledge the demands of morality and then fail to act as he believes he should. It is, rather, that his commitment to morality is less wholehearted, or more patchy, than that of the virtuous person. When the demands of morality conflict with his other aims he is too willing to allow the latter to override the former. He may, of course, deceive himself into believing that his actions conform entirely to the dictates of morality. More interestingly, he may allow that the demands of morality have some force, but insist that they have to take their proper place in the scheme of things; they must not be allowed an absolute veto on a proposed course of action. Such a person often sees himself as a hard-nosed man of the world; those who like to portray themselves as men of action – business men, politicians and the military – are, perhaps, particularly prone to take this stance. It is all very well, they imply, for idealists to insist on impossibly stringent rules of behaviour, but if things are going to get done, if wars are to be won or money made, then there is no room for moral squeamishness.

This argument has point. It appeals to something we have already conceded – that moral considerations can, on occasion, be overridden by other claims. There are also, of course, occasions on which morality makes demands that cannot be ignored. Distinguishing these occasions calls for judgement, but there can clearly be error in both directions. The morally overscrupulous person is inhibited by his over-active conscience; one type of bad person may be insufficiently inhibited by moral scruples. Do either of our theories have difficulty in accommodating this type of badness? I think not.

For the non-cognitivist, the morally good person is seen as someone who has a reflective commitment to promoting the aims with which morality is concerned. There are, however, degrees of commitment. At the one end we have the amoralist, who is not committed to morality at all, and at the other the virtuous person, whose commitment is complete and unwavering (which is not to say that she has no room for other commitments in their own place). There is plenty of room in the middle for people who have some commitment to morality, and so see moral considerations as providing some reason for acting, but who allow other commitments to play a larger role in their lives than they should.

On a realist account the bad person, though sensitive to a degree to moral concerns, is insufficiently sensitive, in that he is prepared to allow other considerations to outweigh moral ones in situations in which a more morally perceptive person would see that the demands of morality were paramount. This is another example of the kind of case, with which we became familiar in the last chapter, in which someone shares the virtuous person's perception of the situation to a limited degree. The bad person shares it sufficiently to see that there are moral considerations which weigh against what he proposes to do, but not sufficiently to see that those considerations are here decisive. This is not to say that such a person may not often come to the right moral conclusions. There may be occasions on which he agrees with the virtuous person that there is a moral requirement to act in a certain way. This may seem strange. How can a not wholly good person share the virtuous person's way of seeing things in one case but not in another? How can his moral perception be patchy?

The solution is implicit in what we have already said about the process of moral learning. In some cases it is easy to see what morality requires; in others a great deal more sensitivity is required. Just as the musical novice can spot simple tunes but not complex ones, so the morally unsophisticated may do well with clear-cut cases while failing to see what is important in the more difficult ones.

It is, of course, a further question whether his failure to see the situation aright is culpable; whether it can be said to be his own fault and something for which he is to be blamed. That would depend on the kind of moral upbringing he had received and the extent to which his failure of vision in this case stemmed from other defects of his, such as arrogance or impulsiveness, for which he might reasonably be held to account. Not all examples of morally bad action are ones for which the agent can be blamed.

FURTHER READING

On 9.1   In the text I ignore the following possibility. A moral realist might accept the possibility of a cognitivist account of motivation. He might acknowledge that the agent's conception of the situation can sometimes be sufficient to motivate the agent without the assistance of a desire, thought of as a non-cognitive state. Yet he might hold that *moral* considerations were not sufficient to supply the agent with reason to act without the presence of a desire. He could thus reject internalism about moral motivation. McDowell (1978, p. 25) suggests that Foot (1972) accepts a cognitive account of prudential motivation, but holds that moral considerations do not provide agents who lack appropriate desires with reason to act.

On 9.2   Hare (1952, pp. 170–5) supplies a clear example of the non-cognitivist appeal to the evaluative/descriptive meaning dichotomy to solve this problem.

On 9.5   Hare (1981, ch. 10) takes a similar line on amoralism to the one in this section.

On 9.6   Midgley (1984) is readable and perceptive about wickedness. The quotations from leading Nazis are taken from an article by Jane Caplan in the *Guardian*, 15 May 1987.

10

Moral Realism and Cultural Diversity

10.1 DISAGREEMENT AND SCEPTICISM

Reflection on the variety of forms of social life which societies, at one time or another, have found acceptable, has long been a source of moral scepticism. The thought that there are many radically different social systems, each of which colours the way its members think about moral and political questions, may serve to undermine confidence in our belief that our way of looking at these questions, or even our way of framing the questions, is the correct one.

So far it is the non-cognitivist who has been accused of falling foul of sceptical arguments. But the realist does not look invulnerable on this score. We saw in 4.6 that one of the marks of truth was convergence. Where there is truth we would expect the opinions of enquirers to converge. Where this fails to happen we may reasonably wonder whether truth is available in this area, unless some convincing explanation of divergence can be found. The study of alien cultures, it is often claimed, reveals a wide divergence between their moral systems. Is there then, a prima facie case for doubting the existence of moral truth? Does the existence of alien moral systems also give us reason to doubt our ability to justify our own?

The realization that there are societies where behaviour which we would find unacceptable is not only tolerated, but even encouraged, can be very disturbing, but does not necessarily lead to moral scepticism. That disturbance can take different forms. It may be the shock of discovering that other human beings could behave in these ways; the Spanish conquistadores were reportedly horrified when they came across evidence of the Inca practice of human sacrifice, and similar outrage was felt by those who first entered Belsen and Buchenwald. Such profoundly unsettling experiences undermine our confidence in the goodness of human beings, but they need have no tendency to undermine our belief in our own moral code. The fact that other people can be wicked is no reason for us to doubt our moral position. Nor need our confidence in our own moral views be dented by the suggestion, horrifying though it may be, that the perpetrators of such deeds believed themselves to be justified in doing what they did. For we may clearly see that their attempt at justification is unsuccessful. What would undermine that confidence would be the suspicion that the members of that society could offer a justification for what they did which, in its own terms, was as acceptable as the one that we are able to offer for our views.

It is in an attempt to put to rest such suspicions that many moral philosophers have sought to discover a set of moral principles that could be seen as rationally acceptable by any human being, no matter what his cultural background. As we saw in 3.6, the internalist realist rejects this approach to moral justification as misguided. His model for the resolution of moral disagreement involves trying to discover which is the correct way of seeing the situation. How we see the situation depends, however, on the kind of training we have received. That training depends in turn on the culture in which we have been brought up. This feature of the realist's account of moral justification may make him seem particularly vulnerable to the suspicion that, while each society can offer a justification of its own moral views in its own terms, there are no terms in which one society can justify its own views to another society. If our perception of moral issues is saturated in the assumptions and outlook of our particular culture, how could we offer a justification of our position that would be accessible to someone in an alien culture?

For where there is a moral disagreement between two people with culturally diverse backgrounds to what can they appeal to resolve their disagreement? Clearly each can attempt to get the other to share his conception of the situation but, given their different trainings, this may well prove unsuccessful. There will be little in the way of common ground between them and so each of them may be left blankly affirming that his is the correct conception. The very same sceptical moves that were used against the simple non-cognitivist account can now be turned against the realist. Each disputant can support his own moral opinion from within his own moral outlook; what he cannot do is provide any reason, that does not beg the question, for believing that his moral opinion on this particular issue is superior to the other's. For any reason he gives will draw on a conception which is not shared by his opponent.

10.2 SOCIAL WORLDS

Reflection on the extraordinary variety of human societies may lead to a radical proposal to resolve this difficulty. So far the realist has assumed that there is one moral reality and that the problem is to justify any particular person's claim to be viewing it correctly. Impressed by the extraordinary differences in culture between, say, medieval Samurai society and our own, we might adopt Bernard Williams's suggestion (1985 pp. 150–1) that there is more than one social world, and hence more than one moral reality. The training of a Samurai warrior would enable him to find his way around his social world, but not around ours.

The suggestion that there is a plurality of moral realities might seem to be little more than a vague and extravagant metaphor. We can begin to flesh it out by appealing to a notion found elsewhere in philosophy, including the philosophy of science, that of *incommensurable conceptual schemes*. We employ a set of interlocking concepts to make sense of the world. That set of concepts determines not only how we divide up our experience but also what is to count as a good reason for what. It seems possible that there might be quite different sets of interrelated concepts that people could use, quite different ways of understanding and interpreting experience. There might be no way of mapping one set of concepts on to the other in a way that allowed us to see any concept in one scheme as having a direct equivalent in the other. Since each scheme uses radically different concepts to describe the world, no statement in one scheme would have the same meaning as any statement in the other scheme. It follows that no statement in one scheme would ever contradict a statement in the other. The schemes would be incommensurable in the sense that there is no common measure by which they can be assessed.

Is there any reason to believe that different societies employ moral and social concepts that are so disparate as to lend support to the claim that there might be incommensurable moral schemes? To answer this we need to distinguish between very general terms of appraisal, such as 'good', 'bad', 'right', 'wrong' and so on, and much more specific moral concepts such as 'courageous', 'honest', 'chaste', 'loyal' and 'just'. The latter, which are used to give a more detailed assessment of some particular agent or action, we might call, following Williams again (1985, pp. 143–5), thick moral concepts to distinguish them from the thinner, more general, evaluative terms which can be employed in almost any circumstance.

It is a striking fact that, when we try to provide a direct translation of thick terms from another language into our own, there is often no word or phrase which captures their meaning precisely. This is an experience familiar to students of Greek ethics. We are told that the Greek terms which are commonly translated as 'justice' or 'virtue' do not really mean exactly what these English terms mean. They divide up the moral world in ways that do not correspond in any straightforward way to the divisions in our own culture. The more striking this phenomenon is the more we may be tempted to say that we are faced with an instance of two incommensurable moral schemes. No judgement in the one scheme contradicts any judgement in the other, for the concepts which each uses differ so markedly. Yet the two schemes exclude one another. They cannot simply be combined together, for to accept one is to live one form of life and to accept the other to live quite another.

If no judgement in the one scheme directly contradicts any judgement in the other then we seem to have allayed the sceptical fear with which we started. The original doubt was raised by the picture of two protagonists making contradictory assertions each of which could be justified in terms of the system to which it belonged. We now see that the differences between diverse cultures are too radical for that to be a possibility. Their moral schemes are not sufficiently close for them to be in direct disagreement on any issue. The two schemes do not engage with each other at all. They describe different social worlds.

10.3 A REALIST RESPONSE

The moral realist may well look on this suggestion not as a helpful proposal but as a wrecking amendment. We have a natural and understandable reluctance to contemplate the thought that there might be a multiplicity of realities. By what right do they all get to be thought of as real? But there are more specific worries which the realist may raise.

Firstly, it sounds as if each society creates its own moral reality, but this makes the proposal look too like our initial description of an irrealist stance. The origins of our debate lay in the contrast between the irrealist, who thinks that we create morality, and the realist, who thinks it is independent of us, waiting to be discovered. On the present proposal the realist appears to have changed sides in that debate.

In reply, it might be said that the present proposal is only an extension of a point which the realist had already conceded. At the end of chapter 5, I pointed out that the realist allows that we may, in framing our picture of reality, use concepts which are only available to creatures like us, creatures who share a lot in common with human beings. There can be no objection in principle, therefore, to allowing that a particular culture, in framing its picture of moral reality, may use concepts that are only available to it.

Secondly, the realist is entitled to ask whether this willingness to embrace a plurality of moral worlds extends to physical worlds as well. If not, then he may reasonably suspect that the difference in treatment of the moral and physical cases is an attempt to reintroduce, in another form, something like that disparity of treatment between factual and evaluative questions that is distinctive of non-cognitivism.

Thirdly, the proposal seems to quell sceptical doubts in one place only for them to reappear in another. Might not reflection on the fact that there are radically different moral schemes available disturb our confidence in our use of our own? What gives us the right to claim that our particular set of concepts is the right one, or even a good one, to use? Once that question is raised, however, it appears to be unsettlable. Normally, when we make an evaluation using a thin moral concept like 'right' or 'good' our answer is guided by our thick concepts. It is because some choice exemplifies admirable characteristics, like candour or compassion, that we judge it to be a good one. In trying to decide whether our thick moral concepts are the best ones to use we cannot appeal to any considerations that make use of those concepts without begging the question. Once we have transcended our own conceptual scheme, and hence our own conception of what is a good reason for what, we have deprived ourselves of any means of answering the question. It looks then as if our attachment to our own moral scheme is one that cannot be justified, except by using the very conceptual resources whose credentials are being questioned.

To this third worry two replies might be made. Firstly, it might be said that, since we do not have a genuine choice between moral schemes the doubt is an idle one. We have to live in the culture in which we find ourselves; we cannot choose to adopt the values of a medieval Samurai, however attractive we might find that prospect. This reply is itself open to objection. It overlooks the fact that such choices do face some people; it is a genuine question for an American Indian whether he continues to live the life of his ancestors, in so far as he is able, or falls in with the dominant culture of the USA.

Secondly, the reflection that we can find no way of justifying our use of our concepts without appeal to what is to be justified should be balanced by the recognition that the same is true of every culture. Since there can be no reasons, at the level of reflection that transcends cultures, for preferring any one set of moral concepts to any other we have no reason not to go on using our present ones with as much right as before. This line of response is a particular example of a standard reply to sceptical doubts.

The sceptic argues that we can produce no reason for thinking that our present beliefs in some area are justified. A favourite sceptical ploy is to show that there are alternative systems of belief which are equally well supported by the evidence. We can, the sceptic claims, find no reason for preferring our system of belief to any of the others. The standard response is that since, by parity of reasoning, we can produce no reason for preferring some other system to our present one we are justified in continuing to make the claims we do. It is doubtful whether this kind of reply adequately meets the sceptical challenge. Fortunately, we can leave the matter open, since there is an important argument, which we owe to Donald Davidson, which shows that there cannot be incommensurable conceptual schemes (see, especially, 1984, ch. 13).

10.4 UNDERSTANDING THE NATIVES

How could we come to recognize that the members of another society are using a moral scheme which is incommensurable with our own? How could a visiting anthropologist from our culture decide that she was living in a society that had an entirely different set of values? The realist argued, in 3.6, that we can only understand the moral practices of others if we either share them or, at least, are sympathetic to them. Since our anthropologist would not share the way of life of the natives she can only make sense of their moral practices if she can see the point of their practices; if she can appreciate their evaluative stance. Yet, if she is to have good grounds for claiming that their value system is really incommensurable with our own, she must find their culture so alien that she cannot find any values that she and they share. There is, therefore, an internal strain in the conditions that would have to be satisfied if a claim to have found such a culture was to be substantiated. The anthropologist has to be sufficiently in tune with that culture to make sense of their evaluative stance. At the same time she has to be so distant from it that she cannot interpret their culture and ours as agreeing or disagreeing about any evaluative issue.

We might suspect that the tension between these demands is irresoluble. This suspicion is confirmed when we consider what would be involved in translating the natives' language – something the anthropologist must do if she is to understand their culture. Where the anthropologist and the natives share no language, how is she to begin to learn theirs? She has to start by observing their behaviour and formulating hypotheses about what their utterances mean, hypotheses which she can test by further observation, and by trying to engage the natives in conversation. Since she does not know, at the beginning, what any utterance means, she must suppose that the utterances which they make when faced with some particular situation are similar to the ones that we would make when faced with that situation. In doing that she is assuming that the natives have similar beliefs to ours. She supposes that, for example, when it is raining, the natives will have a belief that it is raining. So she may tentatively interpret some remark which they make when the sky darkens as meaning 'It is about to rain.'

Davidson calls this constraint on interpretation – the assumption that the natives agree with us in many of their beliefs – the principle of charity (1984, pp. 196–7):

Since charity is not an option, but a condition of having a workable theory, it is meaningless to suggest that we might fall into massive error by endorsing it. Until we have successfully established a systematic correlation of sentences held true with sentences held true, there are no mistakes to make. Charity is forced on us; whether we like it or not, if we want to understand others, we must count them right in most matters. .... The method is not designed to eliminate disagreement, nor can it; its purpose is to make meaningful disagreement possible, and this depends entirely on a foundation – *some* foundation – in agreement.

In short, we make people intelligible by agreeing with them.

Since interpretation can only take place if we suppose that there is a large measure of agreement in belief between us and the natives there can be no interpretation of the natives' language under which they turn out to have a scheme of beliefs that is radically incommensurable with our own.

Nothing in the theory of interpretation rules out the possibility that some of the natives' concepts do not correspond directly to our own. In deciding whether or not this is the case we have to recognize that meanings and beliefs are sensitive to each other. That is, faced with some puzzling remark, we always have the choice of supposing that we have correctly understood the meaning of the remark but that the speaker has strange beliefs about the matter in question, or that the speaker has more orthodox beliefs but that we have misunderstood the meaning of some of his words. Such a choice is illustrated in the case of someone who is trying to make sense of Greek ethics. Having decided to translate some Greek word as, say, 'justice' he may then find Plato making some remark using that word which strikes him as odd. He has the choice of supposing either that Plato had false beliefs about justice or that the Greek concept in question is not quite the same as the one we denote by the word 'justice'. The fact that we may decide that some of the natives' concepts do not correspond to our own does not show that we cannot communicate with them. On the contrary, we could not arrive at this conclusion unless we could communicate with them.

There can be no hard and fast rule about how we make such decisions; our aim, as always in interpretation, must be to make most sense of the alien speaker's position *as a whole*. Any choices we make in one area of interpretation are bound to have a knock-on effect in other areas. Interpretation is a *holistic* enterprise; no part of the web of belief and meaning can be dealt with on its own.

Understanding their morality

The argument from the nature of interpretation is designed to show that there cannot be wholly incommensurable conceptual schemes. Still, it might be argued, that does not show that there might not be incommensurable *moral* schemes. Could not our anthropologist see the natives as sharing with us many beliefs about the physical world while employing quite alien moral concepts?

A combination of three views might encourage the thought that, in the case of moral views, we do not have to agree with others to make them intelligible. The first is the view that interpretation requires only agreement in belief and not agreement in desire. The second is that we know what desires people have simply by observing their behaviour. The third is that a moral view is essentially a matter of having a pro or con attitude to some type of action; that is, wanting actions of that type performed or not performed. Given this combination of doctrines it is held that we simply find out what the locals' moral views are by watching how they behave. All three claims, which are typical of moral non-cognitivism, are mistaken.

The first is mistaken because desires and beliefs are also sensitive to each other. As I argued in 7.2, in ascribing a desire to another we must make it intelligible that he should have that desire, and this must involve our understanding how someone could find this state attractive. We can only do this by making sense of that desire in the light of other beliefs that he has about the object. In so far as we fail to do this we have reason to doubt that we have correctly interpreted his desires. The second is false for similar reasons. In order to see how someone's action is an expression of his desires in a way that is explanatory we need to have an account of what he believes as well. The native may draw a sketch of a buffalo on a cave wall. We may say, trivially, that he must have wanted to sketch a buffalo, but without reference to his beliefs we cannot say what other beliefs underlay his action in a way that enables us to see its point.

The third claim is also mistaken. The view that to have a favourable moral attitude towards something is just to want it to happen is too simple. There are not just two moral attitudes to anything, pro and con, but a whole complex range of evaluations that we make in moral assessment. This is why we employ thick moral concepts. Any proper understanding of the natives' position must take account of what kind of moral assessment they give of different activities. We cannot discover the moral views of an alien society simply by watching what they do and seeing what practices they encourage or discourage. A moral attitude is one for which its proponents can give reasons of a certain sort; according to the principles of interpretation, we must see those reasons as being the right sort of reasons before we can see their attitude as a moral one. There are, after all, lots of activities, such as playing sport or giving tea-parties, that are encouraged in our society but which it would be bizarre to think of as being motivated by moral concerns.

To sum up: the suggestion that our moral commitments can vary independently of our other beliefs is characteristic of non-cognitivism. The realist has shown that this suggestion must be rejected; we need to understand the other beliefs of the agent in order to make sense of his moral beliefs. The enterprise of interpretation is holistic; no one part of the natives' thought can be excluded from it. Since the principles of interpretation rule out the possibility of incommensurable conceptual schemes in general they also rule out, therefore, the possibility that there are incommensurable moral schemes.

10.5 CRITICAL REFLECTION

The lesson of the previous section is that disagreement can only take place against a background of agreement. Disagreement can nevertheless be widespread, significant and hard to resolve. The existence and persistence of disagreement is one of the factors that may spark off critical reflection about our methods of justification. How can we go about assessing those methods, detecting inadequate ones and replacing them? The history of philosophy supplies two models of critical reflection.

The first, which is found most notably in Descartes, is impressed by the fact that no method of justification can be immune from critical scrutiny if the job is to be done thoroughly. To attempt to justify one of those methods by appeal to another would be to try to pull ourselves up by our own bootstraps. We must suspend belief in all of them and then subject each to radical rational inspection, only allowing it back into our belief system if it is guaranteed flawless. The difficulty is that, having temporarily forsworn the use of all our methods of justification until they have been shown to be sound, we have left ourselves with nothing to which we can appeal when we come to subject each method to rational test. We cannot transcend our scheme of justification and try to examine it, as a whole, from the outside because there is no point that we can occupy from which this scrutiny could take place.

The second account, convinced by this objection to the first model, recognizes that we cannot question all of our beliefs and principles at once. We can question, adjust or reject some of our beliefs, but only in the light of others to which we hold fast, and which cannot themselves be under examination at the same time. No belief, however, is immune from criticism, although some beliefs are much better entrenched than others. Our system of beliefs may be compared, in an image we owe to the Austrian philosopher Otto Neurath, to a ship at sea. Any rotten plank can be repaired or replaced, but to take up all the planks at once in order to check them for rot would bring the voyage to a speedy end. If we adopt, as I think we should, this second model of critical reflection then we shall have adopted a holistic model of justification. Each belief is supported by the other beliefs in the set. If a belief is justified it is by its place in the whole set; there is nothing external to the set in terms of which it can be assessed.

Let us return to the difficulty with which we started this chapter. When I am in disagreement with someone else about a moral issue there will be many things which we have in common and to which we can appeal in an attempt to resolve our disagreement. On those matters where we disagree there can, however, be a symmetry, with respect to justification, between my opponent's position and my own. Each of us has reasons for holding to his conclusion and rejecting the other's. Each takes his opponent to be mistaken and may be able to give some reasonable explanation of his error. Each claims that he is seeing the matter aright and that he is able to justify that claim from within his own position. Suppose that we are unable to settle our disagreement; reasons that seem compelling to me fail to impress him, and vice versa.

Should not the recognition of the symmetry of our positions shake the confidence of each that his view is correct, or even that there is one right way of seeing the matter?

There is a harmless way of acceding to this point and an unacceptable one. Let us recall that, since there are no incommensurable conceptual schemes, disagreement is going to occur against a background of agreement. The reasons which my opponent uses to justify his position are not, therefore, going to be totally alien. It is perfectly proper for me to be led to re-examine my own view by the recognition that someone, who is normally sensitive to many of the same considerations as myself, is here disagreeing with me. This is critical reflection occurring in its proper place, within the network of my own current beliefs. The result of that reflection may be a reaffirmation of my own position, and my reasons for holding it, or it may be a change in some of my opinions.

The improper thought is the claim that the recognition of symmetry is itself a reason for me to doubt, or even to withdraw, my claim to see things aright, even though I cannot see any force in the other position. This is to succumb to the despairing counsels of the first model of justification. In vainly trying to transcend my own viewpoint I lose all reason for preferring my position to any other. The suggestion that there were incommensurable moral schemes forced this first model on us. Apparently faced with a moral scheme so alien that no part of it could be absorbed into our own, we were left with a straight choice between accepting or rejecting the other scheme. Since there was no common ground in terms of which that choice could be rationally made, we were left with the impression that critical reflection merely disturbed our present beliefs without offering anything in their place. Since there are no incommensurable schemes, critical reflection should be construed on the lines of the second model. There is common ground from which discussion can take off. Critical reflection can lead us to adapt our own views in the light of what seems good in the moral views of another culture. If, however, we have re-examined our own views and found them satisfactory there are no good grounds for losing confidence in them simply because others do not agree with us.

10.6 PARTICULARISM AND JUSTIFICATION

While we have found that there can be genuine critical reflection about our own moral beliefs, which can lead us either to change them, or to place renewed confidence in them, it may still be felt that this response has not addressed the central worry about realist epistemology with which we started – the extent to which our moral views are the product of cultural training. We have seen that whether someone can see some consideration as giving him reason to act may itself depend on his having had appropriate training. Can we regard a moral stance that is only available to those with a certain cultural conditioning as being rationally grounded? We may be tempted to resurrect the symmetry argument; if I had received the same training as my opponent, then I would share his position, and vice versa. What grounds can I have for regarding the training that I have received as superior to his, as more likely to enable me to get at the moral truth?

It is worth pointing out that, if this is a genuine epistemological worry, then it is not confined to ethics. It has been argued that all our beliefs, and our methods of justifying them, are grounded in community agreement about what counts as evidence for what. New members have to be trained in this system so that they can learn what is the correct move to make at some particular juncture. Since, as we have seen, there is nothing outside the system of belief to which we can appeal in order to justify it, our confidence in it must ultimately rest on the shared view that these beliefs are reasons for those, that this is the correct move to make at this point, and so on.

The symmetry argument only gets a grip when there is no route by which a member of one culture can reach a position from which he can form a reasonable assessment of the beliefs of another culture. In that case there would simply be two systems of belief blankly opposing each other, each rejecting the other from its own stronghold. But this is not the position we are in. We can extend our sensitivity by suitable training and practice so that we can come to appreciate whole areas of human experience to which we were previously blind. Aesthetic sensitivity provides a striking example. We can extend our range of appreciation to include the music, painting and drama of cultures very different from our own. Once someone has extended his range, he is then in a position to draw illuminating parallels and contrasts between art forms in different cultures. He can make reasoned comparative assessments which do not merely reflect the unexamined prejudices of his own society.

Are there any reasons why a similar extension of our sensitivity should not be possible in the moral case? One disanalogy might strike us. In the aesthetic case there is no direct conflict between our taste in, say, music and that of others – the Chinese or the Indians, for example. The existence of other aesthetic sensibilities does nothing to threaten the validity of our own. We can develop oriental tastes in music without losing our occidental ones. In the moral case it does not seem so easy to extend our appreciation of the merits of some other way of life without abandoning, or at least modifying, our commitment to our own. It may be much harder, therefore, to come to a position in which a reasoned comparison of the competing moral stances can be made. There will remain the doubt that, if we reject the moral position of another culture, it is merely because we cannot sufficiently distance ourselves from our own.

It is easy to exaggerate these disanalogies. On the one hand, there are genuine disputes in aesthetic matters; not every view can be accommodated. Moreover, the development of new sensitivities may threaten one's existing tastes. An increasing appreciation of classical music may make one's earlier liking for pop music seem misplaced – it may now seem banal and 'unimaginative. On the other hand, not all differences in moral outlook need be viewed as confrontational. One may become sensitive to the good points of some other way of life without revising one's assessment of the value of one's own. In order to be in a good position to judge it is not necessary to adopt the evaluative stance of the other culture; it is enough that one has insight into its strengths and weaknesses.

10.7 INSIGHT AND TOLERANCE

It is all too easy to condemn what is alien in other cultures. Where one society is in a position to dominate and conquer others that attitude can lead to the intolerant suppression of the way of life of others, where it differs in any way from one's own. Victorian missionaries believed one of their first tasks, on converting the natives of the British Empire to Christianity, was to persuade them to wear more 'modest' clothing and to abandon polygamy. An understandable distaste for this brand of cultural imperialism can produce an equally undiscriminating backlash – an insistence that the social and moral practices of other societies are beyond criticism.

Behind this latter attitude there often lurks some version of the thought that, in an extreme form, leads to the claim that there are incommensurable moral systems – the thought that each way of life is justified in its own terms. But trying to extract a principle of universal toleration from that thought is doubly mistaken. Firstly because, as we have seen, it is not the case that there are a plurality of totally independent schemes each offering its own separate standards of justification. Secondly, even if it were true, such a claim could not be used as an argument for a foreign relations policy of live and let live. If a society could justify, 'in its own terms', a policy of cultural imperialism, then it would not be reasonable to expect it to be deterred by the thought that another society might be able to justify the rejection of such a policy, in *its* own terms. For, *ex hypothesi*, the imperialist society does not recognize the justificatory systems of other societies. There are no quick knock-down arguments to universal toleration by this route.

These two extreme positions – the outright condemnation of any ways of life other than our own and the total refusal to pass any judgement on other moral practices – are equally unattractive. We need to be able to accept that some ways of life offer acceptable alternative forms of human society and that some do not. We may, for example, have considerable admiration for the way of life practised by aboriginal bushmen while condemning the racism of present-day white South Africa. Our preparedness to draw these distinctions must rest on a detailed and careful consideration of the particular case before us and not on some blanket principle as to how we are to judge other societies. One general point does, however, apply. To the usual complexities of making moral judgements is added the difficulty that the society in question is not our own and we may have failed fully to grasp their point of view. Here, even more than usual, we need to be open to correction and to resist the human urge to rush to judgement.

The suggestion that we might find other ways of life acceptable may raise a puzzle about consistency. How, for example, could an American condemn bigamy in his own society but think it acceptable among the natives of Polynesia? This position is surely either straight-forwardly incoherent or, at best, patronizing, in that it implies that the Polynesians know no better and so can be forgiven their wayward marital arrangements.

Such a judgement need be neither muddled nor condescending. For the very different social structures in the two societies make the taking of a second wife a very different act in each case. In the USA the bigamous relationship has no legal expression and will find no social recognition. Even where no deceit is involved, such an arrangement will almost inevitably bring considerable pain to at least some of the people involved. In a society where such practices find their proper place no such unpleasant consequences will follow a polygamous marriage, which will seem quite suitable to all involved. It is a mistake to think that marriage in one society is just like marriage in any other society, so that whatever judgement is made in the one case should be made in them all. Similar remarks apply in other cases where different social institutions are in place.

One final qualification needs to be made. So far, for ease of exposition, I have maintained the myth that societies are comparatively homogeneous and that the boundary between one society and another is clearly delineated. Both assumptions are false. Within even the most uniform of societies there are complex webs of sub-cultures. Many factors, especially the spread of western influence, have blurred the boundaries between one culture and another. So people in our own society can, on occasion, seem quite alien, and distant cultures can suddenly appear disconcertingly familiar. Such considerations only serve to underline the point that there is no position so close to our own that it does not require some sympathetic interpretation in order to understand it, and no viewpoint so distant from us that it is completely opaque.

Our relation with other societies and cultures is a complex area and I have only scratched the surface. Even if we do feel justified in condemning racism or the use of torture in other countries, as well as in our own, it is a further step to decide that we are justified in interfering to prevent those practices. This problem is perhaps particularly acute where members of more than one culture live in close proximity. What steps, if any, should members of one community take to prevent members of the other community doing things of which they disapprove? These issues have been raised in British society with regard to such practices among minority groups as ritual animal slaughter and female circumcision. Conversely, should those who are living in a foreign society live by the adage 'When in Rome do as the Romans do', and themselves engage in activities which they find unacceptable in order not to cause offence to their hosts? These difficult questions cannot even be sensibly aired until we recognize that, with care and imagination, we can extend our moral sensibilities well beyond the boundary of our own culture. Only when we understand others have we earned the right to applaud or condemn their way of life.

FURTHER READING

Some of the ideas in this chapter stem from a seminar on moral realism, run by John McDowell and Donald Davidson, held at Oxford University in the summer term of 1985. My main target in this chapter is Williams (1985, ch. 8), but I have over-simplified his position considerably. Davidson (1984) is tough going. Dancy (1985, ch. 7) provides a good introduction to the whole question of translation. Kuhn (1962) is the classic source of the claim that there can be incommensurable scientific theories. Lurking behind these thoughts is the problem of relativism. For a good introduction to that topic see Williams (1973b). Williams (1985, ch. 9) deals with the issue in a more sophisticated, and more controversial, way.

11

Non-Cognitivism and Utilitarianism

11.1 ETHICS AND MORAL THEORY

It is commonly thought that the debate between moral non-cognitivism and realism, although of considerable theoretical interest, has no practical consequences; in terms of how one lives one's life it makes little difference which ethical theory one embraces. This view is mistaken. Questions of high theory can have a bearing on the nature of everyday moral thinking. As we saw in 4.4, it is a fallacy to claim that discussions about the nature of moral thought can have no bearing on first-order, practical moral issues. More specifically, in terms of the distinction which I drew in 1.7, our choice of ethical theory can have consequences for our conception of moral justification, and hence for our assessment of the prospects of moral theory. Ethical theories, of which non-cognitivism and realism are two examples, are concerned with questions about the nature and status of moral judgements and properties. Moral theories seek to provide a general method of resolving particular moral questions – a justified procedure for determining which kinds of action are right and which wrong.

The ideal spectator theory is a case in point; it seemed that adopting it as an analysis of the nature of the moral point of view committed one to a particular moral theory – namely utilitarianism. This claim has been endorsed by Rawls (1971, p. 185) and by Hare (1973, and in Daniels, 1975, p. 94).

The most attractive kind of moral realism also has connections with moral theory, though of a different kind. For it naturally leads to moral particularism (3.6) which, since it claims that our moral practice can never be codified, denies that such a thing as a systematized moral theory is possible. In the remaining chapters I want to explore these connections in more detail, beginning with that between non-cognitivism and utilitarianism.

These connections between ethical and moral theory are controversial. Bernard Williams, for example, though sympathetic to some version of non-cognitivism, is extremely hostile to utilitarianism. By contrast, some moral realists, such as Brink (1988) and Sturgeon (1986) believe that utilitarianism is the correct moral theory. We cannot assess these claims and counter-claims until we have a clearer idea of what utilitarianism is.

11.2 UTILITARIANISM

In broad terms, utilitarianism is the easiest of moral theories to define; it tells us that our moral duty is to produce as much happiness as possible. When it comes to the fine detail, however, several different accounts emerge depending on our answers to certain key questions. Some concern the scope of the theory: for example, whose happiness is to be taken into account – just that of human beings, or that of all sentient beings including animals? Some concern the nature of our moral duty – are we to try to produce as much happiness as possible each time we act, or are we to live by rules which are designed to increase happiness in the majority of cases? Others concern the definition of happiness – does happiness consist in getting what one needs, or having one's interests furthered, or having lots of pleasure or enjoyment, or having one's desires satisfied? Different answers to these questions will produce versions of utilitarianism that are importantly different from each other, but I shall disregard these complications for the moment.

Structurally, utilitarianism is a *monistic* theory; that is, it claims that there is only one morally relevant property, happiness, and only one basic moral principle, to maximize happiness. It is also a *consequentialist* theory; it judges the rightness or wrongness of an action purely by its consequences; the right action is the one which has better consequences, in terms of human happiness, than any of the alternatives. (These two components are separable; some monists have not been consequentialists, and vice versa.)

The main opposition to utilitarianism is provided by theories which are pluralist and non-consequentialist in structure. The pluralist believes that more than one property is morally relevant. Traditionally, he also holds that there are a number of moral principles which are independent of each other and cannot be reduced to, or derived from, one basic principle. (The particularist is an exception here; he is a pluralist who does not believe in moral principles.) Examples from our ordinary moral thought would include 'Don't tell lies'; 'Don't steal';

'Keep your promises'. According to the pluralist such principles can stand on their own feet and do not need to be backed up by appeal to the basic utilitarian principle. In following these principles we are often justified in acting in ways that we know will not maximize happiness. Similarly, he may hold that there is a plurality of values. Beauty, truth, justice, for example, may be among the things we value, even when the pursuit of them does not necessarily maximize human happiness.

Perhaps the feature of utilitarianism which generates the most antagonism among its opponents is its *consequentialism*. The guiding principle of consequentialism appears to be the dictum that the end justifies the means. Any action, including disloyalty, lying, cheating and even murder, is permissible, indeed obligatory, if it needs to be done to achieve some good result and if the good achieved in the end outweighs the harm done on the way. What matters is not *how* the good result is brought about, or *who* brings it about, but simply that it is brought about. Consequentialism is only concerned with securing the best outcome.

In opposition to consequentialist theories are *agent-centred* moralities. On such accounts the primary responsibility of each agent is to ensure that his own actions do not fall below certain moral standards, nor breach particular obligations he has to a specific person or group of people, even if he knows that the consequences will be worse if he refuses to compromise his principles. He has only a secondary duty to prevent others from doing wrong. In particular, he must not allow himself to be tempted to act wrongly in order to frustrate the evil plans of others. If he acts rightly but others act wrongly, so that bad consequences flow from his choice, he is not responsible for the harm done; those who acted wrongly are.

Acts of terrorism often raise this problem in a painful form. Suppose a group of plane hijackers are threatening to kill all the passengers unless the British government agrees to hand over three of their opponents who have been granted political asylum in Britain. The government knows that, if the exiles are handed over to the hijackers, they will be tortured and executed. There is also good reason to believe that the hijackers will carry out their threat to kill the passengers since other members of their group have done so in past hijackings. On consequentialist reasoning, there is clearly a case for handing over the three exiles in order to save the lives of a much larger number of passengers. But there are obvious moral objections to doing so. In granting exile to these three the government has placed them under its protection so that it would be a breach of trust to hand them over. Indeed, the government would be guilty of complicity in their murder.

An agent-centred morality could insist that the primary duty of the government was to behave in a morally honourable way and to refuse to hand over the men, even if, as a result, more murders will be committed than if the government had complied with the hijackers' demands. This does not mean that an agent should give no weight to preventing bad consequences and evil deeds. It means that his efforts to attain those desirable ends should be limited by the constraint that he do nothing wrong himself. In other words, the agent should act with integrity, refusing to sink to the level of immoral people, even in order to frustrate their bad designs. The consequentialist holds that the primary task of each agent is to prevent bad things *happening*; agent-centred morality maintains that his main concern is not to *do* wrong actions himself.

We can put the point in a slightly different way. Although utilitarianism is both monist and consequentialist there can be pluralist versions of consequentialism. A pluralist consequentialist moral theory might list various desirable outcomes: that there be less deceit, less coercion, a fairer distribution of goods and so on. On a consequentialist view of morality each agent should try and ensure that we end up with the most desirable outcome. So each agent should try to make it the case that there is less coercion, less deceit and a more fair distribution of goods in the world. Consequentialism thus gives a common aim to all agents. Each agent should try and secure the same outcome. An agent-centred pluralist morality could agree that deceit, coercion and injustice are bad. But it differs from consequentialism in giving each agent different aims; each of us should have the aim that *he* should not coerce or deceive other people. On this view it would be wrong for me to coerce other people, even if my doing so would make it the case that there was less coercion overall than there would otherwise have been. I shall follow tradition in describing agent-centred pluralist moral systems as *deontological* theories.

11.3 UTILITARIANISM AND THE IDEAL SPECTATOR THEORY

There is no direct connection between non-cognitivism as such and any particular theory of moral justification. Indeed, simple non-cognitivism led most naturally to moral scepticism – to the view that there is no way of justifying our moral views. The alleged connection only emerged when we moved to the ideal spectator theory in an attempt, among other things, to supply a decision-procedure for resolving moral disputes, thus evading moral scepticism.

The ideal spectator theory aims to set a standard of correct judgement, within a non-cognitivist framework, by defining the right attitude as the one that would be adopted by an ideal spectator. So far, what we have is merely the *form* of a theory, which would be as applicable to, say, aesthetic attitudes as to moral ones. We have no idea what moral judgements the ideal spectator would make until we have given it content. That content is provided by reflection on what distinguishes a moral attitude from other kinds of attitude. To adopt the moral point of view, it was suggested, is to have a disinterested concern with the welfare of all.

The ideal spectator is thus sympathetic and impartial. He will also, it was argued, be a utilitarian. His sympathy will lead him to desire people's happiness and his impartiality will ensure that he is equally concerned with the happiness of each. He will therefore approve most of those actions which bring the greatest possible happiness to those affected by them.

We would be right to be sceptical about this quick argument. Firstly, we might raise questions about the defining features of the ideal spectator; are sympathy and impartiality the best, or the only, features to include? I shall leave such doubts aside; it could reasonably be held that these two properties are required features of any stance that we could recognize as a moral one. Secondly, and more damagingly, we may well doubt whether a spectator with these two qualities need be a utilitarian. If, as I have just suggested, an impartial sympathetic concern for others is the hallmark of *any* viewpoint that we could recognize as a moral one, how could appeal to that feature be decisive in favour of utilitarianism, as against its rivals?

The utilitarian is a monist and a consequentialist. But the impartial sympathetic spectator need not adopt either of these positions. It is simply question-begging to assume that his concern or sympathy for the well-being of humans would lead him to regard happiness as the only morally relevant property. He might well think that other values, such as justice, are important to human flourishing. Many critics of utilitarianism have pointed out that we are not only concerned with the amount of happiness but also with its just distribution. The ideal spectator could prefer a course of action which produced considerable happiness, fairly distributed, to one which would produce slightly more happiness, but at the expense of great unfairness in the way it was shared out.

Nor need his impartiality lead the ideal spectator to adopt a consequentialist approach to moral reasoning. The stipulation of impartiality was introduced to cope with the natural human tendency to favouritism – that is, giving greater weight to one's own claims, or the claims of those to whom one is close, than is justified. One might suppose that an impartial spectator could not approve of an agent fulfilling a particular obligation to a specified person – keeping a promise to a friend, for example – when some other course of action the agent might have taken would have had better consequences overall. Wouldn't the promiser be showing favouritism towards the promisee?

This supposition is mistaken. The spectator's impartiality requires only that he gives equal weight to equal claims; he must not favour the claims of one person over the equally strong claims of another. This is quite compatible with his holding that, because of the relation between them, *any* promisee has a special claim on the promiser which cannot be set aside simply because the promiser can think of another action which would have better consequences. In general, an impartial spectator could acknowledge the existence of special claims deriving from the specific relations between people, provided that he did not favour one claim over another, on the grounds that he happened to care more about one of the people involved than another. The impartial sympathetic spectator could be a deontologist.

11.4 CONSISTENCY AND UTILITARIANISM

Other non-cognitivists have also argued that moral reasoning must be utilitarian in nature. The most famous of these is Hare (1963, esp. ch. 7, 1976, 1981) who claims to arrive at utilitarianism via considerations about consistency. Consistency requires that, whatever moral judgement I make in one case, I should make the same judgement in any case which is similar in all the relevant respects. This constraint applies to possible as well as to actual cases. In real life it may be difficult to find actual cases that are similar in all the morally relevant respects, in order to test someone's consistency. But we can easily construct a hypothetical example, which is morally exactly similar to the one we are discussing, by imagining a case where everything remains the same, except that the people involved exchange roles. In order to test the correctness of my belief that the action I propose to take is morally right, I should put myself, in turn, in the position of each person who will be affected by my action and ask whether, in that position, I am prepared to make my original moral judgement. What will determine the answer to that question?

According to Hare, it will depend on how the proposed action affects my desires or preferences in the hypothetical case. If, on balance, the action would frustrate my preferences in the position in which I imagine myself, then I will not, in that position, be prepared to reaffirm my original judgement. But what determines what preferences I have in the hypothetical situation? Since the actual case and the hypothetical case are to be exactly alike, except for the fact that the participants occupy different roles, the preferences I would have in the other person's place will be identical with his actual present preferences. So the moral judgement I make in the hypothetical case, where I put myself in the position of another, is determined by the present preferences of that person.

It is likely that, when I emerge from the process of putting myself in the place of each person affected by my action, I will have discovered that in some positions I can endorse that action and in others I cannot. How can I consolidate these different judgements into one final and consistent conclusion about what should be done? The method I should adopt, Hare suggests, is analogous to the one I would use in deciding what to do when my own preferences about some course of action are divided, namely to weigh them up and opt for the action which, on balance, most satisfies my preferences. I must, therefore, weigh the preferences I had in all the positions in which I placed myself. Since the preferences I acquired in the course of putting myself in each person's place will be the sum of the preferences of all of them, this method amounts to weighing up the preferences of all the affected parties. To maximize preference satisfaction is, however, on certain assumptions, to maximize happiness among the parties affected. To seek to maximize happiness is to adopt utilitarianism. So, Hare argues, the constraint of moral consistency can be made to yield utilitarianism.

I shall later return to the last part of Hare's claim – that happiness consists in having one's preferences satisfied – but we need first to look at a standard objection to his claim that the judgement I make when I put myself in the position of another should be determined by the present preferences of the other person. If I am convinced that my judgement is correct why can't I, in consistency, hold to that judgement even when I have put myself in the position of others who would prefer me to do something else?

To use an example of Pettit's (1987, pp. 75–6): suppose Socrates, on the night he is to take the hemlock, were to reflect on the fact that his friends wish him not to take it. It looks as if his action will not maximize the satisfaction of preferences. He is satisfied that, having been sentenced to death by a properly constituted court, he is required to accept the verdict. Moreover, he believes that death is not fearful, and that his friends' distress at the thought of his death is due to their failure, exacerbated by their grief, to see the situation aright. He admits that, if he were in their position, he would not endorse the decision to take the hemlock. But why should this realization affect his present moral judgement when he believes that their opposition is due to an inadequate appreciation of the situation? He is quite consistent in sticking to his original decision.

Consistency alone does not require me to withdraw a moral judgement in a case where the majority of those affected by it would prefer me not to act on it. If, after putting myself in the other people's position, I remain convinced by the reasoning that led me to believe that the action was right in the first place, then I need not withdraw it. Hare's argument appears to have been no more successful than the ideal spectator theory in showing that a non-cognitivist theory of moral reasoning must be a utilitarian one.

This objection to Hare only succeeds, however, because it makes an assumption which Hare denies. Socrates was unmoved by the recognition that his action would not maximize preference satisfaction because he believed his moral conviction to be well grounded. But is he entitled, at this stage of the argument, to that belief? Hare thinks not. On Hare's view, at the initial stage of moral thinking, before the action has been subjected to his test, Socrates' moral conviction is just one preference among others. The purpose of critical moral thinking, which for Hare is subjecting proposed actions to his test, is to discover which of our moral intuitions are acceptable. 'To insist on the *prior* authority of the moral intuitions that one starts with is simply to refuse to think critically' (Hare, 1981, p. 179).

If we take the agent's moral intuitions to be merely preferences of his, then Hare's test looks much more convincing. I can no longer claim that the difference in our preferences lies in your failure to see the force of the reasons which make my decision the right one. The sole difference between us is purely one of preference. Suppose my only grounds for holding that anyone in my present position ought to do a, an action which will cause great unhappiness to the large number of people whom it affects, is simply that I prefer to do a when I am in the position of the agent. It would surely be relevant, in deciding whether a is the right action, to take into account the fact that my preferences would be frustrated if I were one of the people on the receiving end of that action. How could it be rational to place such weight on the satisfaction of my preferences when I am the agent, and yet discount them when I am in the position of someone affected by the act?

Consistency alone is not enough to generate utilitarianism; we need to add the premise that each person's moral views are to be regarded (until they have been through the test) as merely preferences of his, with no special authority. If we accept this extra premise then the objection to Hare falls; it does appear that his theory leads to utilitarianism. What about the ideal spectator theory? Can we defend the view that it leads to utilitarianism by importing the extra premise? It seems that we can.

In arguing that the ideal spectator could be a deontologist we ascribed to him some substantive views as to what is of value, and what moral claims are appropriate. If we are to forbid him to import any evaluative opinions of his own, then it would seem that he must give equal weight to the satisfaction of the preferences of each person affected by any action. He is, after all, to give equal weight to the claims of each. Without a substantive view of which claims are important he must give equal weight to every claim; that is, to the preferences of all the affected parties. So he will approve of actions that maximize preference satisfaction.

11.5 PREFERENCES, DECISION PROCEDURES AND HAPPINESS

Two different approaches to moral reasoning, within a non-cognitivist framework, have led to utilitarianism, once they have been allowed to use the extra premise – the premise that each person's moral views are initially to be regarded as mere preferences, having no special authority. This raises two questions. Is the non-cognitivist entitled to that premise? Will any attempt to find a decision procedure for settling moral disputes which starts with that premise end up with utilitarianism? A case can be made for answering both in the affirmative.

Both approaches can be seen as seeking, in their different ways, to escape from the scepticism engendered by simple non-cognitivism. The difficulty was that there seemed to be no model to which the non-cognitivist could appeal in constructing a rationally acceptable decision procedure in the case of moral disagreements. We do have procedures for resolving disagreements in belief, in which an appeal to empirical evidence plays a central role. But the non-cognitivist cannot appeal to such procedures as a model because he considers moral attitudes to be primarily desires or preferences, rather than beliefs. There is thus no question of our being able to settle moral questions by appeal to observable facts.

How then are we to resolve evaluative disputes, which are disagreements in preference, disagreements about what is to be done? What is required is some procedure which stands a chance of being generally acceptable to all the disputants. If it is to succeed it must avoid invoking any arbitrary principles or making any arbitrary exclusions. Insisting on that condition appears, however, to have brought us to an impasse. Any test that we might propose which would enable us to classify some desires, and hence some attitudes, as better than others would inevitably be question-begging. For any criterion we might light on would presuppose some standard of value by which desires could be assessed, and that is just what is in question. In the absence of such a criterion the only escape from this impasse is to treat all preferences on a level, not judging any one to be more justified than any other. To rule out any preferences as unacceptable, at this stage, would be to breach the condition that the procedure be non-arbitrary.

If we make the assumption that no preference can initially be judged to be *qualitatively* superior to any other, the only other possible measure is *quantitative* superiority. That is, faced with some clash of preferences, we should give the verdict to the course for which there is a greater preference. This method has obvious attractions in non-moral cases where a group of people is trying to decide what to do. If they are divided about whether to go to the cinema or the theatre then an obvious way of settling the matter is to choose the option that will satisfy the most preferences.

How are we to find which course that is? We could simply count heads, each vote counting for one, and thus choose by simple majority. But that method overlooks the possibility that those in the minority may have very strong feelings about the matter, whereas those in the majority may have only a very slight preference for their choice, and might be almost equally content if the opposite decision were reached. Thus, in deciding by simple majority, we might fail to choose the course which had the strongest total weight of desire in its favour. To allow for this possibility we could introduce some sort of weighting to the voting so that strong preferences counted for more than weak ones. Exactly how this could be done is a matter of some controversy, but the easiest approach involves an application of what is involved in deciding what to buy out of a limited budget. The strength of the purchaser's desire for any commodity could be measured by the amount of that budget he is prepared to expend on purchasing it. Similarly, we could ask people to put a 'price' on various activities to see how much they value them. The more someone would be prepared to pay for any activity – the more things he values that he would be prepared to give up to get it – the more he values it.

Happiness and Preference Satisfaction

So far we have been going along with the suggestion that happiness consists in the satisfaction of preferences or desires. The objection to defining happiness as the satisfaction of desire is that it does not always seem to be true that people are happy when their desires are satisfied. For example, lots of people want very much to win huge sums of money in lotteries, or on the football pools, and expend quite a lot of time and money in trying to achieve this goal; yet, notoriously, many of those who win a fortune are not happy and regret having been successful. Giving someone what he wants is not, therefore, a reliable method of making him happy.

We need not abandon the thought that there is a link between the satisfaction of desire and happiness. We can modify our account to incorporate the point behind the objection. People are often unreflective about their desires; they have not thought clearly about what it would be like to have the desire satisfied. If someone who is filling in his pools coupon or buying his lottery ticket thought through what would happen if he won – the begging letters, the publicity, the envy of the neighbours, the sudden change in life style – then he might well decide that he did not want to win. Examples where the satisfaction of desire does not lead to happiness are, it might be argued, cases where the consequences of satisfying the desire have not been thought through. Happiness does consist in the satisfaction of desires, but only of desires that would survive this kind of scrutiny – let us call them *fully informed* desires.

A similar response can be made to a further, and similar, objection. When deciding what to do, most of us give greater weight to immediate pleasures and pains than to distant ones. This is not necessarily irrational; often the immediate consequences are certain whereas the distant consequences are more difficult to determine. We are right to give less weight to consequences that may not happen. Often, however, we discount the effects of distant consequences to a degree that is not justified by their comparative uncertainty. We smoke, even though we know that the present enjoyment is likely to be more than outweighed by future suffering and the shortening of our lives. We put off going to the dentist for a check up, even though we know we may suffer worse toothache than any pain the dentist might inflict. In short, we are imprudent. And we disapprove of imprudent behaviour precisely because it often leads to less happiness in the future than prudent behaviour would have done. If we ask people to rank their desires in order of importance, they are likely to show an undue bias towards the satisfaction of desires for short-term consequences, at the expense of desires whose satisfaction is a more distant prospect. If we took their rankings at face value, therefore, and tried to satisfy as many as possible, we might not make them as happy as we could have done. The response to this objection, as before, is to amend our account of happiness to incorporate it. Happiness, on our final account, consists in the satisfaction of fully informed and prudent desires.

If we return to our suggested decision procedure for settling evaluative disputes we see that using it is not equivalent to adopting a utilitarian decision procedure in ethics. For seeking to give as many people as possible what they want will not necessarily maximize happiness. Are there reasons for preferring a decision procedure which aims instead at satisfying as many fully informed and prudent desires as possible? I think there are. The very arguments which showed that happiness could not be identified with the satisfaction of whatever desires the agent happened to have, are also reasons for amending our decision procedure along similar lines. Normally, I seek to satisfy a desire because I believe that I shall be happier in the state of affairs in which what I desire comes about than in one in which it does not. But we have just seen that I can be mistaken in that belief. Where I am mistaken, and my desire is satisfied, I will have good reason to wish that it had not been satisfied.

In cases where I come to realize that I would not be happier in the state of affairs in which my desire is satisfied, the desire often ceases. But desires cannot always be removed by reflection. A desire that persists, even in the face of the realization that I would not be happier in the state of affairs in which it is satisfied, is a prime example of an *irrational* desire. Even where it persists, I have good reason to prefer that my irrational desire be not satisfied.

To sum up: we have good reason to prefer that only our rational desires, that is, only our informed and prudent desires, be satisfied. In other words, we have good reason to have a second-order desire that only informed and prudent desires be satisfied. There seems, therefore, also to be good reason to prefer a decision procedure for settling evaluative disputes that maximizes the satisfaction of informed and prudent desires, rather than of the desires the disputants happen to have. Such a decision procedure will be a utilitarian one for, in maximizing the satisfaction of informed and prudent desires, it will maximize happiness.

It might seem that this amendment infringes the initial stipulation that our decision procedure should not be arbitrary. No desire was to be thought of as qualitatively superior to any other. But now it is proposed that only informed and prudent desires be given weight in the calculations. Can this preferential treatment be squared with the stipulation? It can. It would have been arbitrary to give the satisfaction of one desire preference over the satisfaction of another, on the grounds that the object of the first desire was more valuable than the object of the second, for we had no criteria for judging which states of affairs were valuable and which were not. No questions of value are begged, however, in ruling out imprudent or ill-informed desires which there is good reason, from the agent's point of view, not to satisfy. What is objectionable about them is not their content, but the fact that the agent would not prefer the state of affairs in which they were satisfied to one in which they were not.

At the initial stage, before any procedure for resolving disputes had emerged, it would have been arbitrary to claim that any desire was better or worse than any other. The emergence of a utilitarian decision procedure, however, not only gives us a standard for judging actions and moral principles but also now provides one for assessing desires. Desires whose satisfaction tends to promote the welfare and happiness of others are to be encouraged; those that have the opposite effect are to be condemned. Similar remarks can be made about character traits: ones such as kindliness, loyalty, compassion and tact which tend to promote happiness are to be applauded; envy, malice, greed and deceitfulness are to be discouraged, because of their pernicious effects on the general happiness.

I have argued that the search for a decision procedure within a non-cognitivist framework leads naturally, given certain plausible assumptions, to utilitarianism. Should the non-cognitivist welcome this conclusion? There are serious objections to utilitarianism. It is said, at worst, to be morally pernicious, at best, to give a distorted picture of our moral thinking. These objections, and the utilitarian response, are easily accessible in the literature, so I shall give a brief sketch of a very complex area.

11.6 THE DEBATE ABOUT UTILITARIANISM

The structure of the debate between utilitarianism and deontology mirrors, to a degree, the dialectic that developed between non-cognitivism and realism. The utilitarian claims superiority for his theory on the grounds of simplicity. A theory with only one basic moral principle is obviously simpler than one with many. It offers to bring order to the bewildering array of moral principles and values that we hold to in ordinary life, reducing them all to one common denominator. The utilitarian explains our apparent pluralism by saying that we value all these different things only because the promotion of each of them contributes in an important way to the increase of human happiness. They have no value in themselves; their value is derivative from the role they have in increasing happiness. Moreover, a pluralistic theory runs the risk of a conflict between competing principles or values which it may not have the resources to resolve. The structure of utilitarianism prevents the generation of moral conflict. Where there is only one value there can be no difficulty in principle in determining what is right, whatever difficulties there may be in practice in calculating the consequences.

The deontologist retorts that simplicity in a theory is only a virtue where the theory genuinely explains and does not distort the phenomena. Utilitarianism claims to explain our moral thought in a satisfyingly simple way, but it cannot do so – for our ordinary moral thought is deontological in character. The deontologist brings two main charges against utilitarianism to substantiate this claim: it often gets the wrong answer; and where it gets the right one it does so for the wrong reasons.

We are already familiar with the first charge. Utilitarianism, because of its consequentialist structure, appears to license any action, however terrible, in order to attain a sufficient good. To this the utilitarian can reply, with considerable force, that it will be much rarer for him to behave in a way that will outrage our ordinary sense of morality than his opponent supposes. A more careful calculation of the likely effects of breaking conventional moral rules will show that doing so is unlikely to lead to an increase in human happiness. To take the hostage example: superficially, it might seem that giving into the terrorists will save more lives than will resistance. If, however, we take the longer-term effects into account we can see that giving in on this occasion will encourage similar terrorist outrages in future, so that the short-term gains will be outweighed by the long-term losses. The utilitarian can easily argue that his method of calculating what is right will yield results much closer to our ordinary moral beliefs than might at first appear.

Even if his opponent concedes this point he can still press the second charge: where utilitarianism gets the right answers it does so for the wrong reasons. It offers a distorted account of moral justification; trying to squeeze our moral reasoning into a monistic and consequentialist framework. The utilitarian agrees with us that we should not lightly breach a moral principle in order to obtain some immediate balance of good consequences over bad. But his explanation differs from ours. He claims, for example, that the government ought not lightly to break its promise to the political refugees because doing so in this case may bring bad consequences in the long run. It may weaken people's confidence in the system of promise-keeping in general, and in the good faith of the government in particular, as well as possibly weakening the government's determination to keep its promises in future. All this may be true (although it does not explain why anyone should keep such a promise in a case where no one would find out) but it leaves out what most of us would feel to be central to the case: the reason I should not break a promise is that it would breach my obligation to the promisee. We do not need to look far afield to the remote and hard to predict consequences of any breach of promise in order to see why I should keep my word. The answer lies closer to home in my relation to the person to whom I made the promise. As Ross (1930, p. 19) elegantly maintains, only a pluralistic non-consequentialist theory can capture the complexities of our moral experience:

[T]he theory of . . . utilitarianism . . . seems to simplify unduly our relations to our fellows. It says, in effect, that the only morally significant relation in which my neighbours stand to me is that of being possible beneficiaries of my action. They do stand in this relation to me, and this relation is morally significant. But they may also stand to me in the relation of promisee to promisor, of creditor to debtor, of wife to husband, of fellow countryman to fellow countryman, and the like; and each of these relations is the foundation of a . . . duty . . .

Two-level utilitarianism

So far the deontologist has been getting the better of this argument. We do not think like utilitarians; it looks, therefore, as if the claim that utilitarianism underpins and explains our moral thinking must lapse. One strategy, however, is still open to the resourceful utilitarian who wishes to maintain that his theory is genuinely explanatory of our current moral thought. Here the parallel with the debate between non-cognitivism and realism is striking. Just as the non-cognitivist developed a more sophisticated theory which fitted better with the moral pheno-menology so the utilitarian can offer a more subtle version of his theory (which we owe to Hare (1976, 1981), among others) which is less at odds with our normal thought.

The trick, as so often in philosophy, is to admit the objection but to modify the theory so that it can accommodate it. The utilitarian can agree that we do not think like utilitarians in our everyday thought, but can claim to provide a utilitarian explanation of why this is so. He achieves this by complicating the structure of moral thought. He claims that there are two levels of moral thinking, critical and everyday. At the level of the everyday, the utilitarian can concede that our thought is as pluralistic and non-consequentialist as his opponent could wish. We do not apply utilitarian criteria directly in each judgement we make about an action or a person. We decide what to do in any particular case by appeal to a variety of principles in just the way that the deontologist describes. Utilitarian considerations come in when we reflect critically on our moral practice, asking whether the moral principles we employ in everyday thought are justified. Good moral principles are those which, if generally followed, would increase the sum of human happiness. The best moral principles are those whose general adoption would increase the sum of happiness more than any other set of principles whose adoption we could reasonably propose.

We are thus offered a two-stage theory of justification. We justify an action by appeal to the relevant principles which informed our choice of that particular action. We justify a principle by showing that, of all the possible principles governing this type of action, this one would, if generally obeyed, produce more happiness than any reasonable alternative.

What reasons can the utilitarian offer to explain why we would adopt this elaborate two-level system? The answer lies in human frailty and human ignorance. It is difficult to do the utilitarian sums in individual cases, because we don't know all the possible consequences of our actions; it is impossible even to try to do them properly when we are under pressure, and tempted to take the easy solution, or the one that intuitively appeals to us. Since we are not perfect utilitarian machines, engaging in utilitarian thinking at the moment of moral decision would almost certainly lead to worse results, utilitarianly speaking, than sticking to a few fairly clear principles. A sensible utilitarian would therefore wish to see people trained to be very reluctant to breach certain moral principles, such as the need to keep one's promises. An attachment to moral principles forms a bulwark against the danger of being tempted into the wrong action by other considerations, including utilitarian considerations. Of course, the behaviour of someone who follows this set of principles will only approximate the behaviour of the perfect utilitarian who could be trusted to do all the calculations for each individual case, and to carry through the decision. But we are not perfect, and a near approximation to perfect utilitarian virtue is the best we can hope for.

Take the case of Sergeant Dixon, an upright policeman of the old school. He has been brought up to believe that it is wrong to torture suspects to get information from them, however desperate the situation or great the temptation. Once in his career, he might come across a situation where, even on the most conservative calculations, torture would be justified on utilitarian grounds. Suppose, for example, a terrorist has planted a bomb in a school playground and, by threatening to pull out his toenails, Dixon might well be able to make him reveal its whereabouts. Given his moral training, however, the thought never even enters his mind. On such very rare occasions, Dixon will not do the action which a perfect utilitarian would calculate to be the right one. But in virtually all the cases he will ever meet he will make the right choice.

Contrast with him the figure of Knacker of the Yard. Inspector Knacker has read a bit of utilitarian philosophy in his spare time and believes that it would be right to torture a prisoner in a case where a good end can only be achieved this way, and where the balance of good to be achieved outweighs the harm done to the prisoner and any alarm that might be caused to the general populace if people were to get to hear about it. He tries to think on utilitarian lines when interviewing suspects. The trouble is, he is an enthusiastic policeman and, like any member of an organization, prone to overrate the importance of his own activities and to underrate the interests of others. So Knacker pulls toenails with alacrity, often in cases where a perfect utilitarian calculator would have seen that such action was unjustified.

What kind of police force is to be preferred, from the utilitarian point of view? People like Inspector Knacker, whose willingness to think as a utilitarian leads him to engage, from splendid utilitarian motives, in needless violence which reduces the general happiness? Or friendly Sergeant Dixon, whose refusal to think on utilitarian lines leads to his behaviour being closer to that of the ideal utilitarian than Knacker's? It is only an apparent paradox that a utilitarian may prefer a world full of people who do not think, when making individual moral decisions, in a utilitarian way.

At the level of critical thinking, however, we justify the choice of moral principles that are to be inculcated into the populace by appealing to utilitarian considerations. If any query arises as to whether we should go on following some principle or amend or even abandon it we must settle that question by seeing what the consequences for the general happiness would be of an amended, or even a different, principle being adopted. In doing this sum we must ensure that the principles chosen are clear and simple enough to be learnt, and acted on, by the people who will have to live by them. A more demanding or more complex principle might, if universally followed, give results nearer to the utilitarian ideal, but we may be able to predict that too many people will be unable to follow it for its adoption to be effective.

Objections to the two-level theory

Difficulties arise for a two-level theory when we ask: How can we keep critical thinking separate from everyday moral thought? The strength of Dixon's position is that he believes in a pluralist and non-consequentialist morality. His staunch attachment to his moral principles stems from his belief that they encapsulate values, such as justice, which deserve to be protected for their own sake. Once he accepts, at the critical level, the utilitarian account of why those moral principles are to be adopted his attitude to them must change. Now his reason for sticking to his principles is that doing so is more likely to produce good utilitarian results than would be achieved by his trying to work out what, in each case, would be the ideal utilitarian solution. It seems unlikely that he will have the same commitment to those principles as someone who does believe in a pluralist and agent-centred morality. If he does breach a moral rule, for example, in order to attain what he believes to be a utilitarianly desirable end, he will not feel the same degree or kind of guilt as would someone who believed that it was wrong in principle to act in that way.

Even if adopting two-level utilitarianism does not undermine the agent's commitment to acting in accordance with his moral principles, the theory still does not do what it set out to do. What it aimed to show was how, on utilitarian principles, it was a good idea to think and reason in a pluralist and non-consequentialist manner. But no one who is committed to utilitarianism can think and reason in a non-utilitarian way. He cannot believe, at any level of thought, that some other system of moral justification is correct. All the theory can show is that it is a good idea to behave in everyday life as if one were not a utilitarian. Precisely because he does not accept the conception of moral choice and human relations which underlies deontology, even the sophisticated utilitarian's attitude to moral issues and problems will be different from that of the deontologist. The utilitarian must regard our non-utilitarian way of moral thinking as deluded, although he accepts that the results of thinking in that way are, in fact, beneficial. To pretend to talk, think and reason like a deontologist would be to engage in a massive campaign of deceit.

Faced with these difficulties some utilitarians have put forward an even more radical proposal. Although utilitarianism is the correct moral theory we should not, they say, proclaim this fact. For the considerations of the previous paragraphs suggest that people are more likely to behave in ways that will advance human happiness if they reject utilitarianism altogether, and think and act like deontologists. Utilitarianism would then become an esoteric doctrine, accepted by only a few philosophers who would, if challenged, deny its truth in public. Indeed, in order to ensure that the right moral principles were selected and followed it might be necessary for an intellectual elite, who were in the know, to propagate as the truth a deontological theory which they believed to be false.

This is a profoundly unattractive picture of the moral life, far removed from our present conception of it. If the non-cognitivist accepts this conclusion he is faced with a series of difficult questions. Can he abandon utilitarianism without abandoning the search for a decision procedure in morals? If he abandons the search for a decision procedure must he not give up the project of quasi-realism? If he abandons the project of quasi-realism is he not admitting the main realist criticism of his position? These questions deserve a chapter of their own.

FURTHER READING

On 11.2   Ross (1930, ch. 2) and Urmson (1975) defend pluralism. Nagel (1986, ch. 9) and Scheffler (1982) are helpful on deontology and agent-centred reasons.

On 11.4   Hare (1976) both provides the easiest route into his argument for utilitarianism and also serves as an introduction to the issues raised in 11.5. Socrates' final conversation with his friends is described in *Phaedo* in Plato 1959.

On 11.6   Williams (1973a; 1973b, ch. 10) attacks utilitarianism. Scheffler (1982) attacks consequentialism. Brink (1988) agrees with Hare, but from a realist perspective, that utilitarianism is defensible. The two-level account has its origins in Hume (1975, esp. appendix 3; 1978, Book III, Part II, sections 2–4) as Rawls (1955) acknowledges in his early defence along these lines.

12

Quasi-Realism

12.1 THE PROSPECTS FOR QUASI-REALISM

Our discussion of non-cognitivism has reached this point. The non-cognitivist has insisted, all along, that there are constraints on which sets of attitudes are acceptable. An initial suggestion was that a set of attitudes had to be consistent; a later one that an acceptable set of attitudes would be the ones that an ideal spectator would embrace. Both of these suggestions have force; the question is: Do these constraints allow room for more than one acceptable set of attitudes, or will a unique best set emerge? If the latter is the case, then the project of quasi-realism will be in good shape. Uniqueness is one of the marks of truth; there is just one set of true beliefs. The possibility of a unique best set of attitudes would provide an analogue for truth in ethics.

The ideal spectator theory, it was originally suggested, led to utilitarianism. So, according to an ingenious argument of Hare's, did the constraint of consistency. Utilitarianism offered a method of deciding questions which would, in principle, yield a determinate answer in every case. But utilitarianism, I argued, is not only incompatible with our present moral thought, but a pretty grisly theory in its own right. Can the non-cognitivist reject it? He can. We found that the requirement that he be consistent in his moral judgements is not enough, on its own, to force him into a utilitarian stance. The additional assumption required to generate utilitarianism is not rationally compelling nor, in view of its outcome, very attractive. The non-cognitivist is not required to put his existing moral attitudes to one side and give equal weight to everyone's preferences. He can simply stick to the attitudes he has, provided they are consistent. Similar remarks apply to the requirements imposed by the ideal spectator theory.

The constraints imposed by consistency, or the ideal spectator theory, do not determine a unique best set of attitudes. This sobering conclusion casts doubt on the quasi-realist project (see 6.1). For it would seem that the assumption that there is one set of correct answers to moral questions, which underlies everyday moral discussion and debate, is unjustified. The non-cognitivist might try to avoid this conclusion by attempting to construct an acceptable decision procedure that would yield determinate answers, but which would not generate utilitarianism. But the prospects of that look bleak; I argued that any attempt to construct a decision procedure, which did not simply beg the question against certain value systems, would lead to utilitarianism.

12.2 QUASI-REALISM DEFENDED

If Blackburn's own account (1984, ch. 6) of quasi-realism is correct this pessimism is unjustified. A major part of the quasi-realist enterpise involves showing why it is natural to treat expressions of attitude as if they were similar to ordinary judgements in having a truth-value. Blackburn does not, however, see this task as requiring us to construct a moral decision procedure which would find acceptance with all reasonable men. What he tries to show is that, built into the structure of our moral thought, there are analogues of the various procedures that we employ in an area where we believe there is truth. To see how this works, take Blackburn's reply to the criticism, levelled by the realist in 3.4, that the non-cognitivist cannot make room for the concept of moral fallibility. Blackburn suggests that we can find a non-cognitivist analogue for fallibility in the thought that my attitudes could be improved. If I can recognize that some of my attitudes might be replaced by better ones then I am, in effect, acknowledging that some of my attitudes may be mistaken. But what, on a non-cognitivist account, is it to have the thought that my attitudes might be improved? To answer that, we need to introduce the concept of a moral *sensibility*.

Each of us, on the non-cognitivist picture, is disposed to respond to various situations with different attitudes – we may, for example, be outraged by cruelty, amused by adultery, exalted by physical bravery and so on. The complete set of such dispositions we may call that person's moral sensibility. It is important that we can not only take up an attitude towards people's actions but also towards their moral sensibilities. These can be coarse or sensitive, inflexible or fickle, admirable or despicable. If we can sensibly take the attitude that Pius's sensibility could do with improvement in various ways, we can also take the attitude that our own may need improvement. So, to return to our original question, the thought that my attitudes could be improved is itself an attitude, an attitude I can take towards my own sensibility. It is an admirable attitude, one which I think each person should take towards his own sensibility; an attitude which will manifest itself in such desirable traits as a willingness to look at other people's moral opinions with an openness of mind, to see if he can learn from them.

Constructing moral truth

Once we have the thought that some sensibilities are better than others we can take on the more ambitious task of providing a quasi-realist definition of moral truth. We can define the 'best possible set of attitudes' as the set that would result from taking all possible opportunities to improve our sensibility. We can then define truth in terms of membership of this set. Call the set M. Then any attitude m is true just if m is a member of M. To test this account we must look at what, in 4.5, I called the marks of truth, to see if this account possesses them. The marks of truth are a set of constraints which we should expect to be met if we are to think of remarks in a certain area of discourse as being candidates for truth. Two of the most important are: uniqueness – there is only one complete set of truths; and consistency – every truth is compatible with every other truth.

Blackburn poses the following objection to his own theory: why should we suppose that there is a unique best possible sensibility? The acknowledgement that a sensibility can be imperfect does not guarantee that there is only one route by which it can be improved; there might be several different paths which it might take, all of them equally admirable. Instead of converging on one set of attitudes, improving sensibilities might diverge at various points. In which case there would be no unique M and so no truth. Nor is it the case that we could simply combine all these admirable sets of attitudes into one system, because the different sets will contain conflicting attitudes that cannot be rendered consistent, thus breaching the second constraint.

We are on ground familiar from chapter 10. It is important to be clear just what objection it is that Blackburn is trying to meet. He is not entertaining the thought that I might encounter a sensibility which shared none of my attitudes but which had as good a claim as my own to be regarded as admirable. For there is a core of central attitudes, such as being opposed to cruelty to children, which I cannot imagine being absent from any sensibility that was an improvement on my own. It is when we turn to attitudes nearer the periphery, ones to which I am less firmly committed, that the problem might arise.

The problem that Blackburn is posing to his own theory is that our picture of improving sensibilities might have the form of a tree structure. The trunk would contain all those attitudes which we are sure would have to be in any sensibility that was as good as, or better than, our own. At various points, branching would occur, where equally admirable but divergent opinions would be possible. It was thus not quite accurate to say that, if this structure were accepted, there would be no moral truth; truth would be confined to the trunk below the first branching, to those attitudes common to all acceptable systems of attitudes.

Blackburn's argument to show that branching is impossible asks us to imagine, in detail, the circumstances that would convince us that we had reached a point where branching might occur. It is not sufficient simply that I hold one attitude, which is not in the trunk, and someone else holds an incompatible one. For I may simply take the attitude that his sensibility is inferior to mine. (A sensibility that was reluctant to condemn any conflicting attitude would clearly not be an admirable one; an attitude of condemnation towards the attitudes of the Nazis is a part of any sensibility that could be regarded as an improvement on my own.) What might convince us that branching could occur would be a case where the view that is divergent from mine stems from a sensibility that I am prepared to acknowledge is every bit as good as my own. We would get the tree structure if we supposed that the following is the correct description. In my set of attitudes we find the judgement, say, that monogamy is better than polygamy. In the other person's set of attitudes I discover the judgement that polygamy is better than monogamy. I also judge that his sensibility is not inferior to mine and that neither could be improved on.

But this set of views is unstable. If I am convinced that each sensibility is equally sound then I should no longer be prepared to endorse my original view that monogamy is better than polygamy. Once I have reached the point where I accept that his view has as much validity as mine, I should recognize that both our sensibilities are flawed; a better one might contain neither judgement, but would regard both kinds of marital arrangement as equally acceptable. So an improved sensibility would not include any branching. Wherever a branch threatens we should recognize that there is an improved sensibility that avoids it.

12.3 A REALIST RESPONSE

The picture of moral reasoning which Blackburn presents is close to that which the realist was advocating in chapter 10. He endorses the second model of critical reflection, in which we have to start with the moral commitments we actually have, but be prepared to modify them by being alert to the possibility of improvement. By contrast, the method Hare advocated in the last chapter is dangerously close to the first, Cartesian, model. It instructs us to put all our moral commitments to one side and then subject them to the scrutiny of his test. Blackburn wisely avoids this dubiously coherent demand.

Blackburn's avoidance of methods of Hare's kind may have another source. The thought that motivated Hare's search for a decision procedure in ethics, and that dictated the form that it took, was one that could only be had from a position external to our moral commitments. We were asked, at the initial stage of critical thinking, to regard our own attitudes as merely preferences, which had no greater claim to authority than any other. But this is not the kind of thought that we are prepared to entertain in our current moral system. That we are not prepared to do so is one of those features of our moral practice that tempts people to realism. To allow that a non-cognitivist has any business entertaining such a thought is already to give up the quasi-realist project, and to play into the hands of the realist.

Blackburn's project is a sustained and highly ingenious attempt to steal the realist's clothes. Does he succeed in stealing *all* of them? Do they fit?

Doubts, some of them quite technical, have been raised about Blackburn's claim that the way we treat moral attitudes can mimic precisely our treatment of truth-claims. One obvious difficulty, the appreciation of which I owe to Sturgeon (1986, pp. 127–34), is that Blackburn has left himself no room for a distinction between my moral assessment of someone's sensibility, and my assessment of it in terms of its success or failure at getting at the moral truth. Yet these two can come apart. Some defects in a sensibility are more morally acceptable than others, even where there is no difference in the degree of error produced by those defects. For example, many people hold 'that it would be more admirable for most of us if we had a moral sensibility which erred on the side of leniency in negative judgements on our fellow humans' (Sturgeon, 1986, p. 132).

Another difficulty might appear to be raised by the notion of convergence, which is one of the marks of truth. What Blackburn is offering is, in effect, a version of the ideal spectator theory – the best set of attitudes is the one that would be adopted by the ideal sensibility. However, unlike the version of the theory with which we are familiar, Blackburn's offers no general account of what the features of the ideal spectator are. Each of us is prepared to improve his own set of attitudes in an attempt to get closer to that ideal, and none of us will allow branching within his own system. But there is no reason to think that we shall all be heading in the same direction. Our respective sets of attitudes may just as well diverge as converge, even if each of us thinks of his own set as improving.

Blackburn can reply that the parallel which the objector draws is inexact. The claim is not that, in areas where there is truth, the opinions of all enquirers will eventually converge, but that the opinions of all *competent* enquirers will converge. Divergence may occur, but it will be explicable in terms of the intellectual or sensory failings of some of the enquirers. The proper parallel in ethics to a competent enquirer is a person with an admirable sensibility. But Blackburn's branching argument shows that the attitudes of people with admirable sensibilities will tend to converge. If they diverge too much from my own I cannot think of them as admirable.

The objector may reply that there is this difference between the two cases. In areas where there is truth, such as science, there are generally agreed tests for distinguishing competent from incompetent enquirers. But there are no such generally agreed criteria as to who possesses an admirable sensibility.

Whether or not this retort is sound, it is one that the moral realist would be ill advised to use. For neither are there any generally agreed criteria for determining who possesses the most discriminating moral sensitivity. On this score, Blackburn and the moral realist sink or swim together. I take this to be a measure of the extent to which the two views have come together.

In 1.5 I raised the question of whether, on the non-cognitivist account, our commitment to our values could survive the recognition that they are created or invented by us. The theory appears to generate a tension, similar to the one I detected in two-level utilitarianism, between what we might call the *internal* and *external standpoints*. In the midst of life – in moral action, argument and thought – our commitment to our central moral values is likely to be firm and even passionate. But if we stand outside our own moral commitments we may see them as simply one set of moral attitudes among others, having no more validity than any other set. Does Blackburn's quasi-realism resolve this tension?

This is not a point on which I find it easy to give a definitive answer. Blackburn insists that we cannot, and should not, adopt a viewpoint from which our commitments can be seen as just one set among other equally valid sets. We are looking for the best set of attitudes, and cannot remain indifferent when faced with a choice between competing sets. The quasi-realist project is, after all, to show that non-cognitivism leaves everything in morality as it is. But can it?

The difficulty, it seems to me, lies in the contrast, that still exists in Blackburn's version of the theory, between factual and evaluative questions. On a question of fact the correct answer is determined by the way the world is; on a question of value it is not. What then is it for there to be a correct anser to a moral question? We could reply that the correct answer is the one reached by a rationally acceptable moral decision procedure. But Blackburn does not take this line. It is difficult to resist the conclusion that, although we talk and think within our moral practice as if there were correct answers to moral questions, Blackburn's theory can make no sense, from the external standpoint, of the notion of a correct moral answer. Once we engage in philosophical reflection about morality then, if Blackburn's projectivism is sound, it looks as if the thought that there are correct answers in morals has turned out to be an illusion after all and we ought to embrace an error theory.

Suppose we agree, for the sake of argument, that Blackburn's project of constructing moral truth succeeds. Are there any remaining differences between his position and the moral realist's? There are three crucial ones, with all of which we are familiar, and all of which favour the realist position. The first two concern phenomenology. In two areas, moral observation and moral choice, the realist's account is in better shape than Blackburn's. First, the metaphor of projection, as I argued in chapter 5, is not cashable. The projectivist cannot provide a satisfying explanation of why we experience the world as containing value. Second, in moral choice, we are faced with authoritative demands; the belief–desire theory, to which Blackburn subscribes, cannot account for that authority.

Third, in the area of moral theory, Blackburn's theoretical apparatus prevents him from being a moral particularist, a position which, as I shall argue in the next chapter, has much to recommend it on independent grounds. The model of the structure of a sensibility which quasi-realism employs rules out particularism. A sensibility is viewed as a processing mechanism which responds to what it finds in the world with a range of affective reactions which form the basis of its possessor's attitudes. '[I]t is defined by a function from *input* of belief to *output* of attitude.' (Blackburn, 1984, p. 192) In other words we understand someone's sensibility, their moral viewpoint, if we can see a pattern in their affective reactions to what is really there in the world, namely the non-moral properties. In so far as we can detect no pattern we must either conclude that we have insufficient data to go on or that there is no consistent pattern of response; that is, that the person occupies no clear moral viewpoint but reacts in a random way. But to say that someone's moral reactions are inconsistent is to criticize him. Any such inconsistencies would have to be eradicated in the ideal sensibility.

So the quest for an ideal sensibility becomes the search for an ideal set of moral principles, conceived of as a set of rules which pick out sets of non-moral features for favourable or unfavourable evaluation. Since the non-evaluative properties of the world are accessible to anyone, irrespective of their evaluative stance, it follows that someone who did not even sympathize with the sensibility that was put forward as the ideal could nevertheless understand it, to the extent of being able to predict accurately with what attitudes it would respond to any given situation. But this is precisely the picture of consistency in one's moral practice which was rejected by the realist in 3.6. He holds that there may be no discernible pattern, at the non-evaluative level, in the responses of the ideal moral observer. There may be no set of moral principles which capture just what he would say in each particular case.

FURTHER READING

On 12.1   Rawls (1971) is the most famous example of an attempt to find an acceptable decision procedure in ethics that does not lead to utilitarianism. I agree with Hare (1973) in finding his attempt unconvincing.

On 12.2   For a further defence of quasi-realism, against the objections of McDowell in particular, see Blackburn (1985).

On 12.3   McDowell (1985, pp. 122–3) is the source of my claim that 'the quest for an ideal sensibility becomes the search for an ideal set of moral principles.'

13

Principles or Particularism?

13.1 THE ROLE OF MORAL PRINCIPLES

In chapter 11 we touched on the long-running dispute in moral theory between monists and pluralists – those who think that there is only one moral principle and those who think there is more than one. Moral realists have, from time to time, been found on both sides of this debate. There is no direct connection between moral realism *as such* and any particular moral theory, any more than there is a direct connection between non-cognitivism and any moral theory. But just as a natural development of non-cognitivism led to utilitarianism so the kind of moral realism which I have been advocating, with its stress on the role of sensitivity to the moral facts of the particular situation, naturally leads to moral particularism.

As I explained in 3.6, the particularist is sceptical about the role of moral principles in moral reasoning and so will reject the very terms in which the traditional debate is held. He believes that we have to judge each particular moral decision on its individual merits; we cannot appeal to general rules to make that decision for us. Moral particularism takes the view that moral principles are at best useless, and at worst a hindrance, in trying to find out which is the right action. What is required is the correct conception of the particular case in hand, with its unique set of properties. There is thus no substitute for a sensitive and detailed examination of each individual case.

Scepticism about the utility of moral principles may seem to strike at the very heart of our conception of morality. The concept of a moral principle appears to play a central, and apparently impregnable, role in our moral thought. To be virtuous is to have acquired, and to live by, a set of good moral principles. Moral education is viewed as the inculcation of the right principles in the young. The suggestion that we can do without moral principles is thus likely to appear unworthy of serious attention. This is certainly the opinion of most of the philosophers who have even bothered to consider the possibility of moral particularism. (For examples, see Dancy, 1983, p. 530.)

The conviction that we cannot manage without moral principles finds its main expression in a concern about how we are to cope when we find ourselves in a new, and perhaps puzzling, situation. We require guidance to help us to do the right thing. What would meet that need for guidance would be a set of tried and tested rules that would enable us to apply what we have learned in the old familiar cases to the new and unfamiliar one. Moral principles appear to fit the bill; they tell us which of the non-moral features of any situation are morally significant and so enable us to reach the right decision.

The conviction that there are moral principles that meet this need has two sources. The first is specific to non-cognitivism and comes from its account of what it is to be consistent in one's moral judgements. If we are to use terms intelligibly we must use them consistently, applying them to the same kinds of object or the same property whenever we use them. Since there are no evaluative properties in the world to which we can respond, our use of evaluative terms will only be intelligible if we consistently pick out the same *non-evaluative* features for approval or disapproval. To understand someone's moral system, on this account, is to grasp which features he picks out for favourable or unfavourable evaluation.

The second source of this conviction is not specific to non-cognitivism but is found in a strangely compelling picture of what it is to make a reasoned decision. In giving reasons for any decision, I am implicitly appealing to something general, to something that could be applied to other cases. If something is a reason in this case it cannot just be a reason in this case; it must be a reason elsewhere. Since we give reasons for our moral opinions we must, explicitly or implicitly, be appealing to general rules or moral principles. A moral principle is, if you like, a moral reason which has had its generality made explicit. Thus, if the reason this action is wrong is that it would involve telling a lie, then the wrongness of acting like that must somehow carry over into other cases which involve the telling of lies.

When I give reasons for my claim that an action is, say, morally wrong, I appeal to other properties of the action which make it wrong. I may appeal to some of its non-moral properties – that it caused pain or that it involved the deliberate telling of an untruth – or to some of its 'thick' moral properties – that it was ungenerous or cowardly. The latter kind of answer appears, however, only to offer a partial justification of my moral opinion. For I may properly be asked to give reasons for believing that it is ungenerous or cowardly and I shall then have to refer to the non-moral properties which make it so. So, in giving the full reasons for my belief that the action was wrong, I shall have to give a list of the non-moral properties that make it wrong. A full justification of my moral views as a whole would thus eventually involve the articulation of all my moral principles, that is, a list of all the non-moral properties of actions which I believe to be generally morally relevant.

The search for the perfect moral theory might thus be seen as a quest for the best set of moral principles which, if followed, would enable the agent to reach the right decision in any case he may encounter. Such a system would provide a complete, finite, check-list of non-moral properties which are morally relevant to the rightness or to the wrongness of an action. With the aid of such a check-list the agent could examine any actual or possible action and determine its rightness or wrongness by consulting his list. How long the list should be, just how many moral principles there are, is a matter for debate. The simplest system is, of course, a monistic one, in which only one property is morally relevant and all others may safely be ignored.

A particularist response

The particularist's objection to this conception of moral reasoning is that what we may want to say about the moral character of a particular action may always outrun any such attempt at codification. We have to be sensitive to the way the features of this individual case come together to determine its moral nature.

He rejects both of the arguments put forward to show that moral reasoning must consist in an appeal to moral principles. As we saw in 3.6, he rejects the non-cognitivist's account of moral consistency. He may agree with the non-cognitivist that, if a moral term is to be used intelligibly, its use must be guided by the way things are. Since, however, he has a richer conception of what the world contains than the non-cognitivist has, he can accept this point without drawing the non-cognitivist's conclusion. His use of a moral term will be consistent if he always uses it to denote the same moral property. He may exhibit a genuine and consistent sensitivity to the presence of some moral property without it being the case that there is any recognizable pattern, at the non-moral level, in the properties of the agents or actions to which he applies the term.

He also rejects the conception of reason to which the second argument appealed. On that picture, whether or not some non-moral feature of an action is a reason for its being morally wrong is quite unaffected by the presence or absence of other properties. If the presence of a non-moral property is a reason for an action's being wrong then, since its being a reason will not be altered one whit by other properties the action may have, whenever an action has that property it will provide a reason for the action's being wrong. The particularist regards this account of reasons as unduly atomistic. It supposes that each reason is insulated from its surroundings so that the effect of each on the rightness or wrongness of the action as a whole can be judged separately. The particularist prefers a holistic account. We cannot judge the effect of the presence of any one feature in isolation from the effect of the others. Whether or not one particular property is morally relevant, and in what way, may depend on the precise nature of the other properties of the action.

To illustrate: I take my nephews and nieces to the circus for a treat. They enjoy it. I have done the right thing. Why? Because I succeeded in giving them pleasure. Because the fact that my action gave pleasure was here the reason for its being right, does it follow that, whenever an action gives pleasure, we shall have reason for thinking it right? No. Consider the following. A government is considering reintroducing hanging, drawing and quartering in public for terrorist murders. If reactions to public hangings in the past are anything to go by a lot of people may enjoy the spectacle. Does that constitute a reason in favour of reintroduction? Is the fact that people would enjoy it here a reason for its being right? It would be perfectly possible to take just the opposite view. The fact that spectators might get a sadistic thrill from the brutal spectacle could be thought to constitute an objection to reintroduction. Whether the fact that an action causes pleasure is a reason for or against doing it is not something that can be settled in isolation from other features of the action. It is only when we know the context in which the pleasure will occur that we are in a position to judge.

In short, the particularist claims that we cannot know, in advance, what contribution any particular non-moral property will make to the moral nature of an action. We cannot know, in advance, whether it will be morally relevant at all and, if so, whether its presence will count for or against doing the action. The contribution that each property makes will depend on the other properties that go along with it in this case. It follows that there is no way of ruling out, in advance, some non-moral properties as being morally irrelevant. Any property may be morally relevant. Whether it is so will depend, once again, on the surrounding properties.

Where does the particularist stand in the debate between monism and pluralism? Sometimes that debate is presented as being between those who hold that there is only one fundamental moral principle and those who hold that there is an irreducible plurality of principles. As we have seen, the particularist rejects the terms of this debate. The issue is sometimes expressed in terms of morally relevant properties; is there one, or more than one, morally relevant property? In this debate the particularist takes an extreme pluralist position for no property can be ruled out, in advance, as never being relevant to the rightness or wrongness of an action.

There are reasons for being a particularist which are independent of moral realism. But the version of moral realism I favour provides a setting in which we can make sense of particularism. If we can be sensitive to the individual moral properties of the particular case then we have no need of moral principles, as they are here conceived, to show us the way. It would provide additional support for particularism if it could be shown that no ideal system of moral principles could deliver what it aspires to: a systematically organized set of moral principles that will tell the agent what to do in any particular case. The crucial test here is the problem of moral conflict.

13.2 MORAL CONFLICT

I argued in chapter 11 that our ordinary moral thought appears to be pluralist rather than monist in character. We appeal to a variety of values and moral principles in our moral reasoning, and utilitarian attempts to show that there is just one ultimate value or one basic moral principle were unconvincing. The obvious difficulty facing a pluralist system is the problem of moral conflict. Where there is a plurality of moral principles there is the possibility that more than one might apply to a particular situation and suggest conflicting answers to the question: Which action is the right one?

In Sartre's famous example, a young man in occupied France during the Second World War was torn between loyalty to his sick and widowed mother and loyalty to his country. He felt that he ought to stay at home and look after her but he also believed that he should join the Free French Army. It is characteristic of such a painful conflict that the person facing it takes himself to be under two obligations, which conflict in this particular case, so that he cannot honour both. The problem that faces a pluralist moral theory is to find a method by which such conflicts can be resolved.

The problem of resolving moral conflicts is certainly a difficulty for a pluralist theory but it is not in itself an objection to pluralism. Indeed, since we do experience moral conflicts, it is a strength of pluralism that it makes room for them. For just that reason, a sophisticated monism will not rule them out either, for it will allow that there can be a plurality of subsidiary moral principles between which conflict can occur. It is a strength of monism that it offers a clear method of resolving such disputes; since there is one basic principle from which all the others derive it must be to it that appeal is made in such cases. The weakness of monism is that it cannot explain the anguish that such conflicts often cause. If the clashing principles are merely secondary ones then it is unclear why the agent should be torn between them. He must regard such a conflict as merely an indication that the system of secondary principles, which he has found it useful to construct, does not always deliver a decisive verdict so that he must resort to his basic principle. For him, conflicts should not even be a cause for unease, let alone anguish.

The pluralist, however, should be in a better position to account for that anguish. The agent is under two distinct obligations, each of which has its own claim on him and each of which, perhaps, represents a distinct value which he is called on to foster. In choosing between them he will necessarily fail to honour one moral claim on him and this is what makes the choice painful.

Stressing the difficulty of such choices on a pluralist view serves to emphasize the problem with which we started: How are such conflicts to be resolved? More particularly, what form will such a resolution take? If, in a particular case, there are two independent but conflicting obligations then one of them will have to give if the conflict is to be resolved. Yet how can one of them give if both genuinely apply in this situation?

One solution is to try and place our moral principles in an order of priority. In any conflict, a principle higher on the priority list would always take precedence over one lower down. This would supply a clear decision procedure for dealing with any conflict; one of the principles that applied would always be higher in the ranking order than the other(s). There are two objections to such a structure. First, we have lost the sense in which, where there is a moral conflict, *both* principles apply to the particular case in question. For the lower ranking principle does not really apply in this case at all; it is superseded by the higher ranking one. A military analogy may help us to see this. If a captain and a colonel issue conflicting orders to a private then the colonel's order takes precedence. In this situation the captain's words do not constitute an order and the private is under no obligation to obey them. True, the captain's utterance would have constituted an order had not the colonel issued a conflicting order at the same time. But that does not make it an order in this case. Similarly, the lower ranking obligation does not apply in the case where it conflicts with a higher one. It would apply if there were no higher obligation, but that is not what we were looking for. On this system only one obligation can apply in any situation – whichever is the higher. So there can never be a genuine conflict of principle.

Secondly, it is totally implausible to suppose that our moral principles can be ranked in an invariable order. It does not have to be the case that either my obligation to my country *always* takes precedence over my obligation to my family, or vice versa. It is much more sensible to suppose that it all depends on the circumstances of the particular case. There is no general answer to the question: Which of these two principles is the most important?

A slightly more plausible variant on this scheme, advocated by Kant, among others, divides principles into two kinds, those which can be overridden and those which cannot. Some principles, such as the one forbidding the taking of innocent human life, are held to be so important that they cannot be overridden by any other principle. Such actions must never be done; the principles forbidding them are absolute. Such schemes can allow more than one absolute principle, provided that it is impossible for there to be a case where two absolute principles conflict. Whether this stringent condition can be met is doubtful. In any case, such schemes will allow the possibility of conflict between non-absolute moral principles and so will require supplementation by some other account to deal with these kinds of conflict.

A different solution sees the existence of moral conflicts as evidence that our moral principles are insufficiently specific and stand in need of fleshing out. Suppose that I am brought up with a set of simple principles: I am not to tell lies, I am to be polite to people I meet, and so on. Comes the embarrassing day when the woman next door asks me if I like her hideous new hat. Here my principles fail me. The principle of politeness dictates that I should lie; the rule against lying forces me to be impolite. On this view, it cannot be the case that both principles are adequately expressed, for they have failed to give me a clear answer in this case. One or the other must be complicated so that a specific answer is forthcoming. One or other principle must be liable to exceptions; in deciding what to do in this case I shall, in effect, be deciding which principle to amend by building the exception into the principle. Either my principle about lying will read: 'Do not lie, except to avoid causing people embarrassment'; or my rule about politeness will read: 'Be polite, except when to do so would involve one in telling a lie.'

There are two objections to this account, similar in structure to the objections to the previous one. The first is that it does not so much explain how conflict can be resolved as show that there was never a conflict in the first place – there only appeared to be one because the principles in question were inadequately specified. Secondly, the conception of a fully worked out principle which it offers is implausible and impractical. As he goes through life and finds himself in a greater variety of circumstances, the agent will have to complicate his original simple principles to a degree that would make them lengthy, ponderous and unmanageable. If, for example, the agent is prepared to admit that it is sometimes right to lie then he is unlikely to believe that this applies only in the case where, by doing so, he can avoid being rude. But just how many specific instances are there in which he might consider it correct to lie? Any rule that would be detailed enough to be any sort of a guide would be too detailed to be useful.

Moral principles and prima facie duties

So far we have looked at two accounts of how a theory which made room for a plurality of moral principles might develop in the face of the problem of moral conflict. Each theory was true to the conception of moral principles as a set of rules that would deliver a determinate verdict in every case. But each theory was completely implausible and also failed to give a satisfying picture of the nature of moral conflict. A third account, which we owe to Ross, meets these objections, but offers a conception in which the set of correct moral principles fails to yield a determinate answer in cases of moral conflict.

Ross (1930, ch. 2) distinguishes between a prima facie duty and a duty proper or an actual duty. An agent has a prima facie duty to do or to forbear doing x in a particular situation if a moral principle enjoining or forbidding x applies to that situation. Thus I have a prima facie duty not to tell my neighbour that I like her hat, since to do so would be to tell a lie, and there is a moral principle against lying. Where more than one moral principle applies then I will have more than one prima facie duty; in cases of moral conflict I will not be able to fulfil all my prima facie duties at once. In our example I also have a prima facie duty not to offend my neighbour, and I shall necessarily be in breach of one of these prima facie duties.

Where only one moral principle applies to my situation then my actual duty – the action that would be the right one in this particular case – is determined by that moral principle. In other words, where I only have one prima facie duty, that duty is also my actual duty. In cases where I am under conflicting prima facie duties then there is no set rule by which I can determine my actual duty. In each such case I have to examine that particular situation and determine which prima facie duty is the most stringent, or carries the greatest weight, in these circumstances. Deciding what to do in a moral conflict is a matter of judgement which cannot be codified. In wondering what to say in response to my neighbour's query I have to weigh the prima facie duty not to lie against the prima facie duty not to be rude. I am not, as on the first account, trying to settle this question once for all; I am only trying to determine which takes precedence in just these circumstances. Nor, as on the second account, am I laying down a rule about when exceptions can be made to the principle; for each new case will have to be judged on its merits. My mastery of a set of moral principles will serve to alert me to the fact that a moral conflict exists in cases such as that of my neighbour's hat, but that is as far as it will carry me. No appeal to moral principles can serve to resolve that conflict – at this point I am on my own.

Ross's theory also makes sense of the thought that, in a moral conflict, the agent is actually under two obligations both of which, in this case, he cannot fulfil. For both prima facie obligations do apply to the agent. Although he can fulfil only one of them, that does not make it any the less true that the other applies to him. It can be a source of genuine regret that he has to breach one of them even if he knows his decision to be the correct one.

The sense in which the defeated obligation lingers on even after the agent has decided that his actual duty lies elsewhere can be given a more concrete form. Suppose I am unable to fulfil an obligation to a friend because a weightier obligation arises. I have promised, say, to pick him up at his house and take him to the cinema. I learn that my father is seriously ill and travel home to be with him. It seems clear that my obligation to my father is weightier than that to my friend in these circumstances. But I am still under an obligation to my friend; it has not lapsed. In having decided to go home, however, I make it impossible for me to fulfil the original obligation to take him to the cinema. In what sense, then, can it be true that my obligation has not lapsed, since it cannot be fulfilled? The answer is that I am still under an obligation to him but its nature has changed. I should now try and contact him as soon as possible and warn him of my non-arrival or, if that fails, I should apologize as soon as I can. I may also need to make it up to him in some other way, perhaps by taking him out at some later time. It is as if my original obligation, of necessity unfulfilled, does not vanish but transforms itself into the obligation to make amends.

It may be impossible, in some cases, to make amends at all or, at least, to make adequate amends. The thought that, whatever the agent does, he will leave some obligation for ever unfulfilled explains the anguish which choices of the type facing Sartre's young man can cause. After the choice has been made, since the defeated obligation does not merely lapse, it is perfectly proper for the agent to feel regret. Yet this may still occasion puzzlement. If he has done the right thing, and would do the same again, how can he rationally feel regret for his choice? What he regrets is not, of course, having done the right thing (that would be an irrational emotion) but having failed to fulfil a genuine obligation. He should not feel *remorse* because, in those circumstances, he did what was best; but he does feel *regret* because that particular obligation remained unfulfilled. Such regret does not make sense on either of the previous accounts of moral conflict because they did not make room for the thought that the unfulfilled obligation continues to apply. Monists, of course, must find such regret unintelligible. If there is only one basic moral principle then, if I acted in accordance with it, I cannot have left any distinct obligations unfulfilled.

Weighing obligations

We saw that Ross did not believe that there was any set rule by which we could judge, where obligations conflict, which is the weightier. Attempts to codify such decisions only reveal the belief that there is some computational procedure by which competing obligations can be precisely weighed – but that is just what Ross and the particularist deny. Such decisions require judgement, and judgement is only possible for someone who has a real insight into the issues involved; it cannot be replicated by the use of a decision procedure which could be grasped by someone who had no appreciation of what was at stake. Yet that is what the original account of moral principles appeared to offer – a set of rules which could be applied by anyone, whatever their sensitivity or experience, to discover the right answer.

Moreover, it is absurd to suppose that there will be a determinate answer, in each particular case, to the question which of two obligations is the weightier. There may be cases where it is impossible to judge. This should not be taken to mean that, in such cases, the two obligations are of exactly equal weight. Nor should it be supposed that there must be an answer in principle but that it is difficult to arrive at it in practice. That would be to revert to the computational model. What it means is that there may be no correct answer or, perhaps better, that the correct answer is: there is no answer. But that does not mean that it does not matter what you do. That realization may increase rather than diminish the anguish of having to choose.

A misunderstanding needs to be guarded against. We should not suppose that, in admitting that there are cases where there is no correct answer to the question 'Which obligation is the stronger?' the realist has admitted that there are at least some moral questions where there is no truth of the matter. In saying that there are cases where that question has no correct answer the pluralist is not saying that any answer to the question will do. He claims that the truth is that neither obligation can sensibly be said to be weightier. In this particular case, the question is unanswerable. Whether or not a particular question can sensibly be said to have an answer is itself a question that calls for judgement, and one on which someone can be mistaken.

13.3 PARTICULARISM AND PRIMA FACIE DUTIES

Ross's understanding of the nature of moral principles is the only one that offers a satisfactory account of moral conflict. In such cases it accords well with what the particularist wishes to maintain. It insists that we can only reach a decision in such cases by looking at the features of the particular case in order to judge which prima facie duty is the weightier in these, and only in these, circumstances. It denies that moral conflicts can be settled by any mechanical decision procedure that could be applied by anyone whether or not he had insight into the moral issues. Such decisions require judgement and sensitivity.

What Ross offers is not, of course, particularism, since moral principles do play a role. First, we appeal to them in showing that there is a moral conflict to be resolved, and in determining which features are relevant to its resolution. Second, the appeal to them is decisive in cases where only one principle applies in that situation. How do I discover these principles?

According to Ross (1939, pp. 170–73) we start with the particular case. We realize, say, that this action is wrong and then, perhaps, that it is so because of some particular feature – that it is a case, say, of telling a lie. Through our experience of particular cases of this kind we are enabled to grasp the *general* truth, that lying is what we might call a wrong-making characteristic. As we have already seen, that does not mean that any action which involves lying is actually wrong, for there may be other, right-making, characteristics of the action which out-weigh this wrong-making characteristic on this occasion. Lying is a wrong-making characteristic in that the fact that something is a lie is *always* a reason against doing it. The fact that some course of action involved telling a lie could never be a morally neutral characteristic of the action, still less a reason in favour of doing it.

The particularist denies that we can generalize from the particular case. We cannot know, in advance, that some non-moral characteristic must be relevant in all cases and always in the same way. The particularist can learn from Ross's hostility to a computational approach to solving moral conflicts, but he is unconvinced by his generalism.

It is important to distinguish three different positions here. First, there is Ross's view that if a characteristic matters in one place it must matter everywhere. Second, there is the weaker view that there must be at least some characteristics which always matter, even if there are others which only matter sometimes. The particularist rejects these positions. Third, there is the much weaker view that there *may* be some characteristics which, as a matter of fact, always count in the same way. The particularist need have no quarrel with this position.

13.4 MORAL PRINCIPLES IN ORDINARY LIFE

At the beginning of this chapter I suggested that scepticism about the utility of moral principles not only undermined a certain kind of moral theory but also appeared at odds with our ordinary moral thinking. Since that scepticism turned out to be almost wholly justified it seems that the particularist has some explaining to do. He needs to show that his theory does not unduly distort our moral thinking.

It turned out, however, that the particularist's scepticism was not about anything that might be called a moral principle, but only about what we might call the check-list conception of what a moral principle is. There may, however, be kinds of moral principle to which the particularist would have no objection. If it turns out that it is to these kinds of principle that people appeal in ordinary life, then particularism can embrace them.

It is, in my view, quite difficult to determine just what moral principles are widely accepted in our society, since the role of moral principles is a good deal more talked about than illustrated. A number of the sayings to which people subscribe, some of them with a biblical basis, are quite general in their purport and themselves require interpretation and moral sensitivity to be applied: 'honour your father and mother'; 'love your neighbour as yourself'; 'be true to yourself'. The purpose of such remarks appears to be to serve to indicate areas of general moral concern, leaving us to work out how, or if, they may have a bearing on any particular case.

In order to know, for example, whether a child's action is genuinely a case of honouring its parents we need to look at all the details of the case. Take the case of the Eskimos who, it is said, used to leave old people to die on the ice once they had become too old to hunt or to make a contribution to the welfare of the tribe in other ways. At first glance such an action appears callous and uncaring in the extreme. But more knowledge of the context can completely reverse that initial impression. When this practice flourished euthanasia was essential for the survival of the tribe as a whole. This was generally recognized and accepted by everyone, including the aged parents themselves, who would initiate the chain of events leading to their own death. I understand that a father would tell his son that he wished to go on one last hunting trip; they would go out together, kill a seal and eat it. After they had talked for a while and said their farewells, the father would tell his son to go home, while he would stretch out on the ice and wait for death. The son's part in this ritual appears to be an example of honouring one's parents.

The particularist need find nothing objectionable in an appeal to such principles. In order to see whether they truly apply we have to look at each case in all its lived detail. Nor is appeal to such a principle decisive. For the principle only gestures towards one area of moral concern; there are others.

The need for precise moral principles is most clearly seen, it is said, in the teaching of children. Even this is doubtful. The role of moral principles in the proper education of the young can easily be exaggerated. Moral lessons are not usually taught by instilling a list of principles into the child's mind. Rather, when the child does something, or witnesses some action, the parent draws attention to the morally important features of this particular action. But let it be admitted that we do teach simple moral principles to children, such as 'don't steal', and that we often pretend that they are exceptionless. Does this undermine the particularist case? Not in the least. It is often necessary, in matters of prudence as well as of morality, to issue blanket rules for the good of the child – 'Never talk to strangers.' It does not follow that, when they grow up, they cannot throw away the leading strings of moral principles and learn to find their own way.

But why, it might be objected, teach them moral principles in the first place if it is better, in the end, if they dispense with them? Because they are useful at the time. When people are learning to write essays they are taught rudimentary rules of style. Later they come to realize that there is no rule of style that has not been broken by some writer to considerable effect. They could not have started without stylistic guidelines of any kind – rules which are, for the most part, acceptable. As their sense of prose rhythm develops they gradually dispense with them. In the end, if they are not discarded, they prove a hindrance to good writing. And so it may be with moral principles.

This line of thinking may suggest a difficulty similar to one that faced the utilitarian. Isn't particularism such a dangerous doctrine that it ought not to be widely promulgated? Once people abandon reliance on any kind of principle and judge each case on its merits are they not liable to do worse than if they stick to a few fairly clearly set out principles? But what is meant by 'doing worse' here? In the case of the utilitarian there was a clear criterion by which we could judge whether people did better or worse if they lived by one set of principles rather than another, namely how much happiness was produced by different systems of moral rules. But the particularist does not think that happiness is the only value. It might be that more moral mistakes would be made if people adopted particularism rather than adhering to their, rather vague, moral principles. Even if this were true, and even if the sum of human happiness were thereby somewhat diminished it is by no means clear that those considerations on their own would justify its suppression. On the contrary, there are many excellent reasons, in terms of the things we value, such as openness and honesty, why people who believe a moral doctrine should be candid about it.

Against the dangers of the doctrine should be set its benefits. Over-reliance on principles encourages serious vices, such as inflexibility and rigidity in one's moral thinking. If we choose to judge a moral system by the good or harm it does to the social fabric then probably more unhappiness has been caused by people 'sticking to their principles', rather than being sensitive to what is called for in a particular case, than would ever be produced by a society of moral particularists.

13.5 MORAL EXPERTS AND MORAL TEACHERS

The demand for moral experts is growing. They are asked to sit on government commissions of enquiry, and on ethics committees set up by hospitals and the like. There is also a feeling that each professional person should become his own amateur moral theorist; no training course in a profession is complete without a course on practical ethics and moral theory. Since the main financial beneficiaries of this demand are professional moral philosophers, it is perhaps both churlish and imprudent for one of their number to question the utility of such employment. Nevertheless, the particularist must surely have doubts about how well, in virtue of his professional training, a moral philosopher is fitted to these new roles. Of course, there is much that he can contribute. Any course of study that makes lawyers and doctors reflect on the ethics of what they are doing is to be welcomed. An introduction to the main problems of moral theory will serve both to reveal the complexities of many moral issues and to help people to understand their own thinking more clearly. The presence on an ethical committee of an educated person who has spent time thinking about moral questions in an intelligent way will normally be helpful. But is there not a danger that moral philosophers will be seen, and even come to see themselves, as moral experts in virtue of their special training? There is, however, no reason on the particularist view why a person who has devoted his time to philosophical reflection on ethical issues should be especially sensitive to the moral truth.

There are, in fact, several reasons why he might be peculiarly ill qualified to give moral advice. Just as someone can only be well qualified to judge in aesthetic matters if he has wide experience of different kinds of art, and the right kind of sensibility to react to them suitably, so judging moral questions aright requires a wide experience of life and a suitable range of emotional response. Academic life neither attracts people with these qualities nor encourages them once they have entered the profession.

But the main drawback, in particularist eyes, stems from the very nature of the moral philosopher's professional training. What the philosopher is offering is expertise in practical ethics, the study of localized moral questions such as abortion or euthanasia. Any claim that he may be in a good position to know what is right in the local case depends on a belief in the validity of moral theory, the existence of a rationally acceptable set of moral principles which can guide us through specific problems in practical ethics. Particularism claims, in effect, that there is no such subject as moral theory, in this sense, and so no such subject as practical ethics. In so far as the teaching of practical ethics encourages both pupils and teacher to believe in the will o' the wisp of moral theory it is pernicious.

If there is no such thing as moral theory, if each case has to be considered on its merits, can there be moral teachers? If they do not teach us what the correct moral principles are, or at least how to work out what they are, what do they teach? What we need to be taught, on the particularist view, is a way of seeing, a way of being sensitive to the moral facts which we can make our own. There can, after all, be art appreciation classes without there being a set of principles for judging paintings. We all have moral blindspots, areas of insensitivity, and so there is always room for improvement. What the great moral teachers of the past, such as Buddha and Christ, have done is to bring us, by parable, story and paradox, to see the world in new and revealing ways. What we need is not a better set of principles but better moral vision.

FURTHER READING

Dancy (1983) defends particularism; Dancy (1981) is also relevant. McDowell (1981, 1985) claims that particularism follows from the account of justification which I outlined in 3.6.

On 13.2 Williams (1965, 1966) argues that a proper understanding of the nature of moral dilemmas raises a difficulty for moral realism. Guttenplan (1980) and Foot (1983) supply realist rebuttals.

On 13.5 Warnock (1985, pp. 95–100) discusses the role of moral experts on government commissions.

References

In the case of works by classic authors such as Aristotle or Hume, there are many reputable editions as well as the ones cited here.

Aristotle 1972: *Nicomachean Ethics*, trans. W. D. Ross. London: Oxford Univ. Press.

Ayer, A. J. 1946: *Language, Truth and Logic*, 2nd edn. London: Gollancz.

Blackburn, S. 1981: Reply: rule following and moral realism. In Holtzman and Leich, 1981, pp. 163–87.

—— 1984: *Spreading the Word*. Oxford: Oxford Univ. Press.

—— 1985: Errors and the phenomenology of value. In Honderich, 1985, pp. 1–22.

Brandt, B. 1954: The definition of an 'ideal observer' theory in ethics. *Philosophy and Phenomenological Research*, 15, 407–13.

Brink, D. O. 1986: Externalist moral realism. *Southern Journal of Philosophy*, 24, supplement, 23–41.

—— 1988: *Moral Realism and the Foundations of Ethics*. Cambridge: Cambridge Univ. Press.

Broad, C. D. 1930: *Five Types of Ethical Theory*. London: Routledge & Kegan Paul.

Campbell, K. 1970: *Body and Mind*. London: Macmillan.

Camus A. 1955: *The Myth of Sisyphus*, trans. J. O'Brien. London: Hamish Hamilton.

Dancy, J. 1981: On moral properties. *Mind*, 90, 367–85.

—— 1983: Ethical particularism and morally relevant properties. *Mind*, 92, 530–547.

—— 1985: *Introduction to Contemporary Epistemology*. Oxford: Basil Blackwell.

—— 1986: Two conceptions of moral realism. *Proceedings of the Aristotelian Society* supp. vol. 60, 167–87.

Daniels, N. (ed.) 1975: *Reading Rawls*. Oxford: Basil Blackwell.

Davidson, D. 1969: How is weakness of the will possible? In Feinberg, 1969, pp. 93–113.

—— 1984: On the very idea of a conceptual scheme. In D. Davidson, *Inquiries into Truth and Interpretation*, Oxford: Clarendon Press. Reprinted from

Proceedings and Addresses of the American Philosophical Association, 47, 1974.

Ewing, A. C. 1962: *Ethics*. London: English Univ. Press Ltd.

Feinberg, J. (ed.) 1969: *Moral Concepts*. London: Oxford Univ. Press.

Finnis, J. 1983: *Fundamentals of Ethics*. Oxford: Oxford Univ. Press.

Firth. R. 1952: Ethical absolutism and the ideal observer. *Philosophy and Phenomenological Research*, 12, 317–45.

Foot, P. 1972: Morality as a system of hypothetical imperatives. *Philosophical Review*, 81.

—— 1983: Moral realism and moral dilemma. *Journal of Philosophy*, 80, 379–98.

Guttenplan, S. 1980: Moral realism and moral dilemmas. *Proceedings of the Aristotelian Society*, 80, 61–80.

Hare, R. M. 1952: *The Language of Morals*. Oxford: Oxford Univ. Press.

—— 1963: *Freedom and Reason*. Oxford: Oxford Univ. Press.

—— 1964: Pain and evil. *Proceedings of the Aristotelian Society*, supplementary volume 38, 91–106. Reprinted in Feinberg, 1969, pp. 29–42.

—— 1973: Rawls' theory of justice. *Philosophical Quarterly*, 23, 144–55; 241–52. Reprinted in Daniels, 1975.

—— 1976: Ethical theory and utilitarianism. In H. D. Lewis (ed.), *Contemporary British Philosophy IV*, London: Allen & Unwin, 113–31.

—— 1981: *Moral Thinking*. Oxford: Oxford Univ. Press.

Harman, G. 1977: *The Nature of Morality*. New York: Oxford Univ. Press.

Holtzman and Leich (eds) 1981: *Wittgenstein: To Follow a Rule*. London: Routledge & Kegan Paul.

Honderich, Ted (ed.) 1985: *Morality and Objectivity*. London: Routledge & Kegan Paul.

Hume, D. 1975: *Enquiry Concerning the Principles of Morals*. First published in 1751. In *Hume's Enquiries*, ed. P. Nidditch, Oxford: Oxford Univ. Press.

—— 1978: *A Treatise of Human Nature*, ed. P. Nidditch. Oxford: Oxford Univ. Press. Books I and II first published in 1739, Book III in 1740.

Kant, I. 1972: *Groundwork of the Metaphysic of Morals*. First published in 1785. Trans. by H. J. Paton as *The Moral Law*, London: Hutchinson.

Kuhn, T. S. 1962: *The Structure of Scientific Revolutions*. Chicago: Univ. of Chicago Press.

Locke, J. 1961: *An Essay Concerning Human Understanding*, vol. 1. London: Dent & Sons. First published in 1690.

Lovibond, S. 1983: *Realism and Imagination in Ethics*. Minneapolis: Univ. of Minnesota Press.

McDowell, J. 1978: Are moral requirements hypothetical imperatives? *Proceedings of the Aristotelian Society*, supp. vol. 52, 13–29.

—— 1979: Virtue and reason. *Monist*, 62, 331–50.

—— 1981: Non-cognitivism and rule-following. In Holtzman and Leich, 1981, pp. 141–62.

—— 1983: Aesthetic value, objectivity and the fabric of the world. In

E. Schaper (ed.), *Pleasure, Preference and Value*, Cambridge: Cambridge Univ. Press, 1–16.

—— 1985: Values and secondary qualities. In Honderich, 1985, pp. 110–29.

McGinn, C. 1983: *The Subjective View*. Oxford: Clarendon Press.

Mackie, J. L. 1977: *Ethics: Inventing Right and Wrong*. Harmondsworth: Penguin.

Midgley, M. 1984: *Wickedness*. London: Routledge & Kegan Paul.

Moore, G. E. 1903: *Principia Ethica*, Cambridge: Cambridge Univ. Press.

Mortimore, G. W. (ed.) 1971: *Weakness of Will*. London: Macmillan.

Murdoch, I. 1970: *Sovereignty of the Good*. London: Routledge & Kegan Paul.

Nagel, T. 1974: What is it like to be a bat? *Philosophical Review*, 83, 435–50. Reprinted in Nagel, 1979, pp. 165–80.

—— 1978: *The Possibility of Altruism*. Princeton, NJ: Princeton Univ. Press.

—— 1979: *Mortal Questions*. Cambridge: Cambridge Univ. Press.

—— 1986: *The View From Nowhere*. New York: Oxford Univ. Press.

Norman, R. 1983: *The Moral Philosophers*. Oxford: Oxford Univ. Press.

Orwell, G. 1961: A hanging. In G. Orwell, *Collected Essays*, London: Heinemann.

Pears, D. 1984: *Motivated Irrationality*. Oxford: Clarendon Press.

Pettit, P. 1987: Universalizability without utilitarianism. *Mind*, 96, 74–82.

Plato 1959: *The Last Days of Socrates*, trans. H. Tredennick. Harmondsworth: Penguin.

—— 1966: *Protagoras and Meno*, trans. W. K. C. Guthrie. Harmondsworth: Penguin.

Platts, M. 1979: *Ways of Meaning*. London: Routledge & Kegan Paul.

—— 1981: Moral reality and the end of desire. In M. Platts (ed.), *Reference, Truth and Reality*, London: Routledge & Kegan Paul, 69–82.

Prior, A. N. 1949: *Logic and the Basis of Ethics*. Oxford: Oxford Univ. Press.

Prichard, H. A. 1968: *Moral Obligation*. Oxford: Oxford Univ. Press.

Putnam, H. 1981: *Reason, Truth and History*. New York: Cambridge Univ. Press.

Rawls, J. 1955: Two concepts of rules. *Philosophical Review*, 64, 3–32. Reprinted in P. Foot (ed.), *Theories of Ethics*, Oxford: Oxford Univ. Press, 144–70.

—— 1971: *A Theory of Justice*. Oxford: Oxford Univ. Press.

Ross, W. D. 1930: *The Right and the Good*. Oxford: Clarendon Press.

—— 1939: *Foundations of Ethics*. Oxford: Clarendon Press.

Sartre, J. P. 1970: *Existentialism and Humanism*. London: Methuen.

Scheffler, S. 1982: *The Rejection of Consequentialism*. Oxford: Clarendon Press.

Smith, A. 1976: *The Theory of Moral Sentiments*. Oxford: Oxford Univ. Press. First published 1776.

Smith, M. 1987: The Humean theory of motivation. *Mind*, 96, 36–61.

Stevenson, C. L. 1937: The emotive meaning of ethical terms, *Mind*, 46, 14–31. Reprinted in Stevenson, 1963.

—— 1938: Persuasive definitions. *Mind*, 47, 331–50. Reprinted in Stevenson, 1963.

—— 1948: The nature of ethical disagreement. *Sigma*, 8–9. Reprinted in Stevenson, 1963.

—— 1963: *Facts and Values*. New Haven: Yale Univ. Press.

Strawson, P. F. 1979: Perception and its objects. In G. F. Macdonald (ed.), *Perception and Identity*, Ithaca, NY: Cornell Univ. Press, 41–60.

Sturgeon, N. 1986: What difference does it make whether moral realism is true? *Southern Journal of Philosophy*, 24, supplement, 115–41.

Swinburne, R. 1979: *The Existence of God*. Oxford: Clarendon Press.

Urmson, J. O. 1968: *The Emotive Theory of Ethics*. Oxford: Oxford Univ. Press.

—— 1975: A defence of intuitionism. *Proceedings of the Aristotelian Society*, 75, 111–19.

Warnock, G. J. 1967: *Contemporary Moral Philosophy*. London: Macmillan.

Warnock, M. 1985: *A Question of Life*. Oxford: Basil Blackwell.

Werner, R. 1983: Ethical Realism. *Ethics*, 93, 653–79.

Wiggins, D. 1976: Truth, invention and the meaning of life. *Proceedings of the British Academy*, vol. 62, Oxford: Oxford Univ. Press, 331–378.

Williams, B. 1965: Ethical Consistency. *Proceedings of the Aristotelian Society*, supp. vol. 39, 103–24. Reprinted in Williams, 1973c.

—— 1966: Consistency and Realism. *Proceedings of the Aristotelian Society*, supp. vol. 40, 1–22. Reprinted in Williams, 1973c.

—— 1973a: A critique of utilitarianism. In J. J. C. Smart and B. Williams, *Utilitarianism: For and Against*, Cambridge: Cambridge Univ. Press.

—— 1973b: *Morality*. Harmondsworth: Penguin Books.

—— 1973c: *Problems of the Self*. Cambridge, Cambridge Univ. Press.

—— 1978: *Descartes: The Project of Pure Enquiry*. Harmondsworth: Penguin.

—— 1985: *Ethics and the Limits of Philosophy*. London: Collins.

Index